Prodigal Daughter

A JOURNEY TO BYZANTIUM

 THE UNIVERSITY OF ALBERTA PRESS

Prodigal Daughter

A JOURNEY TO BYZANTIUM · Myrna Kostash

Published by
The University of Alberta Press
Ring House 2
Edmonton, Alberta, Canada T6G 2E1

LIBRARY AND ARCHIVES CANADA CATALOGUING IN PUBLICATION

Kostash, Myrna
    Prodigal daughter : a journey to Byzantium / Myrna Kostash.

Includes bibliographical references and index.
ISBN 978-0-88864-534-0

    1. Kostash, Myrna—Travel—Balkan Peninsula. 2. Kostash, Myrna—Religion. 3. Balkan
Peninsula—Description and travel. I. Title.

DR16.K68 2010   914.96'04   C2010-904238-7

All rights reserved.
First edition, first printing, 2010.
Printed and bound in Canada by Houghton Boston Printers, Saskatoon, Saskatchewan.
Map by Wendy Johnson.
Copyediting and Proofreading by Meaghan Craven.
Indexing by Judy Dunlop.

The University of Alberta Press is committed to protecting our natural environment. As part
of our efforts, this book is printed on Enviro Paper: it contains 100% post-consumer recycled
fibres and is acid- and chlorine-free.

The University of Alberta Press gratefully acknowledges the support received for its publishing
program from The Canada Council for the Arts. The University of Alberta Press also gratefully
acknowledges the financial support of the Government of Canada through the Book Publishing
Industry Development Program (BPIDP) and from the Alberta Foundation for the Arts for its
publishing activities.

This book is for Peter Deyman, witness.

"simplicity, fearlessness, triumph, love"

Is it here on the eastern frontier of Western civilization that all wisdom is to be found, like buried treasure, a paradise once lost?

—JAKOB PHILIPP FALLMERAYER

(in *Icons: The Fascination and the Reality*)

Contents

PART ONE

Demetrius among the Slavs

:: *Grade Four class, Delton Elementary School,*
   northeast Edmonton, mid-1950s

I WAS NINE YEARS OLD, seated at a worn wooden desk in a handsome brick school that was much the most important building in this
immigrant and blue-collar neighbourhood. My teacher, Miss Clarke,
was asking us, kindly, one after another: "And where do you come
from?" No one was Canadian yet, not even those born in Canada. It
was understood we all "started" from some other country. Now it
was my turn. "I'm Greek," I said.

With precocious subterfuge, a little Ukrainian-Canadian girl had
made the link between the "onion"-domed churches of the Canadian
prairie and her source in Byzantium. In that Grade Four moment I
was already testifying, through a kind of tapping into a collective
memory, that I came from a very large world indeed, the world
of eastern Christianity.

Well, perhaps not; rather, I was unwittingly tapping a reservoir
of cultural shame. In that multi-ethnic classroom in Edmonton, I
was laying desperate claim to an origin that was not Ukrainian, for
I already knew, had sensed by osmosis from my western Canadian
surroundings, that Ukrainian, or any Slavic, identity was less desirable than most others, although a notch up from the Cree Indians

and what we then called the half-breeds. But what could I get away with? There were kids in that classroom who were Ukrainian like me, and Polish, and German, and Dutch. We all knew who the "English" kids were, and they weren't us. I knew I couldn't claim to be Scottish, Irish, or Welsh because they were "English" too. And that's when I hit on it. I went to a church that called itself Ukrainian Greek Orthodox. There was no substantial Greek immigration into Edmonton yet (well, there was that radio announcer, Ernie Afaganis, but nobody called him anything but a radio announcer), so all our references to Greeks were to gods and goddesses on Mount Olympus, and heroes who went to the Trojan War.

"I'm Greek," I said.

BEFORE SUNDAY SCHOOL, we children sat with our parents upstairs in the church, for the first hour of the Divine Liturgy. The church was named for St. John Chrysostom, the Golden Mouth, Patriarch of Constantinople, the Liturgy's putative writer, who died in 407. In his icon, he stands in episcopal garb, carrying a Gospel and flanked by the other fourth-century Father-Theologians of the early church: Basil the Great, Metropolitan of Caesarea, and Gregory of Nazianzus, for a time Bishop of Constantinople. In the fourth century, it was all one Church still, Greek and Latin, and these patriarchs commanded all the faithful of West and East. Yet such figures seemed weird and exotic even to me, unnatural, alien, so used was I to the way things were "supposed" to look in the workaday world. In this world, their bodies had disappeared within the stiff brocade from which their skinny necks emerged, topped by inexpressive faces, mild and joyless.

The Liturgy was celebrated in the modern Ukrainian language, although this was not of much help to me as I didn't speak the language in any version. We spoke only English at home. Now I can read, in the Pryiatel' Ditei (prayer book for children), its small pages worn thin at the corners, that, with the priest's opening utterance, "Blessed be the kingdom of the Father, the Son and the Holy Spirit, now and forever, unto ages of ages," we have the first of many, many repetitions of that triad. Father, Son, and Holy Spirit—this was the cue to cross ourselves, in the Orthodox style, thumb, index, and middle

fingers bunched up, the hand moving *from right to left* shoulder. This
gesture was one of the first things we learned in Sunday school: it
separated us from the Catholics, who used their whole hand to move
from left to right. And then we were into the first of the Litanies ("Lord
have mercy"), our signal to sit down. Also included were prayers for
Queen Elizabeth II, the government and the armed forces, for our
"God-beloved and God-protected country, Canada, and for our
God-beloved and God-protected ancestral homeland, Ukraine."

St. John's was the cathedral church, many-domed, cavernous,
its ornamentation forever being upgraded (my father would point
out the church's embellishments—banners, stained glass windows,
bronze candle stands—with a sarcastic poke in the ribs). The priest
officiated way up there in the sanctuary (it was understood that
the front pews were reserved for the parish bigwigs, although
they were not always present), separated from us by the ornately
carved and painted screen of icons, the *iconostasis*, which shielded
the sanctuary and all the mysteries performed within it from
our gaze. I stared at it, year in and year out, until these images—
eikon = image—of saints, prophets, archangels, martyrs, kings and
queens, the Holy Trinity, the annunciatory Angel Gabriel and the
girl, Mary, leaning in toward each other seemed like a gallery of
relatives lined up for an anniversary photograph on the farm. But
through the open doors of the screen I could see Fr. Chomiak moving
about in his several layers of gold-and-white vestments, performing
mysterious rites at the altar, attended by sacristan and altar boys.
All males, of course. Technically, I was one of the God-beloved
people, but I would never be admitted into the precinct of the sanctuary, at least not until I had stopped the monthly bleeding.

Later I will learn that the consecrated altar is considered to be
the sacred place of Christ's sacrifice and therefore must be physically separated from the unconsecrated people in the nave. But I saw
all kinds of unconsecrated people moving in and out of that space—
old men, pimply boys—and I did not yet bleed, yet I stood meekly
at the door opening to the sacristy, offering up the basket in which
the congregation had slipped their loose change for the Children's
Collection, not daring to "pollute" even with my gaze that men's

clubhouse that lies beyond the space—the world—in which men and women mingle, though I sensed furtively the gold plate, the brocades, the beeswax, the box of matches, the overcoats. Decades later this prohibition is still so strong in me that, even utterly alone in rustic Greek chapels and miles away from town or village, I allow myself only a peek behind the faded cloth that hangs from the humble iconostasis, cobwebs shielding the sanctuary from me.

In the pews I sat with my father, the great skeptic of our family, the reader of history books and the thinker of "what ifs," who would whisper flippant asides during the course of the sermon, even though he was the son of pious immigrants and was himself a faithful servant of the Church, who departed weekly on mysterious errands having to do with Boards, Consistories, and Assemblies of the Ukrainian Greek Orthodox Church of Canada, Edmonton division.

At fifteen, I announced to my parents one Sunday morning while we were all dressing for church that I did not believe in God and would no longer accompany them to church services. My mother said that I was far too young to decide any such thing, and that seems to have been that. There were many more Sundays of "church": the, to me, interminable Liturgies; unintelligible sequence of kneeling, standing, and sitting; mournful choral music of the Slavonic service, no musical instruments allowed. I envied my Protestant friends who were in and out of church in an hour, having enjoyed themselves thoroughly with cheerful hymns you could tap your toes to, jolly organ interludes, and sermons about good citizenship.

On Sundays we were no longer in the Anglo world, which was the world of Protestants in all their bewildering variety, though I lumped them all together, especially the Anglicans, as "English." They were the public face of religious belief in western Canada well into the 1960s, along with the Roman Catholics, but RCS (as we called them) had their own schools where they were taught by nuns ("penguins") and said a lot of Latin mumbo-jumbo, so they were not quite "normal" even though public.

I knew much about the non-Ukrainian Christians—what their churches looked like inside and out, what they sang in there, what their weddings were like, how their "Reverends" and "Pastors" dressed, how they celebrated Christmas: they built crèches and ate roast turkey. But they needed to know nothing about me (or about Jews in their synagogues, for that matter, or Muslims in their mosques, Edmonton's Al-Rashid, the first in Canada). After all, how would they learn it? There were no public texts except the annual and obligatory story in the *Edmonton Journal* about "our fellow Edmontonians who observe the Julian calendar," accompanied by a photo of the mother of the household in her embroidered blouse setting the table with the traditional twelve dishes, meatless and milkless. The stage had been set for the dogged representation of Ukrainians as *pyrohy* eaters.

On December 18, St. Nicholas Day in the Julian calendar, we were packed into the church basement along with all the other kids for a St. Nicholas Day concert that climaxed with the arrival of the Saint himself in his episcopal vestments and crown borrowed from the vestry, looking just like his icon. He carried a great sack from which he dispensed gifts, harassed all the while by a cackling *chortyk*, a little devil in black-face, who maligned us all, good or bad. There was always the chance that St. Nicholas would believe him and put our beribboned gift back into his sack, leaving us reduced to tears of mortification.

St. Nicholas is a much-loved saint of the Eastern Church, the kindly Bishop who threw gold into the bedroom of the three daughters of a poor man to save them from prostitution, rescued three innocents from death by decapitation, saved Patriarch Anastasius from drowning, returned a son who had been kidnapped by Arab slavers to his family. I found myself in a tumult of confused desires when I considered this stately Bishop of Myra—bald and grey-bearded and wrinkle-browed, who never made an appearance outside the church but who somehow represented how "we" did Christmas— and that other herald of the Christmas season, Santa Claus—the fat man in the red snowsuit waving at us from his float in the Santa Claus parade trundling down Jasper Avenue, his cheeks and nose, like ours, pink and prickly with frost. Later, he was transported to his throne in the Hudson's Bay Company department store and tilted his head not for our prayers but for our wish list of childish goodies that we were pretty sure he would deliver, no questions asked. He was also popularly known as "jolly St. Nick," but I never made the connection. Jolly St. Nick was *English*. It was as though all public space was secular, while Ukrainian Orthodox space was reserved for devotion.

I sensed that, among my relatives and my parents' friends who went to church, there was a kind of piety, or at least a seriousness about the enterprise, both the city women, in exuberantly flowered Easter hats—my mother in a broad-brimmed, white-straw boater trimmed with navy blue silk around the crown, tilted rakishly now that I think of it—who prepared the elaborate wicker baskets filled with Easter foods for blessing, and also my relatives on the farm, the men who took wives and children to church but themselves stood outside the building, leaning on their wagons, smoking, and talking about grain prices. My childhood Confessions were always a bafflement as I did not understand what the aged, spidery, unilingual priest from the Old Country was saying to me, but he and I endured, his brocade stole laid carefully over my bowed head as I whispered my repentance for not having always obeyed *Mamo* and *Tato*. Every Sunday a tiny black-scarved crone, bent over at a right angle from her waist in permanent paralysis, kissed and stroked the icons laid on the altar in a routine of Old Country veneration. I would encounter her again in Russian novels.

I am told my paternal *baba* was a woman of great piety, although I have no memory of any particular instance of it, unless it were her remark that her one wish at the end of her life was to die when it was warm, for how were the poor gravediggers to dig her grave in the blasted heath that is the Canadian parkland in the winter? (She died one February.) My paternal grandfather died in the 1930s, before my parents were married, but I did come across, in the cigar box with the hinged lid that so fascinated me, a small black and white photograph of his funeral: it was taken outside the church in Vegreville, my father was one of the pallbearers, hatless though stout in his winter coat, my grandfather laid out in the open coffin, his hands crossed over his dark-suited chest, his face bearing a large moustache. Fortunately, Baba had borne a family of sons; she did not have to sell the family farm.

Is this what constituted our piety, a church for the rites of passage, the twelve dishes of Christmas Eve for the twelve Apostles, a bowl of crudely painted Easter eggs on the table for the Resurrection, and a prayer at the end of life not to be a burden to anyone, not even in one's coffin?

My maternal grandparents were something else altogether. What I know of their religious attitudes I know from my mother's familiar anecdotes, as well as from what I sensed in their home: they never went to church and hung no icons. Arguments between my father and my *dido*, my grandfather, were as often as not provoked by the brandishing of their respective newspapers, the *Ukrainian Voice* versus *Farm and Life*. Dido was not my biological grandfather—that man had died in his early thirties from pneumonia contracted from one walk too many on the long, dark, cold road home from the rending plant in east Edmonton. Dido was his younger brother, a bug-eyed, gristly bearded man in coveralls and long johns who spoke no English and who had married, as was expected, his brother's pregnant widow. She lost that child, but ever after it was Dido's bitter complaint that once more in life he had inherited another man's hand-me-downs, including my mother. As the story goes, he forced Baba, whose best subject in four years of school in Galicia had been religion, to give up her Bible, whereupon he placed it in the outhouse. For this was the same householder who spat invective against priests and hung large portraits of Lenin and Stalin in the front room.

He frightened me, this angry, unhappy, half-literate man who bore no relationship to the world I was growing up in. His alienation from it made me cringe.

Dido read magazines from Soviet Ukraine, the ones that Canadians made fun of, their ink-bleeding pages of photos of brawny "Russki" workers on collective farms in love not with buxom dairymaids but with their tractors, pride and joy of the Red October factory. I remember snickering at these smudgy photo-spreads myself, ruddy-cheeked collective farm workers beaming with pleasure, the women in battalions in the beet fields, brandishing hoes, while the men sat enthroned on the tractors. I had a vague awareness that

some Ukrainian-Canadians had acquitted themselves well in political protests during the Dirty Thirties and had even got themselves
killed for their efforts (although it would be years before I read the
whole story of Ukrainian-Canadian militancy in the Communist
Party of Canada), but the only story my pro-Communist grandfather
seemed to have is that he was scooped up accidentally by the police in
Edmonton who were breaking up a demonstration, and landed in Fort
Saskatchewan jail, terrified and humiliated and bewildered and eventually extricated and brought home by Baba, whose own emotions are
not accounted for.

This was the Left—or rather the Communism—routinely
denounced in the church as the ideology that had fuelled the revolution that had torn down the churches and monasteries of Soviet
Ukraine and killed their priests and nuns or sent them "to Siberia,"
had enslaved the Ukrainian people in a godless collectivity, without
hope or agency, and was now spreading its tentacles in the New
World.

The arguments failed to convince me, but I knew how to "interpret" the emotions and body language in which they were delivered:
short men in bad haircuts and carefully preserved suits, DPs in fact,
displaced persons who spoke English only under duress and with a
thick accent embarrassing to hear, who, I was told, had been citizens
of substance in pre-war western Ukraine (then still part of Poland),
educated professionals (or at least schoolteachers) now reduced in
Canada to work as school janitors. I would creep past them in my own
schools, casting a guilty glance into their little cubicles in the basement, where they sat among their mops and pails, as if we shared the
secret fact of their lost prestige.

My mother married into this world—"All that Orthodox clap-
trap and folderol," as she put it years later. Here's what she had still
to learn: how to address the priests and their wives, how to prepare
the home for the New Year's blessing by holy water, whether to
offer carollers tea or rye whisky, how to be useful in the Women's
Association. She would make thousands of *holubtsi* for weddings,
serve at the weddings, do the dishes: my sister and I would sit at
the long, white-clothed banquet tables in the National Hall, kicking

each other under the linen skirts as my mother scurried back and forth between tables and kitchen, her apron her badge of belonging, her hair damp from the steam coming from the cauldrons of water boiling for the *pyrohy*. When I thought about this later, I regretted that by leaving the *other* Hall (the Farm-Labour Temple), my mother had effectively deprived me of an interesting legacy. I could have had a parent who marched in May Day parades, belted out labour songs, and thrilled to speeches by Ukrainian-Canadian Communist militants, who memorized proletarian verses by Ukrainian poets and saluted the hammer-and-sickle flag and...whatever subversive or at least alternative culture was incubated away from the churches.

Instead, in the church basement, as we sat in our rows at the tables now cleared of the bowls of *holubtsi* and *pyrohy*, and the priest and his wife and the deacon sat at the head table facing us, up would stand this small, taut figure; this school janitor, beside the head table, in his lovingly pressed suit and in his own language, would become transformed into a tribune of a people. As a teenager, he had seen his home and family and neighbours engulfed by war, ground between two titanic armies, yet he had taken up his puny arms—a hunting rifle, a confession of faith, a suppressed anthem—and lost everything, only to land in our Ukrainian-Canadian midst, with me, scowling and fidgeting and yawning, complaining I was bored.

Edmonton 1960: One afternoon, I wandered out into the backyard where my father was seated in the lawn chair reading—I myself had been reading Aldous Huxley—and asked him point blank if there was a God. He took the pipe out of his mouth: "Is there a God? If there is, He's a principle of energy, of the eternal cycles of nature and of the cosmos..." There was more, I think—the "I Am" of God as a mathematical theorem. Was this an answer?

As a teenager, what had been pulling at my heartstrings were issues of what we now call social justice. I did not yet suspect that I might be called on to act in the world, but Lord, I believed.

I cheered Fidel Castro, I read George Orwell with deep conviction, Anne Frank's story crushed my heart, and Audrey Hepburn's self-sacrifice as a waifish nurse-nun alluring in her virginal vestments inspired the ideal of the unmarried childless life. Hungarian refugees, tossed up in my elementary school, haunted me with images of their desperate flight from Russian tanks in the cobblestoned streets of the Old Country behind the Iron Curtain, as did the display of United Nations' black and white photographs in the windows of the Hudson's Bay Company store on Jasper Avenue of the wretched camps of the Palestinians dispossessed of their land. Stories of tormented animals left me distraught, and I mourned the untimely deaths of the UN Secretary-General Dag Hammarskjold and American President John Kennedy with paroxysms of real grief. As soon as I was able to conceptualize the meaning of what had happened at Hiroshima, of Jim Crow laws in the southern United States, and of pass laws in South Africa, I knew that the world I wanted to live in was the world of impassioned reason, as represented by arguments, texts, and exposés, all in the service of righting wrongs by the power of language out and about in the world.

As a part-time hippy in the 1960s, in Seattle, San Francisco, Toronto, London, I lived among people who, home from the anti-war demonstration, sat in lotus position during solemn rituals of getting stoned. They seemed demonstrably more evolved than me, outside any particular Christian practices, so I became interested in the books they kept in their Afghan tote bags: Alan Watts's *Nature, Man and Woman*, Herman Hesse's *Siddhartha*, and the *I Ching*, around which we gathered to throw Chinese coins, over and over and over again, until we decoded something that made sense. Leonard Cohen's first album, the one with the image of St. Kateri Tekakwitha in flames, provided the soundtrack.

I am impressed now by how many more hours I devoted to the cryptic runes of an exotic Asian sage—"he who crosses the great water knows good fortune"—than I was ever prepared to give to the sages of my own tradition. St. John Chrysostom, St. John of the Golden Mouth, for instance, Bishop of Constantinople, who wrote in the fifth century: "When you discover the door of your heart, you discover the gate of heaven"—which I now have written on a Post-It note at my desk, as it seems immeasurably more helpful.

For a couple of months of Sundays, I made my way over to the Bethune Centre in Toronto to join a reading circle poring over the classics of Marxism-Leninism. To my own library I added the cheap paperbacks of New Left critiques of the world order, and Malcolm X, Regis Debray, and eventually Germaine Greer and Kate Millett from feminist reading groups. I had made my getaway from the Ukrainian-Canadian ghetto of my childhood and headlong into what could be called "modernity," the conviction that the enlightened mind is a capacious enough organ to enable me to live life as a good and just person, leavened by pleasurable sensation. It had nothing to do with what went on in churches, unless it were a "radical" church somewhere in the Third World or American South, or the places where the anti-war Catholics, such as the Berrigan brothers, Daniel and Philip, prayed. I knew nothing of the persecuted of the churches of Soviet Ukraine; it was her martyred intellectuals and artists who aroused me. History, not God, was keeping the accounts.

For Ukrainians to deny the Byzantine, the Greek, is to perform a kind of suicide, it's to pronounce oneself illegitimate, to humiliate oneself. To reject the "Greek" in one's name is to renounce one's own father and mother, it's to betray our entire history and one's nation!

—ILARION, Metropolitan of Canada, 1953

It is true that while I was growing up, the church my family attended was known as St. John's Ukrainian Greek Orthodox Church. But we did not for a moment confuse ourselves with *Greek* Greeks. For one thing, we couldn't understand their language (although much of our lofty liturgical and theological lexicon was a literal translation of the Greek) and for another the Orthodox Church among the Ukrainian-Canadians was a production site of intense ethnic, even national, Ukrainian pride.

But, outside the church, who were we, we Ukrainians of the Canadian prairie? Take the city of Saskatoon, Saskatchewan, for instance, where 180-some disgruntled adherents of the Greek Catholic and Russian Orthodox churches, not to mention disenchanted socialists and Presbyterians, met in the summer of 1918 to establish the Ukrainian Greek Orthodox Church of Canada, a momentous event widely seen as the rebirth of Ukrainian Orthodoxy outside its homeland on the free lands of Canada. Saskatoon's Holy Trinity Cathedral, located in what used to be a mainly East European working-class neighbourhood, now raises its coppery bulbous domes over the mainly Aboriginal so-called Core Neighbourhood: Goodbye Dnipro Café, Hello White Buffalo Youth Lodge. The church has a very good choir, well-executed Byzantine-style frescoes, and a youngish priest who grew up on a Manitoba farm and decided to join the priest-hood the day his boss on the oil rig in Alberta wouldn't let him go home for Ukrainian Easter. I learn this over coffee in the church hall, where a bulletin board announces Orthodox Youth Missions to Greece and volunteers are setting up the tables for tonight's community bingo game.

But Ukrainian-Canadians have become more complicated than this benign image would suggest. Formerly and officially deeply grateful to the institutions of Canada for inviting us in, giving us a break on homestead land, sending our kids to school, and assimilating us into Anglo-Canadian culture, and, in the nick of time, promulgating the *Multiculturalism Act*, we also became victims, that excruciating condi-tion of mixed shame and indignation—the shame and indignation of being among those interned as "enemy aliens" during the First World War, of the everyday epithets and gestures directed against us, Bohunks, and the stereotyping in the press as either Reds, Commies, pinkos, or nationalists, fascists, and anti-Semites. All of it reinforced our resentment that our historical traumas, rehearsed in ethnic rituals of communal remembrance, were somehow discreditable.

In a recent photo in a community newspaper, of dancers performing at a Ukrainian arts festival in Toronto, I see both "good" and "bad" Ukrainians. Good Ukrainians do not make anyone uncom-fortable: the six smiling young women in ravishing costumes of heavily embroidered red velvet, their lovely heads bearing wreaths and ribbons, project innocence, laughter, beauty, the idealized village maidens of universal folklore. The men's group of dancers typifies the "bad" Ukraine: eight youthful males in Cossack military dress (long blue tunics and ballooning red trousers) hoist rifles with the blue-and-yellow national flag unfurled on bayonets. We see heroic soldiers defending the people from their oppressors. The rest of the world sees rabid violence unleashed on the hapless "others"—Poles, Jews, Russians.

I have traced the palpable borders of Slavs' anxiety about whether they are truly Western, "inside Europe." "Here is where Europe ends," I've been told, in Zagreb, Belgrade, Prague, Warsaw, Lviv. "Over there," among their immediate neighbours to the east (Turks, Serbs, Bulgarians, Ukrainians, Russians, Tatars), it ends.

Ukrainians, for example, are not European-Europeans. They never had a Renaissance or Reformation or Industrial Revolution (as these were experienced in capital letters in the West). They lived mainly in small towns and villages. Jews, Russians, and Poles, and assimilated intelligentsia, were the Europeans in their cities. The notion that Ukrainian heritage is somehow *Eurocentric*, that dirty word of the culture wars of the late twentieth century, is misplaced: the centre of which Europe, exactly? The frontiers of Europe have been sensationally porous, letting in Huns, Mongols, Tatars, Pechenegs, Slavs, Ottoman Turks, and have shifted in slithery lines from Constantinople/Istanbul all the way west to Vienna and then way east to Moscow or way west to Moorish Spain. Turkish muezzins have sung from minarets in Bosnia. Turks rounded up Ukrainian peasants for the slave markets of Crimea. Tatars waved their sabres at the miraculous icon of Our Lady of Czestochowa.

I call this *Euroeccentricity*.

In the post-Soviet and post-Yugoslav wars of the 1990s, I found myself in profound identification with the resurfaced peoples of the East-of-West, but in a cringing sort of way. These were my near relations who stood within the West's gaze once more as denizens of exotic or sinister hinterlands: Balkan, Byzantine, Slavic, Cyrillic, Orthodox, Asian.

After centuries of disapproval if not outright contempt as Byzantines, Asiatics, and Communists, here they were again, spilling over into Western consciousness as the new barbarians at the gates. Fired up by "ancient ethnic hatred," they stormed from village to village; full of vodka and slivovic, they cleansed the ancestral lands of strangers; they drunkenly brandished mountaineers' rifles, aiming them at their neighbours across the fence, with the blessings of a scruffy Orthodox priest with soup stains on his cassock, and a fat wife.

FOR SOME YEARS NOW I have been reading topics in what I think of as "Where does Europe end?" Full of anticipation, I pick up a new book on interlibrary loan, which seems hardly to have been cracked open. It is *The Barbarian Conversion: From Paganism to Christianity*, by Richard Fletcher, of the University of York. He writes in the Preface: "The scope of the book is confined for the most part to western, Latin and Roman Christendom." Fletcher includes the western Slavs, Czechs, and Poles, for they appear in Latin texts. But, "the history of eastern, Greek or Orthodox Christendom is not my concern, let alone the history of those exotic Christian communities, Ethiopic, Indian and Nestorian, which lay beyond the eastern Mediterranean hinterland."

A scholar may write about whatever he chooses. But I am struck by the fact that this book, written in 1993, in that dismal decade of wars and social collapses featuring Europeans of Orthodox Christendom, even these sensational events in former Yugoslavia and in former Soviet Union a mere fifty years after the Second World War, could not drag the West's "hinterland" into scholarly view. My *Concise Oxford Dictionary* defines hinterland as "district behind coast or river's banks, freq. with suggestion of sparse population or inferior civilization."

There you have it: the cultural and spiritual zone to which the Ukrainian-Canadian Archbishop Ilarion exhorted me to swear my loyalty—my source in the Christian Empire of Byzantium—is outside the concern of the interpreters of our shared European space. Yet, after the fall of Rome in the fifth century, for the next thousand years, Byzantium *was* civilization: it radiated wealth, power, and splendour around the eastern Mediterranean world from its home in Constantinople.

In the West's sense of itself, the eastern Mediterranean is a parenthetical text, a bibliographical reference, an inferior culture at the borderland of the normal (that "let alone"). I read this now as a wound, an insult, an aggression against me. I startle myself. I did not know that I was taking it so personally.

In a review of *Pushing Time Away*, Peter Singer's memoir of his grandfather in Jewish Vienna, Jeremy Adler writes, "For a generation after the Second World War it was difficult to discuss one's German-Jewish origins or the Holocaust without embarrassment. Even children whose families had been murdered in the camps found it hard to speak about their loss....Today, by contrast, a scarred identity earns almost universal respect." If you're by descent a Jew or Armenian or Cambodian or Rwandan, perhaps. And if, like Singer, your European forebears lived in a city where "it was not difficult to earn an income sufficient for a comfortable apartment with a live-in maid." Such people left behind memorabilia—Singer found family papers and letters in his aunt's home in Melbourne. Where do you find the letters and family papers of Galician peasants who vanished, speechless, behind Soviet borders, or who tossed up equally speechless on the margins of Canadian enterprise?

On Sundays during my youth, I had stared at an icon that hung on the wall to the left of the sanctuary. It showed two people, a man and a woman in Slavic medieval dress and wearing crowns, with the letters of their names floating around their heads like a nimbus of Cyrillic calligraphy. Volodymyr and Ol'ha. The rest of the world knew them as Vladimir and Olga, and said they were Russian royalty, but inside that church we knew they were Ukrainians, and saints, our very own. The Greeks had Saints Constantine and Helen, emperor and mother, who lived at the very dawn of the established Christian church in Byzantium; we venerated those who came almost a thousand years later, from among the pagan Slavs.

Volodymyr and Ol'ha were regents of the people of Rus, ruling from the holy city of Kyiv on the Dnipro River in what is now modern Ukraine. Ol'ha was Volodymyr's mother. In 957 CE, she paid a state visit to Constantinople and was baptized a Christian by the Greek Patriarch himself. In 988, her son followed suit. Marriage had forced his hand. The Byzantine emperor, Basil II, although keen for a political alliance with Rus, would betroth his sister, Anna, to this barbarian chieftain only on condition that the bridegroom convert to Christianity. Anna *porphyrogennete*, she who was born into the purple, born in the porphyry-lined birthing-room of the great palace, walked solemnly out the gates of Constantinople accompanied by a retinue of priests and a loud and eloquent lamentation that she was being married to no better than an idol worshipper and slave trader.

Up to now, the people of Rus had been satisfied with a cosmology personified by forces—Hors, the sun god; Volos, god of cattle; Striboh, wind god; Dazhboh, god of abundance and fertility; and mightiest of all, capped with silver, Perun, god of thunder and lightning—whom they venerated and placated. With the ardour of the newly converted, Volodymyr ordered that the idols be overthrown. His people fell upon them with axes—they tilted woefully on the riverbank, awaiting their fate—and built a pyre of them and burnt them. Almighty Perun was tied to a horse's tail and dragged about the city, bashed pitilessly by citizens wielding sticks seeking vengeance on the Fiend who had chosen this attractive form—the silver cap, the golden moustache— in which to walk among them, before being tossed ignominiously into the river and disappearing over a waterfall.

My copy of Serge Zenkovsky's *Medieval Russia's Epics, Chronicles and Tales* has been in my library since 1967, a fat little paperback that cost $3.30. This is where I read for the first time the legendary account of how the barbarians of Rus became Orthodox Christians. It all began when Prince Volodymyr summoned elders and vassals to a council that advised him to dispatch ten wise men to visit the lands of the neighbours of Rus so that they might see with their own eyes how others worshipped. And that they return with a recom- mendation about which faith should become the new faith of Rus. And so it was done. "The Bulgarian," they reported, "bows, sits down, looks hither and thither like one possessed, and there is no happi- ness among them, instead only sorrow and a dreadful stench. Then we went among the Germans, and saw them performing many cere- monies in their temples, but we beheld no glory there. Then we went on to Greece [Constantinople], and the Greeks led us to the edifices where they worship their God, and we knew not whether we were in heaven or on earth."

Why wouldn't I have wanted to be someone else, say, at least, a Greek?

Decades later, I was dedicated to my work as a secular humanist in the arts, by which I mean I wrote magazine articles, books, lectures, and radio documentaries about topics dear to the heart of one who had come of age in the 1960s and 1970s—the social movements, the cultures of "resistance," the sense of a global generation. I wrote from within the heat of the women's liberation movement in Toronto and within the passionate creativity of what would be called "cultural nationalism," but which we knew briefly as the Canadian Liberation Movement. Yet I preserved alongside these the older verities of the American New Left (Tom Hayden's manifesto, *The Port Huron Statement*, with pages shrivelled from the steam in the bath), the anti-Vietnam War struggles (the manila folder with pamphlets from the University of Toronto's Teach-In), and all of Bob Dylan's albums.

In 1975 I returned to my roots, to Alberta, and to the small town of Two Hills northeast of Edmonton in the Ukrainian bloc settlement area. The idea was to research a book about my parents' generation of Ukrainian-Canadians, the first one born in Canada, by examining the lives of the people of Two Hills, of all descriptions. The book that resulted, *All of Baba's Children*, changed my life, re-routing me from Toronto, English Canada's power centre, to the western Canadian parkland, and to the community I acknowledged as my "people," the Ukrainian-Canadians. I was urged from all sides to write the "sequel," by which they meant a book about Ukraine herself. "When are you going to go back there?" they asked presumptuously, and I took note of that "back," when in fact neither I nor my parents had ever been to Ukraine.

But in the 1980s I did go "back," not once but twice, to Ukraine and also to other Slavic lands of Europe, Poland, Czechoslovakia, and Yugoslavia, several times, not only tracking identities of ethnicity but also those of history and politics. These were the lands of "actually existing socialism," and I thought it my obligation as a New Leftist of the West—and as the author of *Long Way From Home: The Story of the Sixties Generation in Canada*—to see how they were doing, especially the people of my generation, the "people" of 1968. Then I wrote

Bloodlines: A Journey into Eastern Europe, by which time my life had
been changed again.

On the one hand, I felt battered by what I learned of the
Communist project in the USSR and its satellite countries since the
Second World War (I finally read Alexander Solzhenitsyn's monumental *Gulag Archipelago* and several exposés of the Ukrainian
Famine); on the other, a whole other "cultural project" was coming
into my view, that of the complex and astonishing civilization, the
Byzantine, which showed itself to me mainly in the churches as I
roamed around southeastern and Eastern Europe, and which I gradually began to understand was the matrix of all that followed in the
region: religion, alphabet, statecraft, commonwealth.

In 293 CE, during the reign of Emperor Diocletian, arguably the
oldest border was drawn between Europe's "east" and "west" when
Diocletian divided the empire into two assignments and between
co-emperors, Gaul and Britain in the west, Syria, Palestine, Egypt in
the east. After the Christianization of the empire under Constantine
and his successors, and the designation of Constantinople as the
Imperial Capital (325 CE), and as more territories were added in the
"east," notably the Balkans, the border eventually became the frontier
between Eastern and Western Christianity, between the Cyrillic and
Latin alphabets, between Byzantium and the Holy Roman Empire. It
even became in part the frontier between Islam (the Ottoman Empire)
and Christianity and the iron gate of Europe's Cold War. Such was the
evolution of "Byzantium" in Europe.

Eventually, I would come upon Metropolitan Ilarion's words
from 1953, warning us Ukrainian-Canadians against the "suicide"
and humiliation and betrayal implicit in our forgetfulness of our
Byzantine origins. But for the moment, as the world turned on the
cusp of a new millennium, I was thinking neutrally about how to do
this: how to write a book about Byzantium as a literary and intellectual project. I knew that Byzantium lay behind all the other
stories I had told about "my" people—we would not have built those
onion-domed churches on the Canadian prairie if we had forgotten
everything—but I wanted to find my own way into that story. I was no
longer impelled by earlier, more immature, psychodramas about the

Ukrainian "cultural cringe," or so I thought. But I did not know where to begin.

"What kind of a name is Kostash?" I had once asked my father.

"Kostash," he told me, "is the Slavic version of the Greek name 'Constantine.'" I thought he was teasing me. Decades later, while travelling in Greece, I was constantly informed by Greeks that I was a Greek: "Kostas," they said, apparently unable to pronounce the *sh*, "is a Greek name; it's short for Konstantinos."

"I'm Greek," I said.

:: *Near Muenster, Saskatchewan, Summer 2000*

ST. PETER'S ABBEY shares borders with farms and ravines. The brothers grow vegetables and flowers, and their bees buzz around making honey for us all. The community was established in 1903 when Benedictine monks joined German Catholic homesteaders in the area. The homesteaders have moved on to the twenty-first century, but the brothers still live by the Rule of St. Benedict, which he wrote in 530 CE in his monastery of Monte Cassino:

> *Rule 20, Reverence at Prayer: ...We realize that we will be heard for our pure and sorrowful hearts, not for the numbers of our spoken words. Our prayer must be heartfelt and to the point. Only a divine inspiration should lengthen it.*

Every summer, writers gather here at a "colony," taking residence in the old convent house known as Scholastica (for St. Benedict's sister, a saint in her own right). We spend hours in silence in our rooms, writing or reading or day-dreaming; we meet at mealtimes. Some of us join the brothers when they are called to prayer from their tasks—checking the beehives, picking the potato crop, harrowing the summer fallow—and who hasten five times a day under the peals of the carillon to sing the Hours in their modern chapel through whose stained-glass windows the hot blaze of the July sun is filtered in streams of blue and rose.

One afternoon, feeling restless and yet enervated by the heat in my room, I wander over to the monastery library. The long yellow blinds on the tall windows are drawn against the sun, and the whirring rotations of the large fans in the corners create a small breeze around the reading tables. I have the place to myself. I decide to look at picture books, the big art books ranged on the lower shelves of several stacks.

For Catholics, they have quite a few books about the art of the Eastern Church, including diverse volumes about icons. I heave these onto the table—they are oversize and printed luxuriously—and open them indiscriminately. It's been some time since I was impressed by the fact that images that once had been wholly "privatized" within the church of my childhood had become objects of serious scholarship and aesthetic appreciation, not to mention worth lots of money. These books show icons in all the great museums of the world, in private collections, and in certain churches. There are icons held in all the monasteries of the Orthodox world, including those sequestered in the monasteries at Mount Athos, the Holy Mountain in northern Greece, locked away from the dreaded female gaze. They are "interesting" icons and "deserving of notice," according to the picture books I consult, and I can stare at them as long as I want.

There are Rules, of unknown origin, for the icon painter quoted in *An Iconographer's Patternbook: The Stroganov Tradition*:

1. *Before starting work, make the sign of the cross. Pray in silence and pardon your enemies.*
2. *Work with care on every detail of your ikon, as if you were working in front of the Lord Himself.*
3. *During work, pray in order to strengthen yourself physically and spiritually; avoid above all useless words, and keep silence.*
4. *Pray in particular to the saint whose face you are painting. Keep your mind from distractions, and the Saint will be close to you.*
5. *When you have to choose a colour, stretch out your hands interiorly to the Lord and ask his counsel.*

From my time among the Benedictines, I recognize that these contemplative, solitary acts are not art-making but a form of spiritual discipline. But what of the (apparent) Eastern rule that all the saints, angels, and Holy Trinity must be posed only frontally, stiff, hieratic, courtly, like this solemn and magisterial procession in mosaic of Justinian and Theodora and their solemn retinues across the walls of the church, reproduced in one art book after another, and which I had once strained to see in the dim light of San Vitale in Ravenna? And never in profile?

It dawns on me that I am looking not at representations of persons or even personalities as at their *spiritualized* self; the flesh—muscle and sinew, rapture and agony—have been burned away, and they are now transfixed on Paradise, or on someone or something just behind me—whose elements have been laid down in the dim past by Byzantine monks. They are passionless (*apatheia* in Greek), having achieved the purity and freedom of detachment from all vice and polluted thought, yet, through their iconographic images, they haunt us still. In his ardent—and very lengthy—polemic in favour of icons in the early eighth century, St. John of Damascus wrote: "The saints in their lifetime were filled with the Holy Spirit, and when they are no more, [God's] grace abides with their spirits and with their bodies in their tombs, and also with their likenesses and holy images, not by nature, but by grace and divine power." Iconographic subjects are not even supposed to be "natural."

I pause at one picture, then another, recognizing some figures from the Orthodox churches I have been in—the Archangels, the Mother of God—and from art books—St. George and the Dragon, the Annunciation, the ethereal Holy Trinity of Andrei Rublev—and also at figures of shaggy prophets (Elijah, St. John the Baptist) and of the unfamiliar portraits of the so-called Church Fathers (Basil, Gregory) with their patriarchal beards and robes. And then, among this gallery of the sanctified, as I turn over the thick and glossy page, one face stops me.

His eyes overwhelm his small face. His nose is long and elegant. He is young and beardless, almost pretty-faced, with thick hair tucked behind his ears. He wears a green tunic and red cloak and holds a round shield and long-armed cross. Is this a soldier? A Martyr? St. Demetrius, the caption reads, the Myrrhbearer and Great Martyr of Thessalonica. He has died young, defenceless, not bristling with armour but bearing a circle of a shield that I do not read as a military sign but as a kind of wheel of life. Was he crucified on that long-armed cross? What torments was he subjected to before he rose to Paradise? He bears no pain on his face. I stare into it, the face of a man "who is what he ought to be," in the lovely phrase of Constantine Cavarnos. Demetrius gazes fixedly back at me with a wide-open, unjudging eye, his self-mastery complete. The nimbus of a halo in gold-leaf—iconographer's gold is the highest form of light—crowns his lovely head.

O my doomed darling.

Who is he? I leave the table to go back to the book stacks and look among the collection of Saints' Lives, hoping for one that includes saints of the Eastern Church. The Benedictines do not let me down: I find the *Book of Saints* as compiled by the Benedictine monks of St. Augustine's Abbey, Ramsgate, 1939, and return to the table to read. *St. Demetrius: Born and educated at Thessalonica where he exercised the profession of Rhetor or Public Speaker, he made many converts to Christianity. Some say that he became a high Officer of State and even a Proconsul, but this is hardly probable. Arrested as a Christian and brought before Diocletian's colleague, Galerius Maximianus, he appears to have been stabbed to death without the formality attending a legal execution. This was in one of the first years of the fourth century. His relics are in great veneration in the East.*

Diocletian. Roman emperor. Persecutions of....Back to the book shelves. Other compilations of Orthodox saints and Feasts mention that Maximian a.k.a. Galerius was fond of gladiatorial games and, among the wrestlers, championed a brute of a barbarian called Lyaeus. Never having been defeated in the ring, Lyaeus boasted of the height and strength of his body, and challenged the youths of Thessalonica to a contest with him. At this point Demetrius was already languishing in the bath house, preparing for death. But his friend, the hothead Nestor, decided to accept the barbarian's challenge. He visited Demetrius in his cell and asked for his blessing. Then sealing himself with the sign of the Cross, Nestor entered the stadium and cried out before Maximian Galerius, "O God of Demetrius, help me!" and threw himself upon Lyaeus. He "smote him with a mortal blow to the heart," leaving the barbarian lifeless upon the earth. Furious, Maximian avenged himself on Demetrius, whose God had felled Lyaeus: he sent his soldiers, clattering with armour and iron, straightaway to murder Demetrius.

Demetrius of Thessalonica was martyred in 304 for the crime of preaching the Gospel of Jesus Christ, speared through the right breast in the basement of the Roman baths, and hastily buried in the red earth where he fell. Eventually, the little shrine marking the spot fell into ruin, but his cult lived on.

His icon has been painted ("written") by Greeks, Russians and Serbs, Romanians and Bulgarians, full-length and clothed in bejew-elled drapery, or just showing his haloed head and armoured shoulders. Sometimes he is accompanied by his virtual twin, St. George, both of them in full regalia as Roman soldiers, each with a crown floating over his head. Or he is mounted on a red horse, a spear in full deploy, casually pinning another soldier to the ground. In a 1990 calendar, *The Feasts of Rus*, I even find him hundreds of miles north of Moscow on an icon from sixteenth-century Vologda, a mere sketch of a warrior piercing a diminutive figure caught beneath his horse's hoofs, the companion image, so to speak, of St. George's contest with the Dragon. This "episode" recalls for us, says the commentary, "the miraculous liberation of Thessalonica from the barbarians [but] also the incessant struggle of self-denial which has to be fought in a man's heart and of which God is the eyewitness."

Barbarians. Liberation. A miracle....Yet Demetrius's relics disappeared and, after a time, the details of his life and death vanished from living memory. But from the early seventh century comes the reminder that war-torn Thessalonica, suffering an inunda-tion of barbarians—who suddenly at the end of the sixth century had arrived from beyond the Danube—came under the protection of their Patron Saint.

The invaders didn't stop until they got all the way through to the Peloponnese. But there was one prize they never did take, though they tried over and over again, assaulting its walls and gates to no avail:

the city of Thessalonica, second only to Constantinople, the jewel on the northern Aegean, fabulously wealthy and infinitely desirable.

The city was impregnable, for the barbarians had no weapon against a miracle.

Dead these three hundred years, vanished in historical dust, the Great Martyr Demetrius reappeared as the Holy Warrior, riding his red horse on the ramparts of the beleaguered city, and confronted the howling hordes beneath. Then he performed the miracle of the defence of the city, and saved it for Greece. The barbarians were repulsed.

Thrilled by this exciting account about which I have hitherto known precisely nothing, I begin to look more closely at the reproductions of his icons in the big folios: his slender figure astride a red horse, his green cloak billowing in a heavenly breeze, he is posed triumphantly on the battlements of Thessalonica while the squat figures of the bedevilled barbarians mill about uselessly at the gates and bury their dead. I look and read more closely still: the barbarians are Slavs.

Demetrius has protected Thessalonians for 1,600 years with the power of his miracles—nothing less than the eternal defence of the city from those who have come pouring down into the Balkans—the barbarians, which is to say the Slavs, which is to say me.

At supper, a new guestmaster, smooth-faced and smiling, a little stooped in his brown cassock, introduces himself to us: his name is Father Demetrius. I take this as a sign and ask to meet with him. In his office, where he sits among icons and family photographs, I ask him: "Who is Saint Demetrius a saint *for*? Slavs or Greeks?" In *history*, I continue while Fr. Demetrius rests his head on his hand, "Demetrius is a Thessalonian who ravaged Slavic barbarians; but Demetrius is also an Orthodox *saint*; how am I supposed to deal with this 'fact'?"

Fr. Demetrius is from rural Saskatchewan, born into a Ukrainian Catholic family, now a Roman Catholic priest with this new name, Demetrius. He leans back in his desk chair, looking more mild than scholarly in his wire-rimmed glasses, and assures me that the "Great Suffering Martyr" is venerated by Ukrainian Catholics and Orthodox alike. Still I ask, "How can Demetrius be a saint for the Greeks *and* Slavs?" He looks perplexed at me, pauses, then says that this has nothing to do with anyone's ethnicity, least of all Demetrius's own. "Whether Demetrius is a saint 'of' the Greeks or Serbs or Ukrainians... I've never looked at him that way. He's one of our own holy people."

Fr. Demetrius, I sense, just isn't "getting" it. I press on, about his namesake—What does he think is the story of his life and martyrdom? Does he think there is a connection with the cult of the coincidentally named Demeter? What does it mean that St. Demetrius rides a red horse?—but he seems genuinely uninterested in these questions, hearing me out but not rising to the bait. "Look," he summarizes, "Demetrius is the monastic name given me by Abbot Jerome from three names I gave him to choose from. Dmytro was a favourite uncle of mine. Demetrius is my Patron Saint—a model, a Great Suffering Martyr for the faith—and it doesn't matter who he was historically.

"I've seen people become obsessive about a saint and I've seen the saint who is obsessive about a person. There have been the sudden enthusiasms about St. Hildegarde and St. John of the Cross, for instance. By the way, the Biblical Demetrius was a silversmith—read Acts 19:23-28. He was in the business of making silver statuettes of the goddess Diana in Ephesus. St. Paul was in the area, making converts and putting Demetrius out of business. Then he went to Thessalonica.

"Keep me posted."

REMEMBER THE SABBATH, *to keep it holy.* I shyly join the brothers in the singing of Lauds, Week 2. They sing canticles, hymns, and psalms in a tuneless drone, except for the golden baritone of Br. Kurt, and read the Gospel from a very plain translation, while a single big fat white candle burns at the lectern. Their stripped-down chapel bears not a single votive image except for a wooden sculpture of a dark Madonna and child carved and painted and standing in a back corner. They are very plain, this diminishing community, the brothers in their dark brown cassocks, who face each other across the aisle, and sing their simple responses with understated conviction. But it makes me happy to be with them, to sing under their responses, and to sit in the light streaming through the blue glass quadrangles of the window. Outside lies the land I love, prairie parkland—this plantation of gaunt trembling aspen whose shaking causes the wind to move—at the time of the last of the roses, the first of their hips, the swellings on the saskatoon bushes, the crows cawing from the ploughed fields at the boundary.

The men are singing. "O God, come to my aid. O Lord, make haste to help me. Glory be to the Father and to the Son and to the Holy Spirit, as it was in the beginning, is now, and ever shall be, world without end. Amen. Alleluia." *Amen.* I look it up in the dictionary. *From the Hebrew.* "*So be it.*"

⸭ *Hiking for Demetrius*

:: **Crete**

I SIT IN THE QUIET LITTLE BAR of the Kriti Hotel in Chania, sip-
ping ouzo. This is as good a place as any to start looking for Demetrius:
I've already noticed a couple of streets named for him, and, in the
numerous shop windows displaying the bric-a-brac of the Orthodox
faith, notably stacks of cheap icons in several sizes, I have seen that
St. Demetrius is always among the saints depicted, although his is not
as popular a figure as the Mother of God.

Behind me a worker is painting "impressions of Knossos" on
panels in the hotel lobby, tuned into Harry Belafonte on his port-
able radio. The Cretans were once Byzantines, sixteen hundred years
ago, and some of their towns and villages, Lissos, Souya, Anopoli,
Leutro, Hora Sfakion, Kantanos, are even earlier sites of ecclesiastical
and archaeological treasures from the spread of Christianity when,
it is believed, although there are scant historical sources for it, that
Apostle Paul appointed his disciple Titus as Crete's first Bishop.

The old town of Chania was built over the ruins of Early Christian
Cydonia. This much I learn at the Byzantine Museum into which
I slip on a somnolent Sunday. There are bits and pieces of frescoes
rescued from disintegrating churches, and on one panel I can make
out two military figures in chain mail vests, blue cloaks clipped at

the throat. St. Theodore, holding a spear in his right hand, is the better preserved; all that is visible of St. Demetrius is his bare head, his brown hair curling at the neck, framed by the golden halo of his distinction. His facial features have been scraped away except for the outline of his beardless chin, but his small, well-formed ears are intact. The ears must be there, or at least the earlobe, because it is the ears that hear our prayers and take them to Heaven.

Two days later, in Paleochora, I decide I want to see the church from which this fresco was taken, the church of St. George near Kantanos, up the road from Paleochora. The only travel agent in business this late in the season—it's November—is posting the exchange rates on a kind of tablet between lazy puffs on a cigarette, as though she has nothing better to do, when I walk in. "You need a guide," she says. "Come back in May." May? Who knows where I'll be in May? I loiter in the little office, examining brochures. Then she has an idea and sends me down the street to the "photo shop" where the shopkeeper is selling a book, "a very big book," all about the "monuments" in the area. Twenty minutes later I am the triumphant owner of an outsize and richly illustrated tome, a project of a historical preservation society in Kantanos to describe the twenty-three surviving Byzantine churches of the area.

It has cost me a small fortune, but now it is in my backpack as I ride the bus to Floria and the church of St. George.

I can see the church, blazingly white, in the dun fields. I can hear the yapping of the village curs behind me while I have stopped in the field to read from the big book: "A big battle with the German Nazi took place in Floria on 23-5-1941, and also in the area of Anavos, adjacent to Floria, when a track [*truck?*] convoy of German Nazi was destroyed by the men of the resistance of the area." Of the church of St. George, painted in 1497, it says that "the wall paintings are in almost good shape."

I walk into the church, a very small, single-vaulted room with iconostasis, lectern, a cross-stitched icon of St. George ("a gift of Dimitra Lionaki, this year"), candle stands. The glory of this little space are the frescoes, much-abused though they are, cemented over in spots, gouged and pitted and scoured by time or design, with here and there the ochre of a cape, a horse's flank, the gold of a crown and halo, the piercing gaze, all that is left of a prophet, the soft mouth and moustache, all that is left of a king, showing through the ravages. If St. Demetrius hadn't been removed to the museum in Chania, he may have looked like this.

I walk back to the main road and on to Kantanos where, in another whitewashed vault, I do see him, in a cheap knock-off "European" painting leaning against the iconostasis; I am practically on my knees to view it. His warrior aspect is favoured here—Demetrius spearing a bearded soldier with bared chest who, arm raised in supplication, is half-reclining, his well-formed leg turned in a dainty boot.

I turn back toward Floria and almost walk by the little, crudely lettered sign tilted on a fence gate indicating "this way to the Archangel." Allured, I creep down a stony path, ducking under the netting strung out to catch the ripening olives, and into the pristine, whitewashed courtyard of St. Michael's. From the radiant whiteness of the outside world I step across the stone threshold and into the cool shadow of the world of the Liturgy. The local worshippers have been and gone—I smell the dissipating wafts of incense even as I open the door—and the interior is as clean as the parish ladies can make it. Fading chrysanthemums in glass jars stand on fresh newspaper lining the window sill, a newly ironed, pure white cloth richly embroidered with the Byzantine motif of the double-headed eagle drapes the altar. (Ah, but they missed the little bit of cobweb dangling in a corner of the window.)

Even though the walls are heavy with the darkened pigment of the Middle Ages, all is lightness here, as if the Angel had found the cele-bration so much to his liking in this modest church among the farms that he decided to stay awhile.

I can make out the frescoed figures easily. Although my poor Demetrius has his face half gouged out of the plaster and thrown away, his shoulders still bear an exhilarating amount of drapery blowing in the breath of the wind. I sit on a creaky, rush-bottomed chair and pull out the big book. "...in this period (13th–16th centuries), these small churches are created that resemble warm thanksgiving prayers and supplication in the villages, in the olive groves, in the ravines and the desolate areas." These little chapels and sanctuaries are modest, the images of the saints are but a ruin of what they once were, but the gods are not dead so long as there remains a villager to come by and refill the votive lamps before the icons.

I rest in profound silence except for the occasional faraway bleat of sheep and goats that reaches me from behind the splutter of beeswax tapers that are always laid out in these chapels. Outside, the wild geraniums bloom in the soft breeze lifting up from the valley. I feel peaceful to the point of stupefaction.

:: *Temenia*

FROM ELENA, the forbearing travel agent, who has been inspired to do a bit of freelance research of her own, I learn of a Demetrius church in another direction altogether. I will need a driver. This turns out to be young Yiorgo from a taxicab stand, and so the very next day off we go, he of the little spoken English and I of the less Greek, with a bottle of water and bag of pistachio nuts on the seat between us. It is a big car, heavy on the road and uncomplaining of the rocky surfaces. I have Elena's annotated map in my hand, showing us where to look for the church. "In the olive grove at the end of the road."

We fail utterly to find it, there in the valley between Moni and Livada. Yiorgo is sure he knows exactly where it is, if not here in this well-kept, shaded grove, then surely at the end of that rocky pathway. We walk around peering through branches, squatting for another perspective, standing on boulders to see farther. No telltale flash of white church plaster to be seen. And yet, when we climb up from the river bottom to the very apex of the neighbouring mountain, we see several splotches of white down in the valley from which we have just ascended.

The drive has taken us high up to an elevation alongside the massif of the White Mountains of the Cretan interior. We make our way over the stony roads that link the villages, winding around moun-tainsides of boulders. Bits of precious earth, ground up between the rocks, clutch the exhausted roots of spiny bushes and dying trees.

Then down we go, hurtling seaward—it glints metallically from every direction—until we hit hardtop again.

In Platanes, a miserable little village, hot and settled under dust, tilted every which way on the stony earth, we do find a church of St. Demetrius, an oasis of shadowy coolness in which I peer around, scribbling notes, aware of Yiorgo patiently lounging outside. "I'm Orthodox," I'd explained as I'd got out of the car, waving my notebook, as though to reassure him this dogged itinerary was not a psychodrama but a cultural obligation.

A painted icon secured onto the iconostasis shows St. Demetrius youthful in splendid military attire, blissfully spearing another soldier. I ask Yiorgo to come in and have a look. "Who is this?" I ask, pointing to the recumbent soldier who seems to have tumbled onto his shield. Yiorgo looks, and pronounces him an enemy, the "same" as St. Demetrius but who has refused to be Orthodox. I don't have enough of his language to be able to pursue this. Similarly, small prints lined up in frames along the iconostasis railing show the same killing taking place, over and over, but now the victim looks more barbarian, wearing long hair, a beard, and a deep frown. Not the "same" as Demetrius at all. Maybe a Goth, a Hun? The interior frescoes are all deeply pitted. "The Turks," explains Yiorgo.

In Agia Irini there are no frescoes—perhaps it is a modern church, or one deserted by its plasterers—but there is a framed painting on the icon screen to the right of the central Holy Doors: Demetrius, wearing a golden breastplate and flaring green cape, sits astride a pretty brown horse and serenely spears what looks like a Cretan with his handlebar moustaches, his arm bent back holding a useless scimitar, blood already pouring out of his throat. Where is the sweet, meek, and mild Martyr who bares his own breast to the sword?

As we climb into the town of Temenia, coming the other way in a battered green car is the priest of the elusive St. Demetrius church of Moni himself, Fr. Panayiotis. We stop in the middle of the road so that he and Yiorgo can have a chat, hanging out the car windows, while traffic piles up behind us. Yiorgo explains that we have not found his church but that this Canadian in the car is hoping to speak with him about it—I push my face forward over Yiorgo's shoulder so Fr.

Panayiotis can see for himself that I am in earnest—and it is decided to pull off the road and convene in the nearest café, a charmless establishment of unpainted cement floors and a scattering of chairs lined up against the peeling walls. A young man sits at a window, watching us with bemusement; another arrives to pick up his newspaper and winks at us.

But I cannot prevail on Fr. Panayiotis to sit with Yiorgo and me at our table. He has leaned up definitively against the opposite wall, tilted back in the chair, as though to be at the farthest possible reach from us. He wears baggy soldier's pants and army boots under his worn-out dark blue cassock, his hands are stubby and callused, and, chubby-cheeked under his beard, he looks no more than thirty years old.

I have enlisted Yiorgo as co-interviewer and supplied him with the basic questions I have managed in my pidgin Greek. *Who was St. Demetrius? How do you celebrate St. Demetrius's Feast Day around here?* He's scribbled them out for himself on a small piece of paper that he grips with a kind of terror. Fr. Panayiotis's thick hands chop the air around him as he speaks, rapidly, loudly, non-stop.

I sit, oblivious, catching only a word or two here and there, among them "Dimitrios" and "Thessaloniki." This is what he is saying (from Elena's translation of Yiorgo's report): "St. Demetrius was in the Roman army in Thessalonica, but refused to collaborate with the Romans in their killing of the Christians. So he and the Romans struggled with each other. He was very young when he was brought to trial and executed. He was tortured, which is why he is a Martyr. He died for his beliefs. That is why Thessalonica has him as their protector. In their times of trouble, the people saw the Saint as a horseman. That's all I know. If you want to know more—how he lived, where he grew up and studied—you have to do research.

"The reason the people go to the church is that they believe, not just to please their parents or the priest or their neighbours. They go for the Saint. They have a conscience. On an average Sunday, fifteen or twenty come. Aren't I lucky, happy, if in a village where there are fifty people, twenty people come?" They come for the Saint. Sweet Martyr Demetrius, Miracle-worker, Myrrh-gusher, whose bones in

Thessalonica, they say, exude an aromatic oil that has healed the sick and dying, body and soul.

Later in the afternoon, when Yiorgo and I drive back through Temenia, we see him again, Fr. Panayiotis Androukalis, priest of Livada, Souya, Kostogeraki, and Moni, cutting up wood with a chainsaw by the side of the road, tossing logs around like bowling pins.

:: *Thessalonica*

Salonica is [the sound of] an argument over a bill of lading, a Ladino greeting
outside a synagogue.

—PATRICK LEIGH FERMOR, 1966

THESSALONICA'S FOUNDATION lies in legend, the place where
the Persian king Xerxes put ashore in the summer of 480 BCE while
his fleet cruised the gulf on the way to ignominious rout at the Battle
of Salamis, and named by King Cassander for his wife, a stepsister
of Alexander the Great. In 279 BCE, a band of Celtic invaders was
crushed outside its walls, only the first in a very long series of (non-
Greek, non-Roman, pagan) barbarians mounting hopeful but doomed
assaults against this queen of Greek cities who withstood them all
until 168 BCE, when, like the rest of the known world, she succumbed
to Roman power. But she flourished, wheeling and dealing in Balkan
trade and traffic: even now, if I felt like it, I could go shopping for
shoes on the Via Egnatia, named for that highway scraped out of rock
between Dyrrhachium (modern Durres in Albania) and
Constantinople.

In April 1995, I sat on a narrow balcony under a struggling vine
resting my swollen feet. I had hoofed it everywhere, along a zigzag of

the small streets that run downhill from the old Turkish Upper Town to the university, the churches, the Roman ruins, the British Council reading room, and to the parks, some of them full of Albanian men in black vinyl jackets and baggy pants sitting on their haunches and talking sombrely.

I went for supper at the neighbourhood taverna where I alternated between the *souvlaki* and the *soutzoukakia*, not having figured out the rest of the menu. This was a rather shabby neighbourhood right under the six-towered Byzantine walls. Shabby, but not squalid, as nineteenth-century reports had it, when "shadows of minarets lay across potholed streets littered with dung and dimly-lit cafés echoed with the screeches of pig-tailed Jewesses weaving through groups of soldiers bristling with sabres, daggers and pistols..." Mustafa Kemal, who would be Kemal Ataturk, Father of modern Turkey, was born on its fringes.

In the cataclysm of nation-building that followed the break-up of the Ottoman Empire, the Greeks would demolish all the minarets. The Greek Orthodox Church and Hellenism became indisputably dominant on these once-shared lands, but I wondered if, now that the past was irreversible, there were nevertheless Thessalonians who regretted the paucity of souvenirs of the Turkish "occupation" (almost five hundred years!): the roofed marketplace that once sheltered drapers' and jewellers' shops, the *dzamis* or mosques built in the fifteenth century with their tiled surfaces and spiralled minarets, the *hamams* or bathhouses, the fountains, the tombs. The ramshackle houses of the Upper Town are actually the remnants of domestic architecture, these stout, two- and three-storied, dormered wooden homes that squat bulkily in the narrow cobbled streets and cul-de-sacs, their bay windows and enclosed balconies typical Byzantine flourishes.

With the conquest of Thessalonica by the Ottoman Turks in 1430, Christian churches, desperately needed for Muslim worship, had been seized and turned into mosques, their icons and frescoes whitewashed or painted over, minarets raised in place of bell towers. At first, the Basilica of St. Demetrius, the city's pride and joy, the main church, the tomb and dwelling-place of its Patron Saint, the Great Martyr and Myrrh-gusher, had been spared. When he first entered the Basilica, the city's conqueror, Sultan Murad II, sacrificed a ram with his own hands and then prayed, and decreed that it should remain a Christian sanctuary, which it was, until 1493, when it became a mosque under the name of Kasimye. Until it disappeared in the great conflagration of 1917, a marble slab told the tale at the entrance of the church: *A dwelling I have put back in service, a good work for God, the Lord of the Worlds, Sultan Bayazid Khan, a creation for the benefit of the Moslems.* The Muslim masses believed Kasimye was identical with Demetrius.

When the Spaniards took Moorish Grenada in 1492, tens of thousands of Arabs and Jews flooded into Ottoman territories, including Thessalonica, and inserted themselves into the layers of Greeks and Turks and Slavs: by the seventeenth century, the city comprised forty-eight Muslim districts, fifty-six Jewish, and sixteen Christian (including Greeks and Armenians), stacked up as though tiered on rising elevations from the sea coast to sloping hills to the massive Byzantine fortifications fitfully defending it. Greeks wore blue turbans, Jews wore yellow, and Turks white. Crowded among the thirty-six large synagogues, forty-eight mosques, and thirty churches were the *medrese* (religious schools), dervish monasteries, baths, caravanserais, fountains, kitchens feeding the poor, the markets and gardens. Inhaling the air delicious with perfumes, aromatic fruits, halvas, and sherbets, the seventeenth-century Turkish travel writer Evliya Celebi swooned: "Whosoever enters this house of commerce is literally dazed and confused by the smell of nutmeg, ginger and other burning spices."

Inside the city limits the prevailing spoken language was Hebrew-Spanish (Ladino); outside the walls in the villages, Slavonic. The city's bootblacks babbled in half a dozen languages, printing presses brought in by Jewish merchants were made to clatter away in any language but Turkish or Arabic, although by the nineteenth-century visitors reported that the privilege of owning a printing press, though accorded to a rabbi, was denied to the Greeks and Bulgarians.

More than half the male population was enrolled in some janissary regiment—elite corps of slave soldiers bound to the sultan's service, gathered or scooped up (*devshirme*, the gathering) by levies from among non-Muslim youth. Its population was periodically cut in half by devastating contagions of plague that reached the energetic Thessalonians along the disease routes from the Middle East. Those who could leave the stricken city, did—pashas, beys, and the wealthy—while the poor were condemned to stay behind. "The only prey of the epidemic left are the poor most of whom are dying," in the observation of an appalled and grieving consul of Venice. But eventually the toxins dissipated, the survivors crept out of their cellars or sauntered back from their villas in the Macedonian hills, the sprawling Ottoman markets reopened, and the gorgeous wares of the Mediterranean hinterland, of Turkey and northern Africa, were displayed once again to the discerning eye of the wealthy, sophisticated, much-travelled, and polyglot urban elites—Salonica cotton; Nile linen; brocades from Bursa in Turkey; woollens coarse and fine from Plovdiv, Bulgaria; and perfumes, soaps, and drugs from the fields and meadows of the Levant.

Christians, however, were forbidden to ride horses or carry arms; they could not build their houses higher than those of their Turkish neighbours nor ring their church bells without official permission. And only Muslims could wear yellow shoes.

That mainstay of worldly British pluckiness, the Victorian traveller, saw it all. Misses Muir Mackenzie and Irby, on a philanthropic trip to the "Slavonic provinces of Turkey-in-Europe" (as they named their book published in 1877), were charmed by Salonica in 1863, which they approached by steamer. They did not much mind the filth of the streets exceeding even that of "the wallowing-ground of swine," for the Turks had the genius to multiply spires "to atone for roofs and whenever they build a house they plant a tree....After a time one consents that nose and feet should suffer offence; if only, when the labours of the day are over, one may recline on the cool, flat house-roof, and feast one's eyes on masses of white and green, pierced by taper cypresses and glistening minarets." They spent two profitable days sightseeing the "antiquities," a Roman arch and remnants of the hippodrome, the Byzantine church-mosques, the "coloured marbles and sculptured stones" of successive eras of artistry, though "all that is of the pagan period has been byzantinized, and all that was Byzantine has been mahommedanized." They are particularly offended by the "mahommedanization" of the Basilica of St. Demetrius: "The nave is supported by columns of precious marble; but these the Turk has painted green, and their capitals strawberry and cream colour. Icons and candles he has banished, and in their stead strings up ostrich eggs to ward off the evil eye.... The altar has been hurled from its site....A little side chapel is purged of its idolatries, and crammed with old mats, rubbish and tools."

Even so, the site felt powerful. Hosts of pilgrims still came to the shrine, attracted by the healing powers of its "miraculous exudations" in the crypt, and Christian visitors gratefully received portions of the earth gathered from Demetrius's tomb. A Methodist missionary visiting in the 1850s, Rev. J. Henry House, wrote a little guided tour of the city for the pious traveller, drawing attention to the Mosque of St. Demetrius (Kasimye), "who is more reverenced today in Salonica than Paul himself." Apostle Paul: letter-writer to the Thessalonians, those former idol-worshippers and now early witnesses and martyrs to the fledgling Christian Church in the Roman Empire. House recalled for his readers the tradition that the mosque formerly known as the Basilica of St. Demetrius was built near the site of the synagogue where Paul had preached.

In the 1930s, H.V. Morton (following Paul's itinerary described in the Acts of the Apostles in the New Testament), found only the most remnant memorabilia: a street called St. Paul's that leads to the Old Town under the walls not far from the complex of the monastery of Vlatadon, which seemed to have "some connection" with the apostle's visit; and the monastery's chapel dedicated to Apostles Peter and Paul, with its cypress-bounded garden. "There is a tradition," Morton goes on, "that when St. Paul came from Philippi to Thessalonica, he visited a house in this part of the old city and knelt in the courtyard to pray." A dark, circular, marble stone marked the spot. When Paul, chased out of the city by his enemies, was forced to spend the night beyond the walls, a stream of holy water sprang forth from his torrent of tears.

Toward the closing of the Ottoman era, in the early twentieth century, travellers reported a waning city, almost asleep within its walled and perfumed gardens, behind its green shutters under red-tiled roofs, shut against the mid-afternoon heat. A Greek woman from Constantinople arrived on a summer afternoon in 1910, down from the invigorating Balkan ranges of Serbia into an enervating "laziness," a city drowsy with the miasma of sleepiness hanging over it. John Foster Fraser, an Australian adventurer who had already bolted across Siberia, Argentina, and western Canada, slowed down in Thessalonica on an afternoon's yachting excursion in 1905 and found the view to the city across the bay from his sailboat, if he limited it to the seaside hotels and boulevards, "entrancing." Back of the boulevards, however, he was trapped in Turkish Salonica, crammed into narrow streets, "gloomy and Oriental and smelly—the more Oriental, the more smelly." Fraser then goes to lunch in a Greek restaurant. He complains about this too, setting the tone for the next several waves of Western travel writer who ventures beyond the eastern approaches to Vienna: "I should have liked [the Greeks] very much if I had not had the misfortune to see so many of them eat. Their table manners were atrocious; they made noises over their soup; they messed the food; they held their fingers and forks pointed star wards; and they shovelled vegetables with their knives. The more I travel the more I am convinced that the manners of England are the best."

The cosmopolitan world of languages, races, creeds in the city, of Greeks and Slavs co-existing in villages, and of merchants and traders criss-crossing the whole Ottoman world, all this was now found to be an "uncouth Tower of Babel." British journalist John Booth in 1905 lists them: "Bulgarians, Servians [Serbians], Albanians, Vlachs, Armenians, Anatolians, Circassians, Greeks, Turks, Jews, infidels and heretics of every land and language. Between and among these are sprinkled the races of civilized Europe." However, by the time of the wars among the Greeks, Serbians, and Bulgarians for supremacy in Macedonia, the Greeks, or Hellenes, had become inducted into these European "races." When the Greeks definitively captured Thessalonica in 1912, the English philhellene, Ronald Burrows, penned a poem:

We too of the younger North
Claim that Hellas brought us forth,

...

We who are of Byron's kin,
We who fought at Navarin.
Salonika! Salonika!
We do seek her! We do seek her!

Polyphonous Ottoman culture was initially much admired by
the Renaissance and Enlightenment diplomats and travellers to the
Balkans and to the Golden Porte in Istanbul: Lady Mary Wortley
Montagu, sojourning in Belgrade in 1717, wrote enthusiastically to
Alexander Pope in London of her host Achmet-Beg, his exposition
on Arabic love poetry, and of her desire to study Arabic: "I do believe
I should learn to read Arabic if I was to stay here [Belgrade] a few
months." But, in its nineteenth-century decline and rot, barbarism
and atrocity were understood singularly as *Turkish*. And, as the
nineteenth-century writer J. Philémon viewed the situation in Greece,
Macedonia "is where Turkish barbarity was most brutish, where
tyranny burdened the Christians most heavily. Their sufferings are
indescribable. Nowhere else were there so many inflictions, ceaseless
demands, arbitrary confiscations, murders, kidnapping and rapes of
boys and girls. The *mouteselim* of Salonica was an absolute scoundrel,
a drinker of blood."

But to a native son of the Mother City, such as the writer Nikos
Pentzikis, who lived through all the versions of Salonica from the
last Ottoman days to the postmodern 1990s, who, while unsuccess-
fully trying to keep the family pharmacy going, wrote Lives of the
Saints and meditated on Byzantine texts, for a Thessalonian the city
remained a panoramic miracle, of sight, and of names, no matter how
vandalized: "The picturesque descents—towards the Sykeon ravine
with the poplars, from the gardens of Eskintelik to Rodokhori with
the vineyards—make up the rear....From the ward of Neapolis, one
can see only what lies on the shoulder. An earring on the ear, the

building above the Mevleane, where at one time Dervishes danced, close to the church of the Martyrs...."

In December 2000, I have returned to Thessalonica, main city of the Greek region of Macedonia and residence of St. Demetrius, to visit his Basilica and make the rounds of the great interior, "the vaulting effort of faith," in the words of Nikos Pentzikis. I buy souvenir booklets and make notes of the stupendous gallery of iconic images of the Saint, on icons and in mosaics, modern and medieval. High up above my head he stands in seventh-century glory, draped in white and gold, his boyish head glowing in an amber halo. He stands before soldiery, their celestial Captain, draped in a Byzantine red gown and blue cloak, preaching with his eyes and hands upraised, while the ramparts and gates of the city form a kind of protective wall for the scene. In a side chapel, a bright new wall mosaic represents him full-length in the prayer or *orans* posture, a long silver and blue cloak falling from a clasp at his shoulder. Near the main door, in his icon on the pedestal, he is silver-haloed, silver-speared, and silver-shielded. This is under glass. We leave our kisses on it, as though on the beloved Wonder-worker himself, until a little misshapen man in a blue smock, quick-footed, with a spray bottle of vinegar, wipes the kisses away.

In several depictions, as I had first seen them myself in the picture books of the Benedictine library in Saskatchewan, Demetrius's slender figure is set astride a red horse, his green cloak billowing in a heavenly breeze, a radiant youth posed triumphantly on the battlements of Thessalonica, while the barbarians drag away their dead. Like the medieval viewer, I stand in front of the mosaics and wall paintings of the Basilica of St. Demetrius, but what she would have known as the barbarian Draguvitae, Sagudati, Belegezitae, Baiounitae, and Berzitae I know as the Slavs. These are, by remote but sure connection, my people. They swarm around the Balkans, driving south from the Danube, along routes forged earlier by Huns, Avars, Bulgars, Pechenegs, and Cumans. Mere plunderers and looters and rapists, they terrorize the Greek world and enter its texts. Byzantine historian Procopius, writing in the sixth century, says they fight on foot with spears and bows and live in or near woods and swamps. Probably they wear animal skins and drag cudgels along the ground.

Slav n [Middle English Sclav, from Medieval Latin Sclavus, from Late Greek Sklabos, from Sklabenoi, Slavs, of Slav origin; akin to Old Church Slavonic Slovene, a Slavic people in the area of Salonika]

Slave n [Middle English from Old French esclave from medieval Latin sclavus, sclava, a captive, identical to Sclavus, Slav, the Slavic peoples having been reduced to a servile state by conquest in the 9th c.]

IN MEDIEVAL EUROPE, the ethnic group, Sclavus, had become synonymous with the notion of an enslaved people, the Slavs being considered as slaves par excellence. Gone are the Latin words for slave, *mancipium* and *servus* yielding to the Spanish, *esclavo*, Portuguese, *escravo*, Catalan, *sclau*, Italian, *schiavo*, German, *Sklave*, English, *slave*, Dutch, *slaaf*.

From their homeland in the Pripet marshes of what is now Ukraine, Slavic tribes began in the fifth century to disperse in several directions. I suppose they walked—cattle, horses, some pots and pans, bedding, herdsmen in rough-spun garments and fur cloaks, bark-soled moccasins, a shaman who carried the secrets of fire and thunder—and perhaps they also rafted down the rivers that lifted them from out of the Carpathians and down to the Danube. There they stayed awhile, unable to cross while the Roman-Byzantine fortresses held the line on the southern bank, but they did go on raids, cannon-fodder for more powerful tribes like the Bulgars and Avars, then slipped back safely to the northern Danube shore. They are hard to trace, for the only objects they left behind them in Greek soil were two urns, and, again according Procopius, "they [Sclaveni] live in pitiful hovels which they set up far apart from one another, but, as a general thing, every man is constantly changing his place of abode." Nor do they leave much of a mark as warriors: "When they enter battle, the majority of them go against their enemy on foot carrying little shields and javelins in their hands, but they never wear corselets. Indeed, some of them do not wear even a shirt or a cloak, but gathering their trews [trousers] up as far as to their private parts they enter into battle with their opponents." Their Byzantine opponents tracked them like rabbits, attacking them in the winter when their footprints could be seen in the snow, "when they cannot easily hide among bare trees...when their household is miserable from exposure, and when it is easy to cross over the rivers on the ice."

In the third century, the Goths cross the Danube, in the fourth the Huns. Finally, it is the Slavs' turn. In a passage as portentous for European cultures as that of the Germanic barbarians who poured out of quarantine over the frozen Rhine in 406 CE into Gaul and never went back, the Slavs crossed the Danube in the sixth century.

They destroyed cities and moved on, through abundantly watered plains of wheat to the northern limits of the olive tree, past battle sites, below wooded hillsides and between mountain ranges. They made use of the superb Roman highway system to spread out from inland cities such as Naissus (Nis) and Serdica (Sofia). And there, at the mouth of the Vardar where it spreads out into the sea from its ascent in the mountains behind Scupi (Skopje), is Thessalonica, commanding the northern Aegean with a massive citadel. When they got there, they would call it *Solun*.

A mosaic panel in the Basilica of St. Demetrius shows the Patron Saint with his arms around the shoulders of two founders of the church, all three in splendid voluminous robes. It bears an inscription in Greek, a flourish to the literate viewer: "You are looking at the builders of this famous house from where the Martyr Demetrius is the one who turns back the barbarian wave of barbarian ships and redeems the city."

And so the barbarians stand at the gates and gawk. Inside are stone mansions and gardens of pomegranates, wagons laden with amber, olive oil and plush brocades and bales of airy cotton, the kiosks of tent-makers, mariners and scribes who ply their trade for merchants, and travellers journeying to the city, the King's City, Constaninople. The Slavs stand and gawk, and want it all. Fine tunics embroidered with gold, slaves pouring rose water in the bath, cooks in the kitchen, barrels of wine in the cellar. What they don't yet see, for they mean nothing, are the tiled roofs and the frescoed piers in the narthex of the basilicas, and they can't hear the chants in the monasteries nor smell the musk of the incense in the crypts, but eventually they will want these, too, and one day also they will want St. Demetrius. Newly baptized Christians, they will call him Dimitri Solunski.

:: *Thessalonica*

ON LEAVING CRETE, *I stopped briefly in Athens to see a fifteenth-century church, perched up on Philopappou Hill, named for St. Demetrius. In the cool of the evening we climbed, my Greek-speaking friend Stephie and I, sniffing the dissipating scent of pine on the soft, polluted November air, and admired the stars that managed to shine through here and there in the electrified firmament.*

Paschali the caretaker agreed to take us around the church, shuffling us toward what remained of fourteenth-century frescoes that—he shrugged apologetically—had been painted over. A generation of ham-fisted restorers had left them horribly pock-marked, although Paschali claimed they had also been disfigured by "the Turks." The eyes of St. Demetrius, for example, had been chiselled out.

But, propped up inside an elaborate frame on the wainscot by the main door stood a fresh, new icon, of that heroic—if murderous—Demetrius skewering an armoured soldier. "Who is he killing?" I asked Paschali. A woman who had been sitting whispering to her friend, as though visiting and minding us at the same time, suddenly popped up out of her seat and shouted out at us. "It's a thief." "He doesn't look like a thief," I objected. "He looks like a Roman soldier." "No, no, the story has always been that he is a thief." And she turned back to her friend.

"Why was this chapel built here in the first place?" I asked Paschali.

"The reason you build a church in a particular place," he replied, "is that it has some connection with a saint. A man has many dreams of the Saint and decides to donate money to build a church. Or an icon is found in the ground."

"Is that what happened here, on Philopappou Hill? Someone dreamed of the icon of St. Demetrius?" He doesn't know. The woman shouts out again. "It's quite common to find icons in the ground." When you dream of finding buried treasure, the Greek Orthodox believe, rise and go to your churchyard and dig there, for the buried gold of the miracle-working icon buried in the earth, and exhume your saint.

IN 1979 the French Byzantinist Paul Lemerle translated and published *Les plus anciens recueils des miracles de St. Démétrius*, fifteen miracle-narratives originally orated as sermons by Archbishop John of Thessalonica in the period 610–640 CE, and mainly touching on events that had occurred in the city some thirty years earlier. Six more narratives are the work of an anonymous author writing later in the seventh century. All together they do not appear as a text until the twelfth century.

To summarize Lemerle: It is 586 CE. The dominant Balkan power is the Turkic Avars with whom the totality of Slavic tribes in the Danube region are in alliance. Under the Avar leader or *khagan* they march some 100,000 strong south to Thessalonica. At four days' march distant from the city it seems nothing will stand in their way—they have crossed lands seemingly emptied of all Byzantine presence and authority. But lucky for the Thessalonians, the enemy have no experience yet of besieging such a fortified town nor the supplies to sustain a siege. Some among the Slavs even desert to the Greeks. Eventually, the besiegers withdraw and the Avars retire back to the Danube. But the Slavs do not quite retreat. The *Recueils* tells us that, two years later, the Peloponnese was inundated by a Slavic flood, the outreach of a wave that had hurled itself on Macedonia and central Greece and never withdrawn. "From which we must conclude," Lemerle comments, "that the invaders encountered nothing but a void before them: military, administrative and demographic," a result of the depredations of the Goths and Huns who had preceded them. By 600 all of the Byzantine Empire's lands north of Thessalonica had been penetrated by the Slavs. But Thessalonica was the prize to be won, "deservedly renowned as the champion of Greek power and of Hellenistic civilization," an historian of the city recounts. "Thessaloniki towered up before the horde of invaders like a rock that did not move."

In 604 the Slavs launch a surprise attack by night on Thessalonica. But these are no longer Slavs subject to the Avars; they are now autonomous and with their own motives. These are not an enemy marching from some featureless Carpathian back-of-beyond but one in the vicinity and suddenly at the gates, whose blood-curdling war cry the barricaded Thessalonians recognize. Archbishop John depicts them as accustomed to winning and battle-hardened by success: they have already overrun all of Macedonia, except, of course, Thessalonica, one of the very few cities, along with Corinth, to have escaped the Slavic torrent. But now she is encircled.

There is a twist to the siege. According to one of the Anonymous Miracles, pillage is no longer the sole objective of the besiegers, for they have brought along with them women, children, and baggage, in expectation of taking the city and living there, as they did at Naissus (now called Nis) and Serdica (now known as Sofia). They have also become sailors; Lemerle refers to that mosaic of St. Demetrius with his arms around the founders of his Basilica: Demetrius, "the one who turns back the barbarian wave of barbarian ships," sailors of the Aegean even if only hugging its shores.

But their assault fails, again.

Move forward to about 615. The Slavs call on their former masters, the Avars, to join them in an attack on Thessalonica. The Avars arrive with the Khagan and artillery (bows, sling, catapults) that they rain upon the city for thirty-three days. But, even though they observe the billowing clouds of dust raised by the collapsing walls of buildings under fire, they do not "dare," wrote Lemerle, to take advantage of the situation, and instead withdraw.

The Thessalonians neither hope for nor receive succor from Constantinople, whose troops and treasury are distracted by Arab armies harrying and overrunning the eastern borders. For the

Thessalonians there is only Demetrius. They pray day and night in the Basilica, they compose hymns and preach homilies, now thunderous, now pleading, they bring icons and ecclesiastical treasures from their own homes and beg for forgiveness and hope for deliverance. They are holed up in their fortress with its cyclopean walls left undefended by any substantial army, a great port city without a navy, a city fed from a large and rich hinterland that has shrunk to the dimensions of a narrow and vulnerable belt around its outer walls. They are under siege.This is what "Thessalonian" meant. And *each time,* the *Recueils* tells us, they are delivered from the barbarians with the intervention of St. Demetrius, dead already for several hundred years.

Take that assault of 586, in the mythical number of 100,000, on a population weakened by a recent plague. The enemy is confounded by the Saint himself who appears on the ramparts and throws the besiegers off their scaling ladders with a kick of his forceful boot. At night the barbarians build huge bonfires and let loose their terrifying yells, but on the second day they feel the first pangs of hunger—they have mismanaged their provisioning. On the third day they fire artillery at the walls but they shoot too far and too short. In spite of the pleas of two angels sent by divine order, that he quit the city while he still can, St. Demetrius remains with his people, reinvigorating them with courage. Some of the Slavs begin to defect to the Greeks and warn the Thessalonians of a massive attack being planned for two days hence. Then the Thessalonians have a dream, a vision of a great army led by the Saint, pouring out of the city through all her gates like a torrent of fire and ferment, and, oh miracle, when they awake, the barbarians are already in full retreat.

In one of the numerous religious bookshops in Thessalonica I have bought a comic book. St. Demetrius is displayed on the cover as a warrior-saint in Roman breastplate and halo, mounted on a sturdy steed, on the crest of a hill, facing the sea, with an expression of beatific resignation to his task, which is the defence of the city laid out below. Inside the book, however, Demetrius is something like the Incredible Hulk of Salonica: he stands up in his stirrups, with his stallion pawing the air above the ramparts, to give an almighty shove to the scaling ladder from which the barbarians, brandishing battleaxes, fall like so many fleas off the back of a dog. A few panels further on, they are back at the city walls, this time with formidable catapult machines and a supply of enormous boulders against which the terrified Thessalonians can only marshall a procession of priests bearing icons and swinging censers until—lo!—St. Demetrius appears hauling a boulder of his own. The Thessalonians load it in their catapult and BOOM! KRAK! it hurtles over the walls and into the barbarians' infernal siege machine, blowing everything to smithereens.

In the thirteenth miracle, the Saint, impatient for battle, clambers over the ramparts as light as a bird, his shield and sword and Roman armour weighing no more than the cape clasped at his throat. FRAP! he swings his sword. OOG! UGH! he spears a barbarian who slithers down the ladder, spraying his blood all over the battlement.

Unexpected blasts of wind ram the besiegers' boats together in the harbour, cutting off the Slavs' escape route; the Thessalonians display their hacked-off heads on the ramparts and move off to the Basilica to give thanks. A violent earthquake overturns the walls of the city, provoking the citizenry to cry out together in terror, "Lord have mercy!" at which the walls are restored upright and intact, to the stupefaction of the enemy. The Saint is sometimes seen dressed simply in his white chlamys, floating above the battlement or walking below on the sea, a vision beheld both by baptized Christians and the Jews of Thessalonica, who saw it from their quarter. Archbishop John: "But if one wanted to recount in detail all the miracles performed by St. Demetrius at each place, at each gate and at the sea coast, all the papyrus of the Nile would not be enough to write all the required books."

The Greek resistance was decisive. "This is most obvious in the Thessalonian phenomenon," Demetrian scholar Lemerle concluded. "The great city remained impregnable, and this alone doomed the successive assaults of the Avars, the Slavs, the Bulgars. This is the deep meaning of the Demetrian legend."

Yes, but what did it mean to the Slavs? What does it mean to me? The now-decomposing medieval walls of Thessalonica had been built, rebuilt, and built again to keep the barbarians at bay. Around me I can almost see the spooks of the Slavic nations, and hear them rattling their bags of bones.

⁝ *History is the Dogma of Scars*

:: **Thessalonica**

I DROPPED IN ON *the Canadian Consul in his office in the Bank of Nova
Scotia near Aristotle Square in downtown Thessalonica. He had a photo of
Ecumenical Patriarch Bartholomew (of Constantinople) on the wall and
many Byzantine art books on shelves, which he opened for my delectation as
he took phone calls in fluent Greek, his mother tongue. I looked for pictures
of Demetrius.*

*I had announced myself as a writer; in response, he offered the informa-
tion that, ever since he was sixteen years old, he has read two to three books
a week, without fail. He seemed fortyish. I did the calculations while he was
on the phone.*

*"It is my belief that reading is a practice of civilization," he resumed.
I explained my "Demetrius" project, about Slavs and Greeks, barbarians
and Byzantines. And, referring to his art books, I asked if he knew who St.
Demetrius is slaying in the popular icon? He did indeed, and I added it to
my list: "When St. George slays the snake, and Demetrius the soldier, it is
the act of killing the 'barbarian' spirit. This used to mean the non-Christians."
He peered at me for emphasis. "Now it is we who are the barbarians, we
who believe that life is only about self-satisfaction." He did not seem very
remorseful, for a barbarian.*

IN SALONICA'S late Ottoman period (the city would revert to its Greek name, Thessalonica, after 1912), trade unionists of railroad workers, Jewish tobacco workers, Bulgarian and Jewish typographers, and Greek bakers communicated with each other with leaflets in four languages, Ladino, Turkish, Greek, and Bulgarian, and massed together, some 12,000 of them, for May Day rallies, to sing *The Internationale* in their own languages, together.

The Ottomans initiated a period of administrative reforms and built a railway connection with the rest of Europe, opened banks, and endured a series of strikes by tobacco workers, shoemakers, tannery workers, carpenters, gas workers, and transport workers in Salonica alone.

But it was too late for the Ottomans; from the bottle of intellectual marvels from the European West, the genii of ethnic nationalism had been let loose and would wreak havoc in Macedonia in all the wars of the twentieth century.

Slavs had lived for many generations in what is now northern Greece, as I had learned from reading the *Miracles of St. Demetrius*, sharing the physical geography of a Balkan zone of mountains, valleys, and watersheds known as Macedonia, lying athwart what would become the modern nations of Greece, Bulgaria, and southern Yugoslavia, and sharing a word, Macedonia, descended from antiquity and the House of Philip of Macedon. In the Roman Empire, they were differentiated as pagans or Christians, in the Byzantine Empire as Slavic-speakers or Greek-speakers, then all of them Orthodox in the Muslim empire of the Ottomans. It took a long, long time before the peoples living in this zone thought of themselves separately as Greeks, Bulgarians, and Macedonians. But when they did, all hell broke loose.

A word about "Macedonia." A map in *The Palgrave Concise Historical Atlas of the Balkans*—Map 2: Political 2001—clearly demarcates "Macedonia" as a small state lying directly north of Greece, south of Serbia, and alongside Albania and Bulgaria, with a capital city, Skopje. It is not here called Former Yugoslav Republic of Macedonia (FYROM), the provisional name assigned it when it was admitted to the United Nations in 1993, to placate Greek anxieties about the new republic's alleged designs on its border with northern Greece, an area also known as Macedonia, and its treasure, Thessalonica. However, the newly independent republic did not wish to be banished behind an acronym, and insisted on the name it claimèd for itself during the vicious struggle for national liberation as the Ottoman Empire declined at the end of the nineteenth century: Macedonia. This was also to make the point that, although its people were Slavic-speakers and Orthodox, they were not Bulgarians. And, although they were Orthodox, they were not Greek either.

I assume all this is pretty much matter-of-fact when I walk into Thessalonica's Museum of the Macedonian Struggle. Its director, Vlasis Vlasidis, declares, as we begin a tour of the rooms, that "this is an institution of historical research, and not of propaganda." The museum receives 30,000 visitors annually, mostly schoolchildren, and the "message" of its exhibits is that "we are Greeks by nation but we have different cultural and historical traditions here because of local communities present during the Ottoman era. There were no nation-states then, just several populations who lived together, Greeks, Slavs, Muslims, Vlachs." So far so correct, although there is no mention of the Jews.

I mention that I am particularly interested in the Slavs of this region. Vlasidis responds that, "There are Slav-*speakers* here in Macedonia, of course. But they are not *ethnic*. We are all Greek by nation." I'm not sure how you get a Slav-speaker without the ethnicity to match, but I let it pass.

Notebook in hand, I follow Vlasidis through the exhibition rooms, writing down his commentary and sometimes getting a word in edgewise.

We stand in front of a diorama illustrating the mass suicide in 1822 of the women of Naoussa (west of Thessalonica), who flung themselves into a waterfall rather than be taken by the Turks into slavery. "The presence of Turkish troops in Salonica thwarted the Greek revolutionaries who hoped to liberate Macedonia and bring it into the Greek fold," I scribble. He is referring to the desperate campaign of Greek guerrilla forces in the south, to extend their war against the Turks northward. "Because the revolutionaries themselves weren't so easy to capture, the Turks also hanged local Greek civilians instead."

We stand in front of a copy of a celebrated painting of the wild-eyed Bulgarian revolutionary, Boris Sarafov, who is driving Macedonian Greeks out of their village and burning their houses down behind them. Like the Greeks, the Bulgarians were desperate to establish an ethnic zone for themselves as Turkish power waned in the Balkans. Because Slavs lived intermingled with Greeks, the effort to prise Slav Orthodox peasants from Greek Orthodox peasants was brutal.

Vlasidis describes the process. "Each village had one church and one school and so the two ethnic groups struggled for control. Where villages were mixed, the people were terrorized first by Greek then by Bulgarian guerrillas. Take a village that belonged to the Greek Patriarchate. The Bulgarians enter the village, meet up with a local follower who informs on the adherents of the patriarchate who are then killed and their houses burnt. The survivors report to the Ottomans that they now belong to the Bulgarian Exarchate. A month later, exactly the same thing happens at the hands of Greek guerrillas."

We move to a diorama that illustrates the arrival of Greek guerrillas into the village of Litorocho in 1878, joyfully welcomed by villagers and their priest. The fidelity of the "Balkan peasant" to his Church was "one continuous martyrdom," wrote H.N. Brailsford, who had been everywhere on behalf of the British Relief Fund in the winter of 1903–1904. Of the towns and villages in the Salonica area more than one hundred went over to the Bulgarian Church, which also operated some six or seven hundred Bulgarian-language schools in the region, and a secondary school right inside Salonica. Seeing the danger to their cause, Vlasidis avers that, between 1904 and 1908, Greek guerrillas operated in clandestine cooperation with the Turks, against the Bulgarians "who were by far the greater threat to Greek Macedonia."

Hopes among revolutionary visionaries, that the various liberated peoples might best live together in a political federation, flared briefly and died, as Macedonia remained in the grip of ethnic cleansers and became a theatre of ethnocide, terrorist assassinations, reprisals, secret societies, conspirators, and plain old-fashioned brigandage repackaged by propagandists as national heroism. As traveller John Foster Fraser summarized the situation in 1906, "Both races [Greeks and Bulgarians] believe they are engaged in a high patriotic mission. They will not listen to reason. They regard the others as vermin deserving only extermination. So the burning of houses, the murder of partisans, is proceeding apace in a more flagrant manner than during the time of Turkish atrocities."

And in Kastoria (Slav *Kostur*) near the Albanian border, the local Bishop, Germanos, a handsome figure of a man in flowing mane and black beard, kept a photograph of the severed head of a Bulgarian guerrilla in his church office. Brailsford saw it there, the head "severed at the neck with a bullet through the jaw, dripping blood." Germanos regularly carried arms for the guerrillas under his robes.

In their pamphlet, which I picked up in the museum lobby, the Friends of the Museum of the Macedonian Struggle describe how "Women in villages made bread for the fighters, washed their clothes and bandaged their wounds. Ladies' societies in the towns organized associations for the poor and gathered supplies. Peasants secretly carried weapons and ammunition. Especially important were the priests, e.g. Germanos Karavangelis, Bishop of Kastoria, who assisted in the formation of armed bands." Undoubtedly, the women in the Slavic villages were doing the same for "their" guerrillas.

In front of another display, Vlasidis and I contemplate a slice of the walnut tree used as a gibbet for the Greek captains, Telos Agras and Antonios Migas, hanged by Bulgarians in 1907 in Vladovo (Greek *Edessa*).

The demise of the Ottomans—the decadent court of the Sultanate replaced in 1908 by the Committee for Union and Progress, disaffected young Turks and officers based in Salonica—if anything acceler- ated the intercommunal violence. The new, young Turks may have promised "Liberty, Equality, Fraternity, Justice" for the peoples of the empire from the balcony of the Olympos Palace Hotel in Salonica, but the enfeebled Ottoman Empire's holdings in the Balkans were now violently seized by a series of wars.

Provinces that had been Ottoman for five centuries were lost in five weeks. In October 1912, to shouts of "Christ is risen!" a Greek army entered Salonica, eight hours ahead of the Bulgarians, and received the official surrender of the city from the Turkish Pasha. It was October 26, Feast Day of St. Demetrius.

And Demetrius had come in a dream to the Greek commander-in-chief, Prince Constantine, to give him "a lion-heart and courage, and superhuman strategic insight." He would need it: not since 1430 had Greeks been the lords of Salonica.

Six weeks later, a Jewish teacher in Salonica wrote back to a Paris correspondent of the "terrible anguish which marked the entry of the Greeks into Salonika. A week of terror and horror one can never easily forget." He meant the massacres, pillaging, and burning of parts of the city not only by army irregulars but also by police and civic officials. Bulgarian residents of Thessalonica had been arrested or left voluntarily, the community's property looted and their Bulgarian church banned.

The Greek army "liberated" Macedonian towns and villages in which Greeks formed a majority: in the Battle of Kilkis they burned entire villages and set fires along whole valleys to drive the Slavs from their homes. In May 1913, an agreement divided Macedonia along its Aegean coast, Vardar River, and Pirin Mountain parts, distributing them among Greece, Serbia, and Bulgaria, respectively. After 1913 the Greeks in their part of Macedonia closed Bulgarian-language schools and changed Slavs' family names and village names to sound more Greek. Greek liturgies were reimposed on the churches and Cyrillic inscriptions erased.

And so a "Greek" Macedonia is confirmed, what anthropologist Anastasia Karakasidou calls the "imagined community of the Hellenes." Until 1974, history textbooks in Greece described Bulgarians as the "eternal enemies of the Greek nation." In 1994 Karakasidou received death threats when she published her research on the Slavic-speakers of Greek Macedonia, and communities where she had interviewed subjects regarded her investigations into their multicultural and multilingual past an "insult" that "traumatized [their] Greek sentiment."

Mark Mazower, the city's most recent historian, summarized: "Saint Dimitrios had triumphed again—over the Slavs."

Vlasidis and I have come to the end of the tour of the museum, without his having once made mention of the ex-Yugoslav Macedonians as a separate ethnic or national identity in the region (they are folded into "Bulgarians") nor of ethnic Slavs in Greece, only, enigmatically, of Slavic-speakers. We are all Greeks now.

I buy a museum postcard before I leave. It is a modern historical version of an icon of a warrior-saint. It bears the text, "Macedonian struggle," and represents a Greek soldier, 1904–1908, in the stiff-limbed posture of a Byzantine warrior-saint, his unsheathed sword held up across his chest. We follow his gaze up toward the right-hand corner of the picture: from behind the stylized sun emerges the hand of God, fingers bent into a blessing. God has chosen the Greeks.

Greek feelings about this are clear: Thessalonica is a Greek city, and many thousands of Thessalonians rallied in the central squares when the former Yugoslav Republic of Macedonia seemed covetous of this queen of the Aegean. "Greece could not accept that the Macedonian name be used by a Slavic state or a Slavic people," to quote a pamphlet in 1994. But I think of all the peoples who have run over Greece— Albanians, Kutrigurs, Avars, Slavs, Goths, Franks, and Serbs—and that there is no Balkan or Mediterranean place that has not hosted legions of strangers.

It is a minefield over which the visitor, however well-read or sympathetic, steps with trepidation. I was not always careful enough. The young man who managed the Internet café I frequented in Thessalonica took an interest in my project but warned: "Do us Greeks a favour and never refer to the people of Skopje as 'Macedonians.'" Only Greeks could be Macedonians. A year later, I would be in hot water with friends in Skopje for referring to them in correspondence as "Slav Macedonians": they are "Macedonians," period.

...On its [Salonica's] south-eastern frontier, it is worthy of notice, the mass of the Slavonic population stops everywhere short of the sea.

—G. MUIR MACKENZIE AND A.P. IRBY

EVEN AFTER the incorporation of Thessalonica into the Greek state after the Great War, the Greeks did not have it entirely to themselves. In his memoir of childhood in Thessalonica in the early 1930s, *Refugee Capital*, Yorgos Ioannou recreates the shock and confusion of Greek refugees from the former Ottoman Empire who have been deported, practically destitute, from their former homes to Thessalonica. They arrived from all the provinces of Greece and, adding themselves to the mix, from Bulgaria, Russia, Thrace, Constantinople, the Black Sea coasts, and Asia Minor.

One day the boy Ioannou is walking along the Egnatia Road, precious biscuits in his pockets, a surprise for his family. The city is finally disengaging from war. The Germans are pulling out by train. Greek guerrillas strut wearing criss-crossed cartridge belts. A Bulgarian soldier stands sentry at the train station. It is the Bulgarian who nonplusses the author: "He was standing at attention, gripping a preposterously long-barrelled rifle with an even more preposterously long bayonet that extended well above his head. That's all they are good for, the bastards, poking holes in people...poking holes." Then he sees another Bulgarian soldier, in dark and abrasive khaki, who is carrying a basket. The narrator takes a peek: a pair of high-heeled women's shoes. He sneers, "must have been taking them to his village, a gift from their beloved city, 'Solun nash.'" *Solun nash.* Slavic for *our Thessalonica*. Recalling the moment, Ioannou is indignant: "The yearning for Thessaloniki has not been expunged from the dreams of our neighbours, who never cease to devise reasons for including it in their ostensibly 'peace-loving,' ostensibly 'non-chauvinistic,' ostensibly 'non-bellicose' plans. And all the while, we are supposed to remain indifferent, we natives of Thessaloniki?"

The immemorial destination: "Sloboda ili smrt! Od Koruna do Soluna!" It is the slogan, in October 2000, of the farmers of Cacak, Serbia, marching to Belgrade to oust President Slobodan Milosevic from power. "Freedom or death! From Kordun [historically Serbian town in Croatia] to Thessalonica!" From the Adriatic to the Aegean, this great swath of Slavic longing.

In 1988 I travelled in the Yugoslav republic of Macedonia to view the medieval monasteries of Ohrid and there met Goce, a young recently graduated art historian who insisted on showing me the sights. Over two days of conversation, what had begun as a discourse on the aesthetics of Byzantine iconography and frescoes developed into impassioned speechifying (on Goce's part) on the subject of historical Macedonian Slav identity. I was mesmerized. The supreme beauty of the icons and architecture, Goce's lyrical rendition of the tragedy, in his view, of Macedonia's defeat by the Greek Byzantines and, later still, by the modern state of Greece, combined with the intoxicating atmosphere of the breezes off Lake Ohrid, the tolling of the Vespers bells and Goce's own voice singing the ballads of the villages of Macedonia, left me swooning in sympathy.

I watched Goce across a café table, his dark face disappearing into the shade of the chestnut tree. While I listened to the sizzle of pieces of lamb, and breathed in jasmine and garlic, lemon and salt, on the grill, around us men drank tumblers of red wine and Goce scribbled a rough map of the southern Balkans on a napkin: it was my first lesson in what constitutes, in these parts at least, Greater Macedonia. It comprises three parts—Vardar (a squiggle of his pen), named for the river as it flows in then-Yugoslavia; Pirin, for the mountain in western Bulgaria; Aegean, for the sea rimming the unrequited, lost home harbour. On Goce's face I saw the aggrieved expression of an ancient disappointment: the Slav who was thrown back by Greeks from the sea at the mouth of the Vardar and who now stands with his back to the lake at Ohrid, which, to comfort himself, he calls the Macedonian Sea. Goce did live once in Solun, or may as well have done, so intensely can he taste the dust off the red Byzantine brick and the salt of the gulf. He had a garden and cultivated gourds and vines, combed the fleece of his sheep, and built a stone altar to his gods. Then a Greek saint threw him out.

The salt water laps at the Aegean. The Slavs would build their cities elsewhere, on Balkan plains, in Balkan valleys, and on the shores of Balkan lakes they would call seas.

Goce and I climbed up the crag surmounting Ohrid, to the old monumental gate and the remnants of ramparts from which Samuil, tsar of the First Bulgarian Kingdom (997–1014 CE), lorded his authority over southern Serbia, Albania, Macedonia, Thessaly, and Epirus, between the Black Sea and the Adriatic. Considered formidable as a ruler and invincible as a soldier by his admirers and a rebel by the Byzantines, who had been expelled from Bulgarian territory, he waged almost incessant warfare with the Byzantines, who were ruled by the equally ambitious and accomplished Emperor Basil II. From Ohrid, his capital, Samuil marched his armies unopposed, up and down valleys and across plains all the way to the Isthmus of Corinth in southern Greece. In 1004 he marched ineffectually to Thessalonica, and in 1009 his forces were defeated by Basil's in a battle east of Thessalonica. Basil pressed his advantage, and both Byzantine and Bulgarian lands lay wasted and exhausted by war. Finally, in 1014, at the Battle of Kleidion in southern Bulgaria, the Byzantine army overwhelmed the Bulgarians. Of the 14,000 prisoners of war, Basil blinded ninety-nine of every hundred, leaving the hundredth with one eye, to guide his comrades home. "The Bulgar-slayer," the Byzantines called their Basil, *Bulgaroktonos*. Samuil died two days after they straggled in through the gates, pawing the air in front of them in a last, despairing gesture of homage to their tsar.

Samuil had built himself a palace of towers ornamented with stone and fresco, and churches of marble and copper, silver and gold. He hung a mantle around his neck, embroidered with pearls, and slid gold bracelets on his wrists, and he wrapped his hips with velvet and slung a sword in a jewelled scabbard. His boyars sat in ranks before him.

He threw himself repeatedly at Thessalonica, but didn't he know? It was under the protection of St. Demetrius, and the seawater was the Saint's.

⋮ Demetrius among the Macedonians

:: *Thessalonica*

SEIZING PERSEPHONE, he [Hades] carried her off despite her struggles. [Her mother] Demeter grew anxious and came hurrying to look for her. Not finding her, she lit two torches and sought for her all over the world. By reason of her mourning, the earth grew desolate and famine-stricken, for without her influence nothing could grow or reach maturity.

AMONG A DISCONCERTING NUMBER of blue glass "eyes" hanging around her desk to ward off the evil eye, I have an interview with Dr. Nora Skouteri-Didaskalou, social anthropologist and folklorist at Aristotle University in Thessalonica. What has brought me here is the pairing of Saints Demetrius and George so often in the icons and frescoes I have seen in museums and churches, and my reading that early Christian Lives of the Saints often simply took over pagan myths holus bolus. Could my Demetrius, Christian Martyr, be related to, say, Demeter, pagan goddess of the fruits of the earth? In some of her cults she was also the great goddess of the underworld: in a study of Greek mythology, Jane Harrison wrote that "the Mother herself keeps ward in the *metropolis* of the dead, and therefore 'the Athenians of old called the dead 'Demeter's people.'" I've read that at Eleusis, where her Mysteries had been celebrated, Christians raised a Church of St.

Demetrius on the site of her temple. Second-century Greek traveller and geographer, Pausanias, an initiate in the Mysteries, mentions that it was the custom of the Eleusinian women "to take the sacrificial barley and to make cakes for the sacrifices out of its produce." By the Byzantine era, this offering to the dead had become *kollyva*, a mixture of grains, fruits, and nuts presented during the Liturgy of Soul Saturdays, as in the Saturday before the Feast of St. Demetrius. And in the nineteenth century, the residents of Eleusis still gave thanks to someone called St. Demetra for the abundance of their fields. There is no such saint as Demetra.

Skouteri-Didaskalou's field work on the folkloric importance of seasonal changes over the passage of the agricultural year has been carried out in the villages of western Macedonia in Greece. I ask about the meaning of the feast days of Saints Demetrius and George in the villages, and about why these two saints are so often paired in church icons, sometimes even standing together in the same image.

SKOUTERI-DIDASKALOU'S ANSWER is loquacious and expansive; while she speaks—of how Demetrius and George are celebrated in the late autumn and the spring, respectively—I feel a rising excitement as I am being drawn into a new Demetrian world of symbol and ritual at least as old as the pious Saint's Lives I've depended on for his story. And there is a darkness here, too, a kind of shadowy Demetrius who insinuates himself into the Christian narrative of sacrificial glory. He is no longer entombed in a silver shrine glinting in a basilica ablaze with light, but walking about the fields on a route to the pitch dark underground.

Autumn and spring, Skouteri-Didaskalou continues, are the "high points" of the revolving wheel of the seasons, both saints riding it around and around as we pass into the cold and dark of winter and then out of it into the sun and the warmth of summer. There is Demetrius at the high point of transition, "signalling, 'We had a good summer, we have our produce, the wheat, and everything is stored away, we are looking ahead to the dark, to the short days and long nights, to the bad weather. But we are also *planting* the winter seed in the cold earth and it is sleeping there until the spring.'" At which point the down-turning of the wheel revolves St. George into place, for the rebirth of light and the new production of wheat.

The two festivals became a means for illiterates to organize their life—to rent land on St. George Day, to bring the flocks down from the alpine meadows on St. Demetrius Day, to plant and to cease planting, to set out on a journey on St. George Day to look for work, and to work until the feast of St. Demetrius. Anthropologist Anastasia Karakasidou, also working among the villagers of western Macedonia in the 1980s, found that negotiations between shepherds and owners of flocks on St. Demetrius Day used always to include a pair of new shoes with the job, and payment was made in pounds of wheat. If the shepherd quit before St. George Day, or was dismissed, he had to give the shoes back. And, in a sense, the Feast of St. Demetrius was a way to organize the dead. "The dead are the ancestors," Skouteri-Didaskalou continued, "and they come out of their graves not as ghosts but as protectors—on the so-called Holy or Spiritual Saturdays, the *Psychosabada*, such as the one before the Feast of St. Demetrius. People go to the cemeteries and eat there, using the graves as tables. This is an old, an *ancient* attitude toward the dead. In the cult of Demeter (in Greek she is Dimitra), the goddess of earth and under-the-earth, the dead souls, the ancestors, the followers of Dimitra are called *Dimitri* in her Eleusinian Mysteries. So it is not by coincidence that we have Demetrius (Dimitrios in Greek), an ancient name meaning a dead man who comes out of the earth to protect the living. As a saint he personifies someone who died for the good of the community, offering up his life for Thessalonica."

> *He is for us food and drink and all things enjoyable to eat; he is the sun, the sky, the earth and the sea, and everything that is essential to us.*
> —ARCHBISHOP ISIDORE OF KYIV, fifteenth century

He is, in fact, a kind of Holy Eucharist.

At that moment, in Skouteri-Didaskalou's office, for all his eternal beauty and youth, Demetrius is one of the ancient ones, a divine companion of the endless generations of the tillers and sowers and reapers, who stands with them, his feet in clods of earth, cupping grains of wheat that sift through his fingers and fall into the furrows, the *chernozom*, the quarters of the dead. The days are getting shorter, the light from a tilting horizon slants toward the exhausted fields, the cold air from the mountains of the upriver interior wraps him like a rough, woollen cloak. The farmers open up a fresh furrow in the soil, he lays himself within, and there they bury him. There is a song, a feast, a dance. For he is young and beautiful and pushes up the green sprouts of spring. The farmers reap this crop, and call it Demetrius.

Agrilution: agriculture's evolution

The beginning

Our priestesses sprinkle seeds
in Demeter's earth. We make it fertile
with blood songs and ceremonies.

Medieval times

On Sainte Demetra's festival days
we light lamps, string her with garlands,
dance sacred circles.

Industrial Revolution

One shaft parts mother's turf
musky folds rise and yield
another to praise St. Demetrius

Today

We are the fodder pigs guttle.
Demented, how multinationals take

our land, our sustenance, move us away from family
traditions of growing vegetables, grain and animals, stop us
from attending dances, fowl suppers, community plays—

We get lost in the concrete and glass,
worship new gods.

—BERNADETTE L. WAGNER

As I get up to leave, I ask Skouteri-Didaskalou, for she must surely
have an idea, who is St. Demetrius killing in all those icons of the man
writhing under the hooves of Demetrius's horse?

"He's a pagan."

"He looks like a soldier to me."

"Yes, but he's like a Goliath. Like a Goliath, his head is big. He's a bit
dark in the face always, looking ugly and menacing. A pagan."

:: *Among the meat-eaters*

THE SHADOWY, skittering images on the videotape came from the
villages of Popajcevo and Jargulica in eastern Macedonia (FYROM)
where, on the eve of the Feast of St. Demetrius, *Mitrovdan*, the villagers slaughtered a bull, cooked it, and ate it.

I take note of the scenes. A family leaves their house and walks to
the church. Wreaths of greenery drip over the icons. The family lights
candles. The camera leaves them and moves back outdoors where
other families have already laid their serving pots in a large circle on
the grass near the church. *Next day.* Men gather on the common, throw
money onto the grass, stomp on it. Apparently one of them has bought
the sacrificial animal. Only the men are involved in the butchering and
the stewing. They auction off the head and hide and then toil together
at large cauldrons. At the end of the day they are sitting around
drinking when the women and children arrive with pots in hand,
which they fill from the cauldron and take home for the family feast.

The television monitor on which I watch the video has been liberated from the staff room of the Museum of Macedonia in Skopje and

trundled out to a corner of the vast entry hall. The videographer, Vladimir Bocev, ethnologist at the museum, provides a running commentary as I make my notes from his awkward English and my bewildered understanding of what I am seeing. Behind us museum staff are decorating a plastic Christmas tree and a group of school kids, on their way to the exhibition rooms of Macedonian folk art, stop en masse to watch with Bocev and me the blood sacrifice of the bull, Demetrius's bull. Not much here of gentle Demeter's sheaves of wheat. On the other hand, we know from Pausanias that, in the temples of Demeter, overlooked by statues of her priestesses, cattle were sacrificed in secret at the hands of four old women at the festival called the Chthonia.

Bocev, youthful, curly-headed, open-faced, then receives me cordially in his barebones office to talk about his little film. Had I noticed that there had been no priest present at the killing of the bull, even though villagers had made a point of going to church? Indeed I had. Well, blood sacrifice may not be Christian but it is sanctified: "Everything in Macedonia is a combination of pagan and Christian." He has researched "all of Macedonia" for this ritual—*kurban*, Turkish for "sacrifice"—and had published a detailed account of the rite as practised in the village of Jablanica in the western range of Struga in the late 1990s. As an ethnologist, his particular interest is agricultural rituals connected with the calendar—November 8, for instance, the Feast Day, or *praznik*, of St. Demetrius according to the old Julian calendar. It celebrates the ushering in of the winter cycle—and even those men and women who have left the village will return, from Skopje, Belgrade, Munich, for the Feast Day. (Vladimir Bocev's relatives in Greek Macedonia, he added in an aside, who call themselves Boces and live in Florina, once named Lerin, celebrate St. George's Feast Day; to join them, he has applied for a Greek visa under the name Vangelios Boces.) The traditions are still alive, much to my expressed amazement; I had assumed that a forty-year-long exposure to official atheism in Yugoslavia would have extirpated such pre-industrial enthusiasms as bull sacrifices. But no, *kurban* on St. Demetrius Day is still a very important holiday for the community.

"Women are the keepers of the rituals and the elders supervise their execution. But everybody knows how to do them because they've been aware of them since childhood. In spite of war and military occupation, the people still observed them. After World War Two the Communist state forbade these 'primitive' ways of living which were bad for progress. It was not uncommon in the 1950s for the police simply to seize the meat that was busily being cooked in the communal pots after the sacrifice of the bull. But government and police saw that they couldn't go against the people's will. Some villages did in fact forget how to do the rituals but they have since revived them.

"The traditional village is connected as an economic and a religious society (even villages that are deserted fill up at *Mitrovdan*). The holidays keep people's consciousness alive and their sense of belonging to one group."

The human community eats its fill while their living cattle, already oblivious to the fate of their brother, slowly pass over the blood-soaked earth of the killing site, the *kurbanishte*, lowing softly on their way to the pasture. It is St. Demetrius's Feast Day, and this is an *agape*, a love-feast.

Bocev gives me a copy of his paper, summarizing *kurban* among the villagers, Christian and Muslim, of Jablanica, an extraordinarily rich mishmash of elements—a sacred wood, fasting, a sacrifice performed at midnight, a Liturgy at the cooking pots accompanied by drums and oboe-like *zurla*, gifts of flatbread, chickens, lambs, socks, shirts, towels, a prayer of gratitude to the sacrificial animal for its death, which renews peace and well-being among the celebrants— choreographed at the ambiguous border between our mortal, sinful, penitent selves and the holy ones whom we propitiate. In his meek submission, head helpfully lowered to the blade of the knife, the bull is the instrument of the magic of the renewal of the ancient cycle of life and death. Bocev: "He is killed, cut into pieces and eaten, and yet here he is again, untouched and hitched to a plough!"

How has a corn god become the patron of an abattoir? Is it somehow Slavic, carried into these mountain valleys by migrating herders of cattle who melded it with the seasonal sacrifice of crops? It is a rite, however garbled, that somehow remembers itself from pre-Christian antiquity, after being suppressed by Christianity, folded into Muslim practice, and reasserted by Yugoslav villagers in church or monastery yards without benefit of clergy of whatever stripe, or at best a priest as disoriented as his flock. Church canons forbid the roasting of animal flesh in churchyards following services, but folklorists have stumbled on Serbian villagers who sacrifice roosters at the opening of ploughing season while their priest reads a special Litany, and Bulgarians who sacrifice young bulls for the dead.

There is only one Christian sacrifice, the Eucharist, so how can this ritual killing in honour of St. Demetrius be a communal good among Christians? Yet they do believe it. *Hadn't St. Haralambos pitilessly struck down in his sleep the man who claimed that the* kourbania *were pagan works?* "O wise Haralambos, you delivered us from the moonless night of idolatry O Blessed one," sings the deacon in church, of the Patron Saint of ploughmen in whose honour they make a sacrifice at the Feast of the Bull. So this must be another kind of churching, acceptable in the eyes of God, this gathering around the dying bull, his head turned east to face the Resurrection, the village's offering to their Saint.

In Ottoman Constantinople, where the Day of Kasim substituted for the powerful St. Demetrius cult, Evliya Celebi wrote in awe of the six hundred beef merchants—"infidels of Moldavia and Wallachia"—who brought 300,000 head of cattle into the city for the provision of the city's faithful on Kasim's Feast Day.

They are not impious, then, who bring their little pot of cooked meat to church for a blessing, filling God's house with the smell of meat. The beef in the pot isn't the point. His sacrifice is.

:: *The city favoured by Justinian*

IN SKOPJE 1995, during Easter week, on my way to the Turkish market in the Old Town for a coffee, I tramped along the riverside promenade, following the waters of the Vardar—which empty among the Greeks into the Gulf of Salonica as the Axios—and enjoyed the contrasting enticements, of the hole-in-the-wall grill shops, for instance, and a Mozart recital announced for the concert hall. The ideologist of the Macedonian national liberation movement against the Ottoman Turks, Goce Delchev, is entombed in a sarcophagus in the yard of the Church of the Holy Saviour, hard by a sixteenth-century Turkish caravanserai, Kursumli An, decorated with intricate woodwork, its yards converted in 1878 for the purposes of executing Macedonian revolutionaries fighting the Ottomans. The canvases of the Yugoslav avant-garde hang on the walls of the exquisite fifteenth-century Daut Pasha Amam (bath) Fortresses abut mosques, pastry shops huddle in the shadow of a scabrous shopping mall in whose forecourt small but ferocious taxicabs churn in frustrated circles, trying to exit from the gridlock around the money-changing kiosks.

Justinian, originally Sabbatius, was born near here, in 482, of a Slavic peasant family, in the village of Tauresium. Educated in Constantinople, he was Byzantine emperor by the age of forty-five. I had had a look at him once, craning my neck up at the mosaics of the Church of San Vitale in Ravenna, where he stands among his retainers, beardless, arch-browed, cloaked in the imperial purple, crowned and haloed, and holds what appears to be a large, round, brown loaf: altogether, the panel seemed to echo the iconography of Christ who offers Communion to the disciples. Justinian was, after all, the builder of Hagia Sophia, Christianity's supreme monument in Constantinople.

He sent his urban planners and architects to his home town, rebuilt and beautified it, gave it the name Justiniania Prima and seated an archbishop there. Was this the future Skopje? The Misses Muir Mackenzie and Irby thought so and cite the historian of Justinian's reign, Procopius, who found it almost beyond his capacities "to describe the churches, the magnificent houses, the pillared halls, the market-places, and fountains, wherewith Skopia was adorned in its Justianea Prima days." Not so, according to the *Cambridge Companion to the Age of Justinian*: ruins near Nis, Serbia, have been identified by archaeologists as the sixth-century city, and even produce a map.

Yet this same flattering, flowery Procopius scandalously wrote a *Secret History*, vituperative and venomous toward his boss. ("A faithless friend, he was a treacherous enemy, insane for murder and plunder....Of the plundering of property or the murder of men, no weariness ever overtook him.") But Skopjans honour him: the university's Faculty of Law is named for him, for his unequalled accomplishment of the codification of Roman law and constitutions, the Codex Justinianus, a model for many other legal systems, and the Corpus Juris Civilis, still the basis of modern civil law in many states.

BUT HE'S NOT ON THE MAPS. Over coffee, I compared maps, for I was here before, in the 1980s, when I assumed Yugoslavia—just because I so admired the idea of it—was eternal. But now the street named for the great Slovenian Communist economist and architect of Yugoslav self-management, Edvard Kardelj, is renamed, preposterously, for Alexander of Macedon, the Red Army's street is now the Macedonian Soldier's, and the Yugoslav National Army's has been turned over to St. Clement of Ohrid. The internationalists, Marx and Engels, yield to the Internal Macedonian Revolutionary Organization for national liberation, and even that great master of Balkan strategies and a founding father of the state of Macedonia within Yugoslavia, Marshall Josip Broz Tito, whose portrait—still a vigorous and handsome man in his old age—was once ubiquitous, has lost the square given over now simply to "Macedonia."

Much of this new Macedonia confounded me. I was told the economy was on freefall, bereft of its old Yugoslav market, yet I saw that the shops were full of every desirable consumer good, that a Peugeot dealership was implanted across the road from a boarded-up Yugoslav-era factory, and I heard that books published in editions of 3,000–5,000 sold out among a population of a mere two million, and journalists who hadn't been paid in months went nevertheless to literary congresses in Istanbul.

On Good Friday, my friends, Ljubica Janeslieva and Violeta Hristovka, in skirts and sandals, lifting their faces to the miraculous sunshine, walked gaily arm in arm with me about the old city. They had long been professors at the university and from their earliest student days had been grateful for the secular (not to say Communist) space opened up to intellectuals in Yugoslavia. Yet, in lock-step with them, I found myself inside the eighteenth-century Church of St. Demetrius, replacing a thirteenth-century structure, just at the edge of the Old Town. It was gloomy within and it took a few seconds for my eyes to adjust. There stood a young, black-bearded priest in black cassock and soft velvet cap, sentinel to a flower-strewn "bier" raised a half-metre off the floor and decorated like a bridal bed that represented, I realized, the tomb of Christ. My friends, to my surprise, were intent upon lighting the fistful of skinny beeswax tapers they had purchased at the gate and setting them in front of the numerous icons placed around the nave—the first act of veneration of the faithful inside an Orthodox church—but I stayed at the doorway, fascinated by the scene at the bier. A steady stream of young couples approached it, genuflected, and then suddenly dropped to their haunches and crawled under it, duck-walk style. When they emerged from under the floral drapery, the priest gave a perfunctory shake of his water-sprinkler with an expression of great forbearance. I guessed this was a fertility rite of pagan predecessors now overlain by Christian symbol.

On Saturday, clutching more fistfuls of beeswax tapers, like all of post-Communist Christian Skopje it seemed, we advanced on the cathedral square for the Midnight Mass. Most of Skopje had probably never gone to church, yet there they were in their thousands, gathering in excited groups as though at a medieval fair. Sucking cans of Coca-Cola, gobbling bags of popcorn, and chomping on kebabs and bread, they milled about with their friends and family while children pestered their parents for balloons and the smoke from a hundred charcoal grills sizzling with lamb and pork fat rose in a silvery drift, swirling around the klieg lights lighting up the platform at the far end of the square where the priests and deacons and altar boys steadfastly performed the rites of the Divine Liturgy. It was only very much later that I thought of the minarets of the mosques just outside our range of vision on that square, piercing the black sky beyond the lights and balloons, slender turrets under Heaven, too.

"You see those villages," he continues, pointing to white smudges on the hill-side in middle-distance. "They all used to be ours." Then he launches into a catalogue of place-names whose Slavonic resonance I immediately recognize: Golishani, Negush, Stredno Selo, Vladovo, Orizari, Vrtikop, Voden, this stream-bed, that church-yard, those hillsides. And suddenly beneath the official map, with its irreproachably Greek names, another map unfolds, a hidden map of a concealed land which now exists only in the memory of old men, and, as I was later to learn, in the bitter resentment of their exiled sons and grandsons. A map whose dimension is time, not space.

—FRED REED, 1996

DECEMBER 2000: I stand on empty platform number six in the train station in Thessalonica, waiting for the night train to Skopje. I am pursuing Demetrius to that Macedonia among the Slavs.

After a few minutes, a short woman in a fake fur coat zigzags her way to me, lugging a very heavy sports bag that has already burst one of its seams. In pidgin Greek she asks if this is the platform for the train to Skopje. On a hunch, I reply in proto-Slav, that I am going to Skopje, too, and she perks up. Do I have friends there, *gosti*? I learn that she has just spent a month with her sister in Ydessa, Greece, and that she herself lives in Veles, Macedonia. And that she doesn't speak Greek.

Another zigzag delivers a middle-aged man in an overcoat, hauling several bags, who inquires in broken English if we speak English. He turns to me: do I know if this is the platform for the train to Belgrade? I say I'm pretty sure it is. Satisfied, he drifts away. Next, a short and stocky man in baggy trousers and fake-leather jacket sidles up, with a roughened, leathery face and brutalized hands, every crease a rivulet of dirt, wondering where to catch the Skopje train. (What is this? Do I look like an information booth?) Then he and the woman from Veles fall into animated conversation. I try to follow for awhile, but they keep dropping their voices confidentially, but I do catch, from their words and agitated and indignant voices, a conversation about the grim nature of the sweatshop jobs in Greece ("...working at her sewing machine day and night...") and the ever-present fear of being thrown out ("They come looking and checking your papers, and whoof! Out you go") and "How much do you make?" and "I am a pensioner, they don't worry about me," and I wonder, as they shift away right out of earshot, if I am eavesdropping on one of those quintessential Euro-moments of the twenty-first century, where people from the European margins exchange work and border experiences as if they were members of an illegal organization.

They call Thessalonica "Bulgaria," those smug Athenians who live in the sun-bleached south, uncompromised by the misery of the Balkan refugees, beggars, and buskers in vinyl jackets and muddied runners, who gather in increasingly despondent huddles in the parks of Thessalonica, hoping for work. Men without women. Men without children. Men making the rounds of the outdoor tavernas, gawking at the life they used to have in their home places.

The train to Skopje is a kind of "Bulgaria" itself, with only second-class coaches on offer and our little band on platform six its only passengers. Nothing seems to have been retooled or replaced in forty years, neither the scabby upholstery nor the curtains bunched sadly in the grimy corners of the windows, and the non-smoking compartments reek still of an eon of Balkan cigarettes smoked in the corridor. I have the compartment to myself. The rising moon outside, dimly lighting the outlines of low-slung mountains pressing in on us passengers, bared branches whizzing past, and creek beds catching the flow of silvery water, carry me forward into winter.

In 1963 an earthquake shattered Skopje in an early morning horror that pulled down its Byzantine churches, crumpled its Ottoman alleyways and its bustling riverfront. Then it was reconstructed. "The disastrous reconstruction, supervised by a Japanese architect, has robbed it of its soul," wrote Sam Vakunin, once a consultant to the economics ministry of the Government of Macedonia, and now in 2000 raging against the irreparable present, this "Socialist metropolis replete with monumentally vainglorious buildings."

Describing Emperor Justinian's city in the seventh century, Procopius had written of its magnificent houses, the pillared public halls, the abundant vegetable markets, the cooling fountains spilling out the mountain water brought down to the hot plain by aqueducts. A fine and opulent city. "In brief, the city is both great and populous and blessed in every way." Now Vakunin pokes around in disgust, at the uncollected garbage, the potholed streets, the "violation" of the city's spirit by three McDonald's restaurants, the variegated but separated urban currents of Albanians, Slavs, Roma. My friends agree that "Skopje is really getting awful," with its new luxury apartment blocks in which the newly rich, with no visible means of support, submerge themselves, arrogant and spendthrift, while squatters living hand-to-mouth in barracks abandoned by construction companies are forcibly removed to the outskirts of town, "absolutely the worst places in the world." It occurs to me that I've never seen that part of Skopje, nor have I ever been introduced to an Albanian.

I take a walk in the dark, in the neighbourhood of my small hotel near the Grand Hotel (later the Holiday Inn). The sidewalk pavement is laid down in large, flat tiles, but suddenly there is a shallow pit just ahead as though someone has torn out a piece of the sidewalk and walked home with it. It's hard to tell what's what in the murk, whether there's a path safe to cut across the open field between some squatters' huts. There's scrap, waste, rubbish, dog shit, plastic bags, all underfoot as I take my evening stroll.

Next morning, Zoran Ancevski, a poet I met at a PEN congress, fetches me at the hostel, and we drive off to the centre of the Old Town, in search of a picturesque venue for a cup of coffee. Skopje in winter. Trees in solemn leaflessness stand in drifts of dried-up, crumbling leaves. A sun like a moon floats wanly in the fumy atmosphere. Zoran's favourite café is closed for Ramadan, its windows shuttered. The whole narrow cobbled picturesque lane is deserted, so we settle for the café *Klub*, hidden behind a thick, leather-padded door in the Brutalist shopping centre by the river. When we leave a little later, at noon, the (recorded) voice of the muezzin rings out from all the minarets around us that rise clean and sleek above the rooftops, as if lifting stodgy Skopje skywards along with our spirits.

At the open-air farmers' market, we saunter around the tightly packed stalls admiring the fresh, dewy spinach, little lettuces, leeks as long as walking sticks propped up in stooks on the ground, the deep ochre of the flesh of giant squashes cleaved open to our scrutiny, vats and tubs of olives, honey from pine resins, homemade rakia, dried figs from Turkey overlapping each other in luscious propinquity. Zoran stops by a mound of white cheeses and asks the cheese-maker, her fists planted on her hips, from which meadow grasses her sheep have fed, for each grass will lend its own aroma to the milk. It seems to me that I can smell them all, lavender and clover, purple vetch and mint, vintages of Balkan husbandry.

Over lunch with poet Kata Kulavkova, we order baked sauerkraut, risotto, fried eggs on spinach, pork and mushrooms in cream sauce, chicken in gravy, a kind of ham quiche, *sarma* (Balkan cabbage rolls), and bottles of red wine. We eat and drink and talk as the meagre daylight seeps away, and leave in the dark.

Before we part, we raise our glasses for one last toast, to Krste Misirkov, died 1926, a champion of Macedonian letters who lived in a kind of orthographic coherence all over the old Cyrillic world: born in a village of Greek Macedonia, he studied in Belgrade (Serbia), Sofia (Bulgaria), Poltava (Ukraine), Petersburg (Russia), and Odessa (Ukraine), and worked in Bitola (Macedonia), Petersburg, Sofia, Odessa, and Kishinev (Moldova). He criss-crossed his own tracks on an itinerary of speech-making, editing, and publishing, agitating for a Macedonian Mother Tongue that had to be prised from its Bulgarian matrix, which eventually led to a ferocious campaign against him in Bulgaria. Government officials collected copies of *On Macedonian Matters*, published in Sofia in 1903, and destroyed them, threatening him with death if he ever set foot in Macedonia. He died in Sofia, in humiliating poverty, an exile to the bitter end.

But his granddaughter lives in Skopje, in fierce defiance of history, and of today's Bulgarians, Greeks, male writers, and publishers. Kata Rumenova, novelist, has baked Violeta and me a huge leek cake in her small kitchen and serves it in fat slices while she announces that "no one" is invited to these rooms, meaning no male person. "My male colleagues hate me. If I had been born a man I'd have had my work collected between hardcover by now. I've done translations and never been paid. I've done translations and then been informed that the publisher was going to use a male Academician's name in my place.

That's why I have nothing to do with that Mafia. And *no one* is invited into this room. When I was young and beautiful they tried other ways..." To top it off, because her illustrious grandfather belonged to an anti-Bulgarian faction of the Macedonian liberation movement, her own books for children have been blacklisted by the current Macedonian government, which harbours pro-Bulgarian elements.

This is all fascinating, but I've been brought here to talk about Thessalonica. Kata Rumenova was born not far from Thessalonica, in Pella, the town that had been the royal seat of the kings of Macedon, Philip among them. It was her family's fields, she claims, which covered the ruins of Pella, the ruins of a court in which poets and musicians were welcome: Euripides, tragedian from Athens, lingered amiably in the palace for months at a time, strolling through arcades of Ionic columns, along floors laid with blue and white mosaic tiles. I notice that Kata has propped up a pen-and-ink sketch of the head of Alexander the Great, who himself must have had the run of Pella. "How can Alexander be Greek?" she asks rhetorically. "Macedonia has always been a territory invaded and settled by all kinds of people, so it's all mixed up, and the worst thing here in the Balkans is that everyone wanted to make us Macedonians slaves. While the kings of Europe were still illiterate we were literate."

This is a line of argument I am familiar with, among some Ukrainians, for instance, who boast of the eleventh-century accomplishments of the rulers of Kyiv: law codes, cathedrals, libraries, school systems, and princesses married to royal heads of Europe, while their neighbours, notably Russians, lived in bear skins and manned trading outposts in the northern forests. It is unclear which historical period Kata is referring to. That classic of Greek history, H.D.F. Kitto's *The Greeks*, describes the Macedonia of Philip, Alexander's father, as a "wild and primitive country, barely united under a royal family that made pretensions to Hellenic descent." And does her "we" and "us" include both Greeks and Slavs of today's Macedonia? In any case, the fused Macedonian world of Illyrians, Hellenes and Slavs has been sundered, and because Kata reads and speaks Greek, "I know what they've said and written about us [Slav Macedonians], so I write about *Greek* atrocities."

One of her novels concerns three women in Yugoslavia, 1945–1990, and how the wars of the 1990s separated them, but her best novel, she says, is linked with historical incidents in her husband's life. He was a Slav from Thessalonica, summoned back to his birthplace to bury his brother. In his youth he had loved a woman, another Thessalonian Slav, whom he now meets again after forty-five years; she hangs herself shortly after the reunion. "This is a very strong metaphor for Macedonian history." She shoves another wedge of cake onto our depleted plates.

:: *Orphans of the borderlands*

ELENA, one of Ljubica's English literature students approached me after my guest lecture: Would I like to meet her father, Kole Mangov, a judge, poet, and activist, born then orphaned in Greece? Put that way, yes.

A few days earlier, Ljubica, her husband, Anatas, and I had been guests of an elderly artist of Skopje who sat shrivelled within a wing-backed chair in the old-fashioned salon of his spacious apartment and spoke in a kind of squeak. As he was also almost stone deaf, our responses were shouted in the vicinity of his left ear by his son, who had invited us, and poured us tea we sipped from the family china. On the way out, the son chattered to me in English, and only half-play-fully suggested a trip together south, to "Solun," to see and hear for myself that he would be able to speak "Slavic" all along the route, even with Greeks, all the way to Thessalonica.

So, I thought, in spite of assimilation, expulsion, and population exchanges suffered by Slavs and Greeks, there remains a kind of Via Slavonica of speech whose track had been laid through old Macedonia a very long time ago.

I am plucked out of the soupy fog by Elena and her father, Kole Mangov, who drive me to their home in a wheezy car coming apart at the seams. The warmth of the family's reception—his wife, Liliana, and another daughter, Ilina, are waiting for us in their flat, at a table dressed in lace and laden with platters of sweets—dispels the melancholy accumulating around me from the persistent, sodden fogs of

Skopje's winter. This may have been Demetrius's season, this tilt of the earth to the gloomy underworld, but it was chilling me to the bone.

I have been invited to hear a story. It is Kole's story, which begins with his birth in 1940 in the village of Banitsa, a mining town in the county of Lerin, to give it the name he assigns it but which is inside Greece. "Lerin" is the Slavic name of the large town that, in 1926, became Florina. Banitsa is a village in northern Greece with a Slavic etymology, now called "Vevi." "A Greek name," says Kole, "but what does it mean?"

Kole lived his early childhood inside the Macedonian language and failed to understand a word of what was being said to him in the Greek-language kindergarten, but soon enough he learned two words: *Pou pate?* They mean, "Where are you going?" It was a Greek policeman who wanted to know.

Late in 1945, Kole, his stepmother, and a passel of village school-children were on the road to Yugoslavia, walking to Zivojno and its open-pit mines. Kole's father had fled to Yugoslavia in April, together with a group of other miners from Banitsa (he shows me the photograph, his father is the one wearing a smart, brimmed hat), following the Greek elections of spring 1945, and the White Terror of the Rightist forces. Because his father had fought with the pro-Communist guerrilla forces during the German occupation of Greece, he now fled for his life to newly socialist Macedonia, a constituent republic of Yugoslavia, twenty-three kilometres from Banitsa. He sent for his son. And there Kole was, five years old and on the road: *Pou pate?*

He was going to his father, the Communist soldier. He had no idea that he had left his home forever: three years later, his father returned to Greece to take up arms again, to fight alongside Greek Communists in that country's ghastly civil war, and was killed. In 1950 Kole was sent to an orphanage in Bitola, south of Skopje. The Greeks had closed the border in 1949. Having been born into the Slavic minority in northern Greece, Kole was now effectively exiled from his ancestral home. But his memory is saturated with what he calls "the spirit of the people of my village. That spirit is alive in me, rustical, sparkling, everlasting, universal."

We have been drinking a succession of cups of Turkish coffee, our fingers are sticky with the honey of the cakes, all the lamps are lighted, the air is heated. I am offered more of everything, and peanuts and oranges. The village is still there and Kole's relatives live there. But their name is now Mangos.

Kole is weeping, Elena as well, and Liljana, with her head in her arms at the dining room table among the cakes. Their grief is raw, even fifty years after Kole's barely remembered but somehow joyous childhood in a Greek village that has lost its Slavic name. Kole has photographs on the wall here in Skopje of the engagement and wedding of his parents. "She's modern, you see?" he says, indicating his girlish mother in Western dress who will die in childbirth. "See, he's wearing a good English suit," he says, of his father's wedding clothes. The groom will die on some unnamed mountain slope of his homeland. In the aftermath of the civil war, with the Left brutally suppressed or in exile throughout the "fraternal socialist" countries of Eastern Europe, a decree forbade the Slavic-speaking people of Greek Macedonia to use the Slavonic form of their family names, peasants were prohibited from leaving their villages bordering Yugoslavia and were compelled to declare publicly, before officials in Kastoria (Slavic: Kostur) and Florina (Lerin), that they did not speak Macedonian. The orphan of Banitsa would not be coming home.

:: *Back to* normalno

I RODE THE BUS from Skopje through southern Serbia, one of the Balkans' most tedious journeys, a trip I had made in reverse a few years earlier. Then, the transition from southern Serbia into Macedonia had seemed like a lurch into a zone of blight and under-development, now it was the other way around.

"What has happened at Leskovac?" I will ask Drinka Gojkovic, a human rights researcher in Belgrade, thinking of the town, soggy under a cold, slate sky, travellers huddled together under a piece of corrugated tin roofing that served as the bus shelter, everyone in black and brown coats and jackets shapeless and bulky with the cheap synthetic fabrics of their construction. The oversized sloppy boots. The pensioners standing motionless, speechless, hands outstretched with their offerings: dried herbs, woollen socks, a clock, its alarm set off to get our attention. Foamy, muddy sloppings splashed from the potholes of the streets. And rubbish everywhere, the plastic bags simply thrown onto wasteland or verges, garbage tipped out of house-hold containers onto the open fields. "Poverty," Drinka will say. "It's poverty that has happened to Leskovac."

Hundreds of transport trucks had pulled up on the highway and there their drivers had left them—a blockade—to stand and warm themselves over fires of burning tires. We had to make wide detours off the highway to get around these roadblocks, a protest by local citizens against military and police ineffectiveness against the depredations of Kosovar insurgents crossing over into Serbia with impunity and agitating among local Muslims. Here and there en route to Belgrade, planted improbably on the bleak plains of the south, rise sudden eruptions of a tycoon's villa, an architectural pomposity complete with stone lions roaring at the gates. There were no signs of life, as if even the *Mafiosi* wouldn't dare to exhibit themselves in such a sad country, leaning out their windows, rifle underarm, jeering at the shivering truckers and farmers plodding along the highway.

The nights were cold in Belgrade. And because of the rotating power blackouts around the city entire neighbourhoods were without traffic lights as well. This was an invitation for drivers to "sauve qui peut," and inevitably they got themselves and their vehicles into terrible jams as each tried to make his or her way forward *no matter what*, impeding everyone else who had exactly the same intention.

Drinka was lucky never to be blacked-out thanks to the bank on the ground floor and all its computers, which must never come unplugged. Her elevator ran smoothly, and we could calmly descend whenever we wished, out to the little street market with its crates of potatoes and cabbage, its hot cheese pies and little bottles of slivovic.

Everything had to be done anew: schools and teacher training, hospitals, social benefits, new jobs for youth, affordable housing, public works, public transportation, resettlement of refugees, truly independent media not tied to political parties, even the "good" ones. I sat, shivering, in the office of Borka Pavicovic, theatre drama-turge and producer, sharing the little zone of warmth radiating from an electric heater, while she, wrapped dramatically in a tomato-red cloak, and applying a generous swath of red lipstick, explained to me that new post-Communist, post-nationalist governments in Eastern Europe are very suspicious of the cultural sector. "They think of us as a place in which Communism and then nationalism took root," she scoffed. Activists such as her, with her Centre for Cultural Decontamination, had laboured, without a break for cynicism, through the darkest nights of the spirit.

So this was liberated Serbia. But, as Drinka observed, everyone was very confused about what it means. What does it mean to be "proud" to be Serbian? We talked in her living room high above 27 March Street, as the light drained out of the room. Drinka is thin and powered by nervous energy, never far from a telephone or computer. If she stopped for a minute, I had the impression she would collapse from despair. The most shocking identity crisis, she said, was the one provoked by the new nationalists who suddenly demonized Communism. "We went from an identity as Yugoslav socialists who were proud of what we'd achieved and what we represented, in and to the world, to an identity that was supposed to assess that past as entirely rotten. Why? Because that past 'failed' the test of nationalism. Yugoslav Communism had 'betrayed' all the nations."

Friends pointed out what had happened to street names. Communist *Supremo* Marshall Tito was the first to go—even though at least one generation had grown up proud of him—when the main artery downtown was renamed for generic "Serbian Rulers." And soon Boulevard of the Revolution was destined to become Prince Alexander. On the name plates at street corners that bore the Yugoslav-era names, vandals had already been at work in anticipation of their unnaming, scratching and gouging and painting over the offending names, just like Turks and Iconoclasts at work on the eyes of Orthodox saints.

It is as though the collective experience of building Yugoslavia over fifty years was now bogus, the public commemoration of Communists a "stain" on Serbian self-regard, kings and princesses and monasteries deemed more authentic and "meaningful" as markers of Serbian identity.

2002: the Intermezzo Internet Café in downtown Belgrade stands only a few metres farther on from Student Square where, in 1968, the June Days of a delirious student protest against the Red Bourgeoisie of the aging Titoist regime ended in most of the students going back to classes.

Across the street: a cosmetics shop, a kiosk doing brisk business in hot and greasy cabbage pies, and Plato Bookstore, the city's most interesting jumble of books, current and superannuated, that services the students at the Philosophy Faculty/Filozofski Fakultet right next door. There are no more student protests, just a lot of grumbling that "nothing has changed" in post-dictator-Milosevic Belgrade: prices are inflationary, jobs have not reappeared, young people still line up at the visa section of the Canadian Embassy on Prince Milos Street with the dream of fleeing. Where once there were kiosks selling kitschy Serbian nationalist memorabilia and pictures of Serb guerrilla-poster boys active in Croatia and Bosnia, there are now postcards showing the destruction of Serbian cities and countryside. And [in English]: "Fuck your Coke, Fuck your pizza, We still have our slivovica [Serbian pronunciation, *sleevoveetsa*]."

To get to the embassy, they walk past the grim dereliction of the bombed-out military buildings that were destroyed by the NATO bombardments of 1999 and remain unrepaired. The NATO bombings are not the liveliest topic of conversation. At a couple of social evenings I attend, non-stop joke-telling substitutes for serious conversation, by which is meant political discussion. "We want to be normal, like you Canadians," explains a friend's husband after one such evening. "We're sick of politics. You want to talk politics? We'll send you Milosevic. Better yet, how about American bombers over Edmonton?"

At the Intermezzo Café on this wan and declining afternoon I watch *The Simpsons* with Serbian subtitles while some sort of boomba-boomba pop music bounces out of the sound system. I look around, at lovely young women in pairs, gesticulating in conversation, twirling blue and pink paper umbrellas in their café frappés. I watch the woman in charge of a mobile telephone sales and service at her perch on a high stool at a countertop, long pink fingernails clicking on her keyboard as she plays Solitaire. There is a litter of magazines no one is reading. VISA *welcome here*, and Diner's Club.

"There are no social democratic economists here," says old friend Milan Nikolic. Nikolic, one-time student militant, political prisoner, and sociologist, now directs a research institute on social policy and never fails to have the Big Picture. I drop in on him at his office in the city centre, up on the second floor of a gloomy building around the corner from the Aeroflot offices. His offices are pleasant rooms, filled with energetic young people to whom the project of correcting shambolic social policies is going to be turned over eventually.

Nikolic sits imposingly at a large desk, leaning back into a broad leather chair into which his girth expands to fill all the available volume, and tells me that no one should underestimate the enormous changes in the year-and-a-bit since the October 5 Revolution drove out Milosevic. "Think of it: We Serbs were isolated and despised in the world, people felt hopeless, criminality and corruption went unchallenged (outside dissident circles), the media were kept on a very short leash, and so on. Now we are more 'normal.' But if you look at what still has to be done the changes seem to have brought us forward only about this much." And he indicates the space between two pinched fingers.

Afterwards, we go for supper in the restaurant favoured by the journalists at the newspaper, *Politika*, across the street. Poking at the cabbage and potatoes, Milan continues with his State of the Union: "Unemployment is at 50 per cent. People still list themselves as employed at plants that haven't operated for years or paid their workers. We have had an out-migration of 200,000 people, our best and brightest, while up to a million refugees are still unsettled. Some of the elderly have returned to villages in Croatia and Bosnia, in order to die 'at home.' There's no money for any of it: reconstruction of social services, transportation, energy infrastructures, schools, hospitals, ecological clean-up, you name it."

A friend, he relates, was offered a few ministries from Hell (including Energy and Social Policy), which he rejected, being able to predict the trajectory of events in such a job. "He would begin with big ideas, work eighteen hours a day, and get nowhere because there's no money. And where do you start? When a house is falling down, what will save it? Propping up the kitchen ceiling? Nailing down the linoleum? People feel disappointed by you and let down, accuse you of theft and cronyism, get mad at you and, to top it off, vandalize your car. You lose your confidence. Who needs this?

"We can't change the past. In the meantime, it's the future that can defeat us."

When I meet anthropologist Ivan Colovic, in an amiable interview one grey afternoon, the collection of his essays, *Politika simbola [The*

Politics of the Symbol], has already been in circulation for some years, published by the independent and sassy radio station B92, at a time when the regime of Slobodan Milosevic had still seemed unassailable. The essays cover topics as diverse as church sermons, lyric verse, tourism, and the use of the phrase "turbulent times." To study the rhetorical, demagogic, and promotional use of symbols in politics, he argues, is to be forearmed against the "exceptionally resilient" nationalist cults and myths of this country in transition to a democratic model of society.

The working class is no longer heard from. Instead, Colovic tells me, the public hears the Serbian Orthodox faithful and the literary critics and historians in tandem with the theologians who construct a Serb "identity" from anti-Communism, anti-Semitism, anti-Americanism. "The dominant discourse has been Serbian victimization and innocence. Even now, to raise the issue in the media of Serbian responsibility for war crimes is to wound national feeling." The more firmly that Serbs refuse to confront their responsibility, the more important becomes the abstraction of Serbianness and nationalist strategies that resort to old mythologies; as a Serbian minister for culture, Zeljko Simic, once put it, after the NATO bombing of Serbia in 1999, "The radiation of the Serb spirit has proved stronger than the radiation of the aggressor's bombs."

"Serbianness," remarks Colovic, "is a kind of spirituality that has replaced the consciousness of the working class."

But this is not the first time that the Christian symbolic order has been in competition for the soul of "Serbianness."

IN BELGRADE, mid-week, I visit two little churches, St. Petka and Ruzica, poised on a high point of Kalemegdan Park with a commanding view, that sunny morning, out over the blue-grey streams of the Sava and Danube. It is quiet up there, no river traffic sailing the Danube, thanks to all the bombed-up urban junk that still lies unrecovered in its depths. I can hear the birdsong, which is immensely cheering. I peek inside St. Petka. It seems to be a communal meeting point: men and women stand in queue to kiss the icons in rotation, light candles, pour out holy water into plastic bottles. I withdraw, suddenly feeling shy.

Next day, St. Demetrius Day in fact, the weather turns nasty. Could this not have been predicted? St. Demetrius Day is the first day of winter, and, according to Serbian folklore, on *Mitrovdan* you can predict the severity of the winter by the way an ox lies down and sticks out its legs—or not. If he lies down with his feet tucked under him, the winter will be hard; if he lies with his leg extended, it will be mild. And if the leg is bent back toward the south, it will be mild, turned north, harsh.

Could someone not have looked at an ox and let us know?

In Serbia, they have a saying: On Mitrovdan [St. Demetrius Day], when it's cloudy, winter will be mild. If snow falls on Mitrovdan, it's because St. Demetrius is riding his white horse. In Serbia, there is a superstition that, on Mitrovdan, everyone in the family has to be at home together, otherwise they will all be scattered for the year.

St. Petka is the parish of the youthful and vigorous Fr. Vladimir Vukasinovic, who is also a professor at Bogoslovije, Belgrade's School of Theology, an imposing collection of buildings miles away from the main action at the University of Belgrade downtown. It takes me several minutes of wandering cluelessly around the substantial corridors and staircases, while young men and women and seminarians rush about from class to class, to find the office at which Fr. Vladimir has told me to present myself. A theologian at the faculty who introduces himself as Bogdan, a man of continental charm in my view, accompanies me to a kind of boardroom, and, while waiting for Fr. Vladimir to show up, explains that, although not every graduate in theology is a priest, it is now required of priests to finish their studies with two or three years of courses at the faculty, "to raise the intellectual level of our priests." I wonder if this will only exacerbate the separation of the worlds in which priests and their flocks live? Well, yes, "but there's such a pressing need for priests that some are allowed out into their ministries with just a beefed-up seminary education, as in the old days."

Fr. Vladimir sweeps into the faculty's conference room in a great volume of black cassock. Over the course of three hours' conversation,

a series of equally tall, broad-shouldered, and handsome priests inter-
rupts us periodically, each greeting me with the utmost pleasantness,
even gallantry, and I will find myself reluctant to take my leave, even
as I know it has become dark and cold outside.

Fr. Vladimir is immensely sympathetic, well-spoken, funny, patient
with my questions, and expansive with his answers. He speaks with
compassion and humour about the shortcomings of his flock. His
approach as a priest is to take people as they are, who they are, when
they come to him, not to condemn their misunderstandings and
imperfections but gently to show them the correct Christian practice.

"A gypsy family once came to me with two large bags of women's
clothing, everything from winter coats to brassieres. They explained
that these were for Sveta Petka. I had to laugh. 'Our saint is a spirit!
How is she to wear these things?' 'Now, don't you worry about
that, Father. No problem.' A woman came to me, enquiring of the
Feast Day, Good Friday, *Velik Petak* [Great Friday], if this were Sveta
Petka's husband? 'No, no,' I told her, 'it's her uncle!' The point being
that you do not move people along spiritually simply by contra-
dicting them and telling them what they should do or believe, like a
commandment.

"People come in with their great big *slavski kolac,* bread to
be blessed for Slava [the Feast Day of the family's Patron Saint],
even though it is not a day of Slava. They dimly remember a daily
blessing of bread and want to practise it again." He makes sure first
to congratulate them for their devotion, for having thought of the
blessing of bread at all.

"I do not criticize them. It is a nostalgia for the communal experience of the Eucharist."

But there is a *theological* problem with this kind of self-assembled
ritual and prayer, and that is that the text is often mixed and mangled,
and "it isn't full prayer, which *always* involves a priest and the people.
Prayer is dialogical! A priest praying alone is not a full prayer either.

"But the genius of the people lies in the fact that the faith and the
sense of being Serbian has been kept."

I mention the little scene I had glimpsed inside his church, glowing
with icons and people's kisses. He does not blush in telling me he blesses

and consecrates all kinds of things in everyday life, not just icons.

"If I consecrate a thing—house, car, icon—it's like activating the thing through prayer, plugging the hair dryer into the socket. The consecrated car is the prayer in everyday life. It's not just for Sunday morning. Prayerful attitude to life is everyday: when we start school, build a house, have an operation. Christianity involves the body as well as the spirit. People want to have a bodily experience of the church—oil on their forehead, the smell of incense, kissing the icons, eating the bread. You cannot understand Christianity without understanding materiality. My spiritual rebirth was when I realized that everything around me could help me communicate with God and to build His house, even the stones in the field."

I remember a scene elsewhere in Serbia that I had watched years earlier with derision: a country priest strode briskly around a blue Volkswagen, all its doors open, wildly swinging a censer while a young couple stood aside respectfully and the white fumes of frankincense drifted over the dashboard and steering wheel. Now it is I who blush, for not understanding a prayer for a car.

Local inhabitants navigated the rivers with dinghies hollowed out from trees and with rafts. They ate millet bread, drank a mead and another drink, from barley.

—FRANJO BARIŠIĆ, 1952

I HAVE BEEN GRANTED ADMISSION to one of the libraries of the Academy of Sciences in downtown Belgrade, a refuge from "normal" Serbia, and with deep pleasure I settle down at the polished table in the small reading room I have to myself except for the hospitable librarian at her desk by the door.

I've asked to see *La vie rurale dans l'Empire Byzantin* by Germaine Rouillard, published in Paris in 1953, to find clues to the mentality of the medieval cultists of St. Demetrius.

The text is shocking. I find myself in the company of unruly peasants in Greece who, perhaps driven by the destitution of their circumstances, have beaten and robbed the owners of the estates on which they have laboured, namely the monks and abbots of vast land-holding monastic orders. They have also refused to perform their obligatory day's work of unpaid labour, and, in the case of the monastery at Lembos, refuse to reimburse money they've borrowed from the monks. The monks have complained directly to the emperor in Constantinople, adding that a mob of peasants has killed a monk, who had declined to hand over some cheese, and have brazenly pastured their cattle in the monastery's meadows.

But it is the peasants' piety I am interested in, these Byzantine kin of the villagers in northwestern Greece who bring down their flocks on St. Demetrius Day, who get paid, who buy new shoes, on St. Demetrius Day, and of the Macedonians who cook and eat the flesh of a farm animal on St. Demetrius Day. "It's true," writes Ms. Rouillard, "that the faith of the peasants who attended the churches and chapels of the towns and large estates wasn't very enlightened and was mixed with superstitions...and one recalls in this regard the reproaches made by Joseph Bryennios [fifteenth-century theologian] against his contemporaries: 'We are convinced that Nereids live in the sea and that spirits reside in every place....Some of us, and these are Orthodox, cense the fig trees, the cucumbers and the spirits of the house....We have recourse to incantations for fertility of the fields, the growth and health of the herds, the success of the hunt, the plentiful harvest of the vines.'"

When the great French Byzantinist of the early twentieth century, Charles Diehl, whom Rouillard cites, stared into a fifteenth-century miniature of peasants on a hunt, he saw there "the Greek with regular and noble features," the Slavs "with slit eyes and red beards in full bloom." But the slitty-eyed Slav and the Greek with the great cheekbones cohabited a spiritual world that included "animalistic elements, totemism, magic, pantheism," according to Dr. Petar Vlahovic, a retired ethnologist still keeping an office at the Philosophy Faculty at the University of Belgrade when I meet him, to ask about early Slavic Christianity in these parts.

The light in the small office is yellowish, the steam radiator rattles and wheezes, the professor is courteous and talkative. "That's how Slavs absorbed Byzantine elements into their cultures. Thanks to Christianity, we abandoned some pagan beliefs but cultural pluralism is part of our mentality." He means both the ten centuries of ecumenical Byzantium and Eastern Orthodoxy when there were no national-linguistic states sequestering people within monolithic identities, and the modern "global culture," which has more meaning now, he argues as an ethnologist, than "pure Serbianness."

Now he looks at how people live in cities and at Christmastime how they put Christmas trees on their apartment radiators not on a hearth and how on the farm they will hang flowers not on the horns of their cattle but on their tractors on the "Green Holiday" after Easter. During the Ottoman centuries, when Orthodox Christians were constantly reminded that their faith was second-class and they could not even ring church bells to summon the people to prayer, the church eased up on its campaign against "paganisms"—after all, many, many villages no longer had either priest or church—and, as a result, says Vlahovic, "Serbianness was preserved in the old traditions revived out of sheer self-defence."

But, uneducated as they were, the peasants knew they had to pray every day and to someone, and they placed their icons on impro-vised altars and said their improvised prayers. "Their life depended on their animals and so they made magic. They made sacrifices to God and asked for His protection. They had no chance to celebrate the Eucharist without a church or priest, so they confessed their sins to a dogwood tree and ate the buds as bread. Country people kept these beliefs right up to World War Two, but villages as such don't exist anymore."

Even their Christian/Orthodox beliefs carry a heavy dose of practicality—a priest may pray for rain during the Divine Liturgy, a congregation may kill a bull on a saint's feast day for good luck—or of confusion, as when they celebrate the Day of the Mice (*Mishjidan*), a day of magic and foolery and incantations, along with St. Demetrius Day (*Mitrovdan*). Mice live through the winter in the farmers' houses and barns, feasting on the stores of wheat. And there is the word *demetriaka*, Greek, for a portion of grain.

Near Leskovac in Serbia, Professor Vlahovic tells me, unmarried boys and girls gather on St. Demetrius Day, special cakes in hand, to walk together out of the village and into the fields, there to build a fire, dance around it, and eat the cakes. "It's a kind of sacrifice to St. Demetrius, if you like, without meat and without a priest." I think of sad, impoverished Leskovac, which I once viewed from the window of the bus I rode north to Belgrade, and I wish I had seen this other scene, tender and bucolic, sweethearts sharing cakes in the stubble fields of winter.

But "Demetrius" is darker than that. When Slavs brought with them into the Balkans their gods for protection, health, and fertility, among them was the one who would become St. Demetrius. "He was first a pagan god and crossed over into Christianity. Some of the characteristics of the pagan gods then moved into him. The idea of protection, for example. It is said St. Demetrius killed ninety-nine people before he was killed. This is the popular story. Actually, he killed one hundred"—he warms to his subject—"but the death of that hundredth is not part of the sin." I want to stop him—wait a minute, I've never heard this before, where did you hear it?—but Olgica Marinkovic, the translator, is translating at such a clip that I can only bend to the task and keep on writing. "That one whom he killed had spread bad tales about the girl he was going to marry, which is a sin. This is a bigger sin than killing ninety-nine men.

"St. Demetrius is the protector of this girl and of mothers. And the sons who treat their mothers badly, he turns to stone. The grandson who loves his grandmother, he turns into a gold pigeon. This is a story told on our terrain about St. Demetrius of Thessalonica." He pauses.

"Here's another specific characteristic: *Mitrovdan* is the beginning of winter. On that day the *hajduks* [mountain bandits] stop fighting and spend the rest of the winter with friends. It's on St. George Day that they go back to the woods to fight. Demetrius is not a warrior-saint." I raise my eyebrows, but the professor rushes on.

Demetrius is a household god. For a week before *Mitrovdan*, women stop their domestic work—weaving, sewing, handiwork in general—because it is prohibited to use scissors. The open blades of the scissors signify the open jaws of wolves, and to use the scissors invites the beasts to attack the flocks. It is forbidden to touch the flock with your bare hands. Nor can an animal be bought or sold.

Demetrius stands at the portals of winter; he is a patron of the dead. On All Souls Day, *Zadusnica*, the Saturday before *Mitrovdan*, the souls of the dead, who have been walking the warm, pulsing, green earth all summer, must return to their graves and to the cold, black earth that is Demetrius's realm, and into which the farmer will sow his winter wheat.

:: *Sofia*

Once upon a time in Bulgaria, a poor fisherman, with a wife but no children,
caught a fish who begged him to release him back to the river. The next day,
the fisherman caught the very same fish who again pleaded to be released.
The third day, when the miraculous fish appeared once again in the fisher-
man's net, the fish told the fisherman that finally it was time to take him
home to his poor wife, to eat him and to bury his bones under the manger of
their mare. Nine months later, the mare gave birth to twin colts and the fish-
erman's wife to twin boys, whom they christened Dimitar and Georgi. The
colts and the boys grew up together and, when it came time to seek out their
separate destinies, the brothers each mounted a horse and promised that,
if one of them should be in trouble, the other would come immediately to
his aid. And so it came to pass. On his own adventure, Dimitar learned that
Georgi was in battle with a ferocious dragon. He rushed to his rescue, and
slew the beast. The grateful brothers dedicated the rest of their lives to Christ
Jesus, and called themselves Saint Dimitar and Saint Georgi.

—RACHKO POPOV, 1991

A YEAR EARLIER, in November, on my first visit to Sofia in 2000,
the city was still basking in the last days of autumn, and I walked
aimlessly through neighbourhoods, enjoying leaves sailing down

from the plane trees and roses still in wrinkled bloom, while feral dogs ran in packs through abandoned lots gone to weed and thistle, and old men curled over chess boards in the parks, which had a weathered sort of colouring in the muted sunshine. This was not far from the vacated pedestal of Georgi Dimitrov, the first premier of the Bulgarian People's Republic. As the author of ruthless Sovietization in the 1950s, he had been blown off this pedestal in the exhilaration of post-Communism. Four years later, I will walk through this park again and in Dimitrov's place will be erected a massive reproduction of a box of Johnny Walker Red.

I've missed Demetrius's Feast Day, old and new calendar, for it's now December.

From the window of the restaurant, The Friends, by Slaveikov Square, I take refuge from the bitter cold. Outside, people bundled up in parkas, hunched against the wind, stand sentinel at the long plank tables where they offer used books for sale—their children's story-books, their old atlases, the collections of Marxism-Leninism, as well as computer manuals and the works of Pencho Slaveikov, the only Bulgarian writer to have been nominated, back in 1912, for the Nobel Prize in Literature.

Through another window I can read the mishmash of shop signs in Cyrillic and Latin scripts, sometimes within the same message. The scrolling display for MTI International—that much is in Latin script—promises—in Cyrillic—Professionalism, Reliability [Konkretnost], and Perfect Service. I wonder how much longer, in a McWorld of American English, these Cyrillicians, as I think of them, can hang onto letters that had been fashioned in medieval Balkan monasteries expressly for them, as they entered Christendom? I return to my reading of the local English-language weekly, the *Sofia Echo*. "Dear Santa," the Editorial begins, "we've decided to come up with our wish list ahead of time as it might take a while for things to make their way to Bulgaria from our lovely friend at the North Pole. Dear Santa Klausov: please bring Driving For Dummies; this fantastic new guide would do wonders for many of Sofia's drivers. It details such important things as stopping at red lights, what a pedestrian crossing is, and why cars should receive maintenance checks more than once every fifteen years." I check the streets outside the windows again; I don't so much see daredevil cars as wobbly trams and a cluster of pedestrians at the tram stop, congealing in the wind.

What a cultural free-for-all. The cinemas proffer the same American movies that the rest of the planet is watching at this very moment, the iconography of Arnold Schwarzenegger, Julia Roberts, and Tom Hanks, to rival that of popular Saints Panteleimon, Paraskeva, and Nicholas. In the bookstores, Sofia's discerning readers can purchase translations of the international bestsellers that now crowd out the thin collections of local starving poets. The Nike "whoosh" logo on sports clothes is a universal "branding" sign among the teenagers, but the old slogans—Onward to Victory with the Five-Year Plan!—are not. Across the street from a cyber café near the university are both the Pitsa Italija restaurant and the Russian Cultural Centre, which looks just like the main Bank of Montreal building in downtown Edmonton. McDonald's renders itself in Cyrillic signage, compounding the confusion: is the Big Mac Bulgarian or not? You can see Bulgarians juggling identities, making up the rules as they go along: McWhoosh, or collapsed Communist, or ethnic, but all of them in crisis.

I compare Soviet and post-Soviet-era street maps. V.I. Lenin Boulevard is Tsarigradsko Shosee (Constantinople Way); Russian Street is now dedicated to Bulgaria's first head of state and constitutional monarch, Prince Alexander Battemberg; Patrice Lumumba, the murdered Congolese left-wing nationalist, and Klement Gottwald, Czechoslovak Stalinist leader, have lost their respective streets but not Graf (Count) Ignatiev, Russian diplomat who fruitfully meddled in Bulgarian affairs during the Ottoman period and the wars of liberation. Marshall Feodor Tolbukhin, of the Red Army's Third Ukrainian Front, scourge of German forces on the southeastern front in 1944, has been stripped from the boulevard now named for Bulgaria's supreme and sublime national hero, the revolutionary martyr of the Ottoman era, Vasil Levski. The monument to the Red Army still stands, though: perhaps the Bulgarians are not ashamed of this, the rapturous gratitude of civilians to the liberating Reds in September 1944, after a war in which, after all, the Bulgarian state had been allied with the

German cause, however warily, and Sofia had been bombed by the Allies.

I'm enjoying my meal, the spicy pasta sauce, the carafe of rough, red wine, but the rest of Bulgaria lies out there, where, according to the newspaper, there are now 100,000 drug addicts, compared to the mere three hundred of a decade earlier. And illiteracy is on the rise again, thanks to the collapse of public investment in the schools and teachers' salaries, and it is estimated that in another decade every seventh Bulgarian will be illiterate. Bulgarians illiterate? The very people to whom the Cyrillic alphabet had been gifted, and from them to my Ukrainian ancestors? Even I feel humiliated.

They must be patient: in six years they will be "inside Europe," along with Romania the last of the post-Soviet, para-capitalist societies to be admitted to the European Union for the time being. In 2001 a reporter goes to the town of Pernik some forty kilometres southeast of Sofia, a ghost town where coal mines and metalurgical and steel industries used to flourish, where now the young people, even the computer programmers, cannot find work nor can they afford to live in Sofia; they tell the reporter they dream simply of leaving Bulgaria altogether. In Vidin, residents of half-ruined apartment blocks sit sunken in the dark because they cannot afford the electricity bills; one by one, the factories have shut down, and now also the Internet café and restaurants. To amuse themselves, youths pitch stones at the blind street lamps while their parents and grandparents sell cigarettes they bring back in shopping bags from Serbia, and wind-up toys and plastic alarm clocks and nylon panties, scraping together a few dollars a day. I've seen them, on the interminable bus ride from Belgrade to Sofia, youngish women in stylish jeans and high-heeled shoes even in this raw winter, big-bellied men in porkpie caps, grandmothers with dark and drawn faces in oversized sweaters, their stumpy legs shoved into plastic boots, all of them with barely a place to sit once they've brought on board an astonishing amount of "cargo" from bargain-shopping in Belgrade.

On yet another very cold morning in Sofia, in an unheated, noisily cheerful café near the university filled with students and artists wrapped up in long wool scarves, I meet Ilia Iliev, a young "ethnological scientist" at Sofia University. "Iliev is one of our most interesting and bright young intellectuals," a retired anthropologist had told me, pointing me to a website and Iliev's paper, "Price and Prejudice." Here Iliev wrote that he had watched the "process of pauperization" as it played in a used-clothing shop, as a teacher, a secretary, and a high-school student each fingered the cast-off finery of the ladies and gentlemen of Europe, which has been funnelled through the Red Cross into their Bulgarian street. Such an enterprise, a *used-clothing shop*, they tell Iliev, would have been unthinkable in "normal" times.

Iliev, huddled deep inside his duffle coat, looks around the freezing café, waving at friends. This is one of those post-Communist spaces that give the lie to the social despair that lurks in the statistics. The students, as everywhere, are more enraptured by their own vitality than by the prognosis for their generation delivered by their elders, in the shape, perhaps, of this elderly farmwoman who grimly makes her rounds of the tables, proferring to each group of rowdies her fistful of parsley for sale, three sprigs at a time. Parsley in December? A miracle. But they shoo her away.

"Normal" means pre-capitalist, Iliev explains, an "echo, a memory of the period when the teacher, the secretary, had a higher revenue and a higher level of consumption," and could buy her clothes new as befit her prestige as a Bulgarian worker. "Normal" was to be Communist, or at least socialist, when one knew what a fashionable suit was and what should be purchased for the modest living room. The teachers and secretaries were thus assured of belonging to the larger group of what they considered to be their counterparts, their peers, smart middle-class women in shopping malls in Western society. What had gone wrong? "The interviewees argued that something wrong had happened to the whole society at a certain point—in the Middle Ages, or with the Ottoman occpuation, or in 1944, or in 1989." This national calamity "explained" why the interviewee could not afford the way of life to which she would have been entitled had she lived elsewhere, somewhere not-the-Balkans.

:: Who are the Bulgarians?

The Bulgarians are distinguished in all essentials from their neighbours—the
Greek, the Rouman, and the Turk....How strongly difference of race can tell
under identical conditions of climate, religion and government, is exempli-
fied in towns where Greeks have been dwelling side by side with Bulgarians
for centuries. The one is commercial, ingenious, and eloquent, but fraudulent,
dirty, and immoral; the other is agricultural, stubborn and slow-tongued; but
honest, cleanly and chaste.

—G. MUIR MACKENZIE AND A.P. IRBY

ILIA ILIEV is also the author of the much-discussed article, "The
Proper Use of Ancestors," published in 1998 in *Ethnologia Balkanica*
and which will send me running around Sofia in urgent enquiry: Who
are the Bulgarians? For all their use of the Cyrillic alphabet and their
adherence to the Orthodox faith, Bulgarians were not Slavs—with
ancestors spilled out of that fertile, fecund, inexhaustible matrix, the
Carpathian Basin—but something like *Bulgars*, who had once been
Turkic but had become *Bulgarians* by some evolutionary process I was
unfamilair with.

What compelled me was the fact that, once the Bulgars settled
permanently on what had been Byzantine lands, controlled the resident Slavic population and assimilated its language, and became a
Christian state when their tsar, Boris, was baptized into the Church
of Constantinople in 865, they acted as a kind of cultural transmission
belt for the pagan east Slavic tribes roaming the Ukrainian steppes.
It was at the monasteries of Preslav that the Cyrillic alphabet was
invented, letters that would open Christian texts to the eastern Slavs.
This First Bulgarian Kingdom was a great success, at its most powerful
a state that, east-west, spread from the Black Sea to Budapest and,
north-south, from the Dnipro River to the Adriatic Sea. As Bulgars,
they had brought new construction and military techniques into
Europe and built a capital city, Pliska, which was among the largest
towns in Europe. In 1018, however, Byzantium annexed the Kingdom
of Bulgaria to its own imperium, toppling good Christian Tsar Boris,

abolishing the Bulgarian bishoprics, and demolishing the state. A catastrophe, if one was a medieval Bulgar(ian).

I begin to see what might lie at the heart of "proper" and "improper" uses of ancestors: the unstanchable psychic wound of enforced political, cultural, and spiritual subordination to power. After Byzantine domination came Ottoman through to the end of the nineteenth century; in the twentieth, Soviet hegemony in Eastern Europe. While Bulgaria was still subsumed within the Turkish Ottoman world, Bulgarian ethnographers argued for the vital importance of the nation's Slavic origin, for Slavs, even the indigenous rabble of the Balkans, "belonged" to Europe, unlike their Asiatic overlords. Bulgarian intellectuals then refined their argument to recover the *proto*-Bulgarians, nomadic warrior non-Slavs from beyond the Black Sea whose "political genius" engendered the first independent barbarian kingdom on Byzantine territory in 681 CE. In this account, the Christian Slavs, once the seminal culture, have now become a formless mass compared to the pagan Bulgars' discipline, organization, and self-consciousness.

Nevertheless, the two peoples mated, and, historically, a Bulgarian identity did consolidate in the merger of Slavs and Bulgars as proto-Bulgarians.

This then was "Bulgaria" until the arrival of the Communist state in 1944 when, as Iliev puts it, "the proto-Bulgarians were removed from circulation." The internationalism of the Communist movement "required" that Bulgarians share ancestry with that most heroic of the Communist states, Slavic Russia.

Then, in 1972, in place of the discredited proto-Bulgarians, arrived another non-Slavic group onto the ethno-historical scene. Bulgarian archaeologists excavating a prehistoric necropolis near the city of Varna on the Black Sea coast exposed what is arguably the oldest hoard of gold artefacts ever unearthed—dated between 4600 and 4200 BCE—objects of great refinement and buried with an evident complexity of ritual. At that date they were neither of proto-Bulgarian nor Slavic origin. Who were these extraordinary craftsmen? The Thracians, apparently, for whose ethno-genesis I resort to the *Handbook of Greek Mythology*: "The Thracians were warlike, barbarous people, though brave. They drank heavily, and made cruel sacrifices of their enemies on the altars of their gods. Since the climate was severe and the people fierce, Thrace was called home of Boreas [the north wind] and Ares [god of war]" This is perhaps the Greek view of things; from the Bulgarian point of view, the contribution of the Thracians to regional civilization was their alleged sensitivity and, above all, their non-Slavic brilliance, such as the figure of the so-called Thracian Horseman, the enigmatic rider represented as a hunter, whose memory among the early Christians of Thessalonica—here's the wonder—would seep, speculatively, into the popular image of St. Demetrius.

This is an ancestry, an antiquity, to rival that of the western Europeans, johnny-come-latelies to the scene. If, from the point of view of the West, Bulgaria and Bulgarians belong to the "East," and therefore outside its interest and concern, well, then, the "East" would establish its cultural *bona fides* in a game of genealogical one-upmanship.

Over congealed cups of cappuccino, Iliev and I pursue the question; in the seven years since he's published his paper, "The Proper Use of Ancestors," I ask Iliev how he would update his account of the politicization of Bulgarian identity. He would emphasize, he replies, the "beauty" of the tri-partite hypothesis—the proto-Bulgarian, the Slavic, *and* the Thracian components—for its "aesthetic coherence," for everyone can identify with at least one of them. This is to be compared with the University of Sofia's Department of Ancient and Medieval History, which now includes Thracian Studies but makes no mention of Slavs as such. (From the department's website: "Of special importance are lecture courses in the history of Hellenism and most of all those in Thracian Studies—areas in which Bulgarian historiography has established traditions and occupies its due place in Europe.") A typical argument for why the Bulgars were absorbed into the Slavic language rather than the reverse goes like this, says Iliev: "The proto-Bulgarians, being cleverer than the Slavs, learned Slavic as a second tongue, while the Slavs were too stupid to learn Bulgarian." These theories have been taken up by the pop media. "This can be compared to the Celtic and Druidic fads in the UK and France."

Iliev calls this a "period of shame" for Bulgarian intellectual life, but there was a brief and scintillating period during the struggle for national liberation from the Ottoman Empire when revolutionary hero Vasil Levski had a vision for the network of revolutionary committees that had sprung up over Bulgaria in the 1860s: a democratic, "pure and sacred" republic based on the principles of law and freedom for all human beings and equality between the peoples in the Bulgarian lands. Instead of an uprising, however, Levski, a former church deacon, was betrayed by an accomplice and hanged in Sofia in 1873, at the age of thirty-six.

A few days after my conversation with Iliev, I stop in downtown Sofia at some remnants of stone Turkish barracks of the sixteenth century and read the little plaque. From these dungeons, "the Apostle of Freedom," Levski, was taken out "to the gallows and his historical immortality." He was buried in the prison's graveyard, a deliberate humiliation, and rumours spread that Levski had not in fact been left to rot in a communal grave. According to legend, on the very night he was hanged, Levski's body was removed to a fifteenth-century church in Sofia. Whether he will pass from urban legend to new historical fact is dubious: during the excavation and removal of artefacts from the church some years ago, right in the middle of a construction zone, the workers lost the bones.

> *The excavator is an expert at mounds.*
> *It has broken the rusty lock and now*
> *the whole treasure is on the road,*
> *a plundered treasure,*
> *bone and stone.*

—TSANKO LALEV, *"Excavations" (translated by Belin Tonchev)*

WRITING IN THE MAGAZINE, *Conde Nast Traveler* in 2002, G.Y. Dryansky drives across the Thracian Plain on his way from Sofia to the historic city of Plovdiv (named Philippopolis by the Greeks, Trimontium by the Romans). In these valleys Thracians had planted their vines and their grain, thriving as a unique culture four millennia before Christ, until they were absorbed as one more element into the mixture of Persian, Macedonian, Roman, and Slav that the very word *Bulgaria* is said to mean. They have left behind the mystery of their culture in the still unexcavated tumuli in the high, grassed-over mounds that tilt on the fields between the slabs of the Balkan and Rhodope mountains. But the National Museum of History, steward of the national consciousness, is on the case.

The museum has been relocated to the edge of Sofia, almost on the flank of Vitosha Mountain. The ordinary public, then, must make a dedicated effort to get there if they don't have a car, but I have been driven there by a friend, linguistics professor Diana Yankova, who has not yet seen it herself in its new quarters. The building is the refurbished conference centre of the old Communist Party; we Lilliputians creep, speaking in intimidated whispers, around its bulk, its grandiloquence, its outsize staircases and salons and chandeliers.

The exhibit rooms are extremely well done, wonderfully lit, the artefacts in open view and tagged in English as well as Bulgarian. There are rooms of pre-history, of Thracians and Greeks and Romans, and then suddenly we are with the proto-Bulgars and medieval Bulgarian state-builders. There seem to be no Slavs here. Maybe the Slavs didn't leave artefacts, or none worth displaying here? I think of Ilia Iliev's reference to a recent Bulgarian excavation of a sod house sunk into the earth, a *zemlianka*: "They recognized that it was a Slavic hut because of its extreme primitivism." Of these embarrassing people, precursor residents of the Bulgarian lands, the Museum of History appears to pass over in silence—Yankova confirms this, as we stand in front of the large wall panels with their texts written only in Bulgarian. The Slavs, until the day before yesterday still one-third of the Bulgarian ethnocultural identity, have been disappeared. In Hall 3, "The Bulgarian State during the Middle Ages 7th–14th centuries," we are whisked from the arrival of Khan Asparuh (681–700) to Khan Omurtag (814–831), the adoption of Christianity (864), and the Golden Age of the First Bulgarian Kingdom without stopping to mention the Slavs.

THE NATIONAL LIBRARY is closed for cleaning the day I have chosen to work there, given over to a brigade of women with mops. I make my way desultorily along Prince Dodunkov Street, happening on a mosque where I stop to fill my plastic water bottle with the warm mineral water gushing out in steaming torrents from a series of pipes—water that had once served the Turkish bath house now being renovated as an art gallery. From where I stand on Maria Louisa Street, I can see the large letters, VMRO [Internal Macedonian Revolutionary Organization], on the side of a building on Pirotska Street. That would be the Macedonia that is claimed as part of the Bulgarian lands, for the anti-Ottoman VMRO revolutionaries of the nineteenth and early twentieth centuries dreamed of placing a Bulgarian governor in Thessalonica, of naming Bulgarian officials and of Bulgarian as an official language alongside Turkish in the region of Macedonia.

I turn the corner off Pirotska and walk through a wide-open door, right into a Soviet-era building whose familiarity only deepens as I ascend the wide staircase in almost complete darkness; I can almost feel the stained and threadbare carpeting through the soles of my boots. I find a light switch and keep climbing, hoping for a sign indicating VMRO, opening doors here and there, faintly outlined in the deep gloom of the corridors, which disclose only warrens of offices. People are rushing about purposefully, from one office to another, none of them in the least curious about my obvious bewilderment.

I walk back down the staircase, this time noticing on the third floor that here the Macedonian Scientific Institute has its offices. That will do.

I enter a small room with very high ceilings and a single large window that, though thoroughly smeared with grime, admits enough light for two elderly gentlemen at very large desks to carry on with the business at hand, working on documents. To one side sits a tiny manual typewriter of honourable vintage. A map of the Balkans' ethnic divisions hangs on one wall, a large cupboard leans against another in a corner. One of the men, Mr. Stoyan Germanov, speaking English rather well, greets me warmly, seemingly satisfied by my introduction of myself as a Canadian writer interested in (unspecified) materials in English. He invites me to take a seat on one of the wobbly chairs by his desk. Perhaps my vague query is the most interest in the institute he's seen in decades. "We're all volunteers here," he explains, although the institute is a venerable body established in the 1920s, suspended under Communism in 1947, then reinstated in 1990.

Mr. Germanov and his institute seem mainly concerned with combating what he calls "Macedonization" in the Balkans—the emergence of a "so-called" Macedonian identity among people who were once satisfied to call themselves Bulgarians from Macedonian lands. He, for example, was born near Bitola, in present-day Republic of Macedonia. He points to a spot on the map near the frontier with Greece. We chat amiably—he had once been to Montreal for a conference—while his colleague is patiently folding a series of weathered papers into a neat pile. So this is what it has come to, almost a hundred years after the Balkan Wars.

Mr. Germanov presses on me a large and heavy volume of texts translated into English under the title, *Documents and Materials on the History of the Bulgarian People*, published by the Bulgarian Academy of Sciences in 1969, now yellowed and massively outdated. I accept it politely and shove it in my knapsack alongside a gift from Greeks in Thessalonica, *The Falsification of Macedonian History*, by a former cabinet minister, published in 1984 and awarded the Prize of the Academy of Athens. "In northern Greece," it is written with an impressive tone of authority, "in Macedonia, there reside today more than two million Greeks but no Slavs."

The Bulgarian documents, for their part, emphasize that the Slav population in Macedonia is Bulgarian, as the Preface declares, reaching as far back as the medieval *Miracles of St. Demetrius*, which mentions the settling of Proto-Bulgarians in the Bitola Valley. Macedonians, on the other hand, are "nowhere" spoken of as a separate people.

I remembered evenings in Skopje, and poems.

I sought you in the accents of unknown languages, in the unsaddled evenings
and empty beds in the field, in the surprise primrose behind the herb-seller's
ear, in the punctuation in the speech of whining children. I'm seeking you in
the wild chance of unification of my scattered nation, in a stalk of sorrel, in
the unused air which annoyed and appeased the neighbouring villages.

—PETRE ANDREEVSKI, 1991

WHO ARE THE BULGARIANS? In the eleventh century, the
Byzantine writer Cecaumenus reports that the Slavs in Macedonia
speak Bulgarian and that the son of Ivan Vladislav, Alusianus, with
"a great multitude of Bulgarians," attacked Thessalonica but all were
repelled: Alusianus's troops were exhausted with fatigue from their
long march to the sea, and they "scattered about, some wanting to
drink water, others to give their horses some rest, and still others
to recover themselves from fatigue." When the Thessalonians from
behind their stupendous walls observed the enemy soldiers "loitering
in a disorderly manner," they rushed out through their opened gates
and routed them.

As for the equally calamitous twentieth century: In 1912 both Greek
and Bulgarian armies streamed for Thessalonica, to be the first to free
her from the Turks. The Greeks entered the city eight hours ahead
of the Bulgarians. But sixteen thousand Bulgarian troops kept on
coming anyway, only to be thrown out two years later in yet another
Balkan War. The Greeks were in charge. The king transferred his court
to Thessalonica and the Mosque of Kasim reverted to the veneration
of St. Demetrius.

:: *Sofia, Veliko Turnovo*

WITH NOTEBOOK IN HAND, *I slip into the Archaeological Museum in Sofia to view the current exhibit, "Christianity in Bulgarian Lands." I peer very closely at icons of St. Demetrius — or Sveti Dimitar — and make notes of what I see, hoping some day to be enlightened. So, for example, an icon relief on wood, with scenes of lives of Saints George and Demetrius, Sozopol, fifteenth or sixteenth century: who was who here? Around the border of the plaque I can make out one or the other Saint being roasted in a furnace, tied to a stake and flogged, prostrated at the chopping block, tormented on a wheel, slung upside down on a pillar. But other little scenes show the two Saints preaching before a king, embracing each other before the wheel, and standing side by side, calm and radiant within their haloes on what seems to be a balcony of a palace...or is it heaven?*

An icon from Veliko Turnovo, 1617: Demetrius in his aspect of warrior-saint, protector and defender, slaying the enemy. Here he is again, that enigmatic figure impaled at the end of Demetrius's spear and here dispro-portionately small compared to the enormous fiery-red horse bearing down on him. In spite of the armour he wears around his breast, Demetrius's sword has pierced his right collarbone and he gazes in perplexity at the Saint, huge on his horse. Demetrius handles the reins in one hand, the spear

in the other, and looks off into the distance, imperturbable as ever. Who is
he killing?

LATER, having found the National Library open for business, I sit in
the gracious stillness of the public reading room, whose procedures
have an eternal changelessness to them that has left me feeling deeply
peaceful: generations of readers have handed over our coats and bags
to the cloakroom attendant, having emptied our pockets of anything
superfluous to the task at hand, and we have been presented the
indispensable numbered cardboard disc with which we may request
books and be assigned a spot at the reading tables.

A sequence of mysterious ciphers on the cards in the library catalogue indicates the shelving position of a book somewhere in the
basement of this great building, fittingly named for Saints Cyril and
Methodius, monks of ninth-century Thessalonica who created an
alphabet for the Slavs, and so I sit at my assigned seating place at the
polished table and wait for the books I've requested to be retrieved.
The hurly-burly of Sofia just outside the windows is muted in the
silence of readers, broken every now and then by the cracking of a
book's spine, pens scratching on paper, the thoughtful turning over of
a stiff page in a portfolio.

The books arrive. In *Bulgarian Contributions to European Civilization*,
in an 1866 icon of St. Demetrius in the Church of the Holy Trinity
in a village near Romania, in the familiar representation of the
triumphant warrior, the blade of Demetrius's spear is embedded in
the forehead of a serene if somewhat downcast armour-plated soldier.
Who is he killing? According to the caption, the Saint is in mortal
combat with the Antichrist. So he, too, may now be added to the list of
Demetrius's prey: St. Demetrius is killing a Turk, a Barbarian, a Thief,
an Enemy, the Antichrist. I look up from my reading as the winter
light seeps into the silent, commodious chamber of readers. I am
disturbed that this representation of a murderer should be venerated
in this Orthodox world I am travelling through, with only my inatten-
tive girlhood learning as a guide. Perhaps this violent image consoled
the suffering Christian subjects of the Ottoman Empire, but I miss the
earlier imagery of Demetrius as the young man in soft, white, Roman

robes and sandaled feet, who, taken prisoner by the governor's men in Thessalonica, lifts his arm so the soldier's sword can do its work.

I dive in again. André Grabar, *La peinture réligieuse en Bulgarie*, Paris, 1928. Grabar, a founding father of modern Byzantine studies who once laboured over an inventory of medieval monuments in Bulgaria, in this book methodically describes the icons present in Byzantine-era Bulgarian churches and monasteries. For instance, here is a fresco of Demetrius in the monastery of Dragalevci, under the inscription, "Great Demetrius, the General." Good. I open my notebook, pick up my pencil. "He is galloping to the right," I copy, "all the while striking at a Roman soldier, curled under the hooves of his horse, with a lance." Ah, the writ of this internationally renowned art historian: so Demetrius is killing a Roman soldier. "From an icono-graphical point of view," I keep on copying, "this figure laid out under the horse is as old as images of the hero-knight."

Yes, that Thracian horseman for example, galloping in from the shores of the Black Sea in the sixth century BCE, overrunning shrines of Apollo, then buried in shrines of his own. These will be the compost for Christian chapels in a place in Bulgaria called Sozopolis, "city of salvation," formerly Apollonia, and will be dedicated to St. Athanas, St. Nicholas, St. Petka, St. Demetrius. Under St. Demetrius in Sozopolis lie the unexcavated foundations of a medieval church and, for all we know, under that is the Thracian Horseman with his cape blowing in the wind of the kingdom of the dead.

I return from my reverie. "This is how victorious Roman emperors were depicted [and] the Balkan saints such as Demetrius of Salonica merely inherited the ancient tradition." So perhaps we are to under-stand this bloody little scene as not from the unrecoverable Thracian past but merely as an echo of late Roman imperial iconography? I think of all the Roman emperors seated on marble horses many times larger than life-size. They are always in armour, insignia of the real source of their power: violence.

"Nevertheless, in the past people have wanted to name the vanquished figure," Grabar goes on, about Bulgarian painting in particular, "and they have seized on the Bulgarian king, Kaloyan. Because, according to the legend, the city of Salonica was delivered from a Bulgarian siege by the miraculous intervention of Saint Demetrius when Kaloyan suddenly fell dead at the walls of the city in the year 1207."

I have not realized I am holding my breath. I let go of it. So, finally, this image of the speared man that has stalked me since I landed in Crete, this enigmatic representation of a warrior who has found his human prey and now murders him, has an explanation. St. Demetrius's writhing victim has a name, and it is Bulgarian: "Beautiful John," or Kaloyan in Greek, Ivanitsa in Bulgarian. Historically, Kaloyan (1168-1207) was a younger brother of the rebels Petar and Asen, who, after them, continued to wage successful campaigns against the Byzantines until he reached the gates of Thessalonica. He called himself Romaioktonos, or, in Bulgarian, Grkoubiets, the slayer of the Greeks, the Byzantines, but in October 1207, while besieging Thessalonica, he was slain by its immortal defender and protector, St. Demetrius. That's Kaloyan, then, whose image I've gazed, peered, and stared at, scrutinized and queried, all along my route of Demetrius: a prince of Bulgaria.

But immediately arises another perplexity: Why would an icon painter in the very important Bulgarian monastery of Dragalevci— an artistic and spiritual centre dating back to the fourteenth century, named for the Mother of God of Vitosha—choose to depict for the veneration of his own people, among all the edifying iconographical subjects available, the death of one of their own Bulgarian kings at the hands of a Greek saint at the gates of a Greek city?

It was time I called on Mme Vasilka Tapkova-Zaimova, doyenne of Bulgarian Byzantinists, author of "The Cult of St. Demetrius in Byzantium and the Balkans," "The City of St. Demetrius in the Demetrian Texts," *Byzantium and the Balkans After the Sixth Century*, and much more.

I have brought flowers from one of the flower sellers in the kiosks lining the road near the Cyril and Methodius library. Madame rather unceremoniously receives them, pitching out a similar bunch, beribboned and now desiccated, from a vase standing on the imposing sideboard in the hallway. I am directed straight into a little sitting room off the entry hall; everything is faded as though, once moved in and situated, it has never been given another moment's thought. A strong portrait of Madame Tapkova as a young woman hangs on the wall behind her where we sit, and I realize that I am sitting surrounded by the bric-a-brac and library of a life that had its sources in a now-vanished Bulgarian world: of Bulgarian ethnicity, my hostess was born in Thessalonica and speaks French rather than English.

Mme Tapkova-Zaimova is very widely published. Bibliographies in several languages and Festschrifts attest to her long and international career. I ask her about Kaloyan and the miracle of St. Demetrius.

"The story is really quite simple," she begins matter-of-factly. "It begins with St. Demetrius as a Martyr. Having become a Martyr, he performs miracles and from this fact becomes the protector of Thessalonica. He is protecting the city from whom? From the Slavs who are coming into the Balkans. Very simple. Even the Slavs, who were settled all around, little by little forgot that they were once enemies of the city. Having been baptized and become Christians, they accepted the church's version of events.

"As for Kaloyan, the story goes like this. Kaloyan moves to take the city of Salonica and finds himself beneath its ramparts. He looks around, sees the Basilica [of St. Demetrius] and says: 'St. Demetrius, if you grant me victory, I will build you an even more beautiful church.' Then, during the night, he is assassinated, that is, someone stabs him in the heart. He shouts, a crowd arrives, and accuses a man named Manastras, one of his bodyguards. Manastras replies: 'No, it wasn't me who stabbed him, it was St. Demetrius!' From that [legend] a whole iconography spread through the Balkans including Bulgaria: St. Demetrius knifing Kaloyan lying prostrate at his feet."

Had I thought of meeting Professor Yordan Andreev, historian of medieval Bulgaria and of Bulgarian-Byzantine relations? Professor Andreev of the university in Veliko Turnovo? Veliko Turnovo, medieval city associated with the cult of St. Demetrius?

Veliko Turnovo, west and north of Sofia, situated over several hills wound around by the meandering Yantra River, was once the splendid capital of the Second Bulgarian Kingdom from the twelfth to fourteenth centuries: it housed royal and patriarchal palaces, an impressive fortress, and an independent bishopric, as well as the

Church of St. Demetrius of Thessalonica. As the bus rumbled along the foothills, I read a tourist pamphlet. Over the ensuing ages, through many vicissitudes, including reincorporation into the Byzantine state and then capitulation to the Ottoman state, Turnovo was the location of a school of literature and the arts, a stronghold of the Bulgarian national spirit, a centre of uprisings and hope of the Bulgarian people in the ages of Turkish slavery, the foremost place of the Bulgarian Renaissance, and so on until 1908 and Prince Ferdinand's proclamation from Tsarevets Hill of the full independence of a new Bulgarian kingdom. Tsarevets Hill: where in 1185 Vassily, Archbishop of Turnovo, had laid the golden wreath on a prince's head and the brocaded robe on his shoulders, and red boots at his feet, and made of him a new Bulgarian king, Petar, brother of Kaloyan.

There was, of course, the Byzantine point of view of these events. Niketas Choniates, thirteenth-century Byzantine chronicler—*O City of Byzantium*—and imperial secretary to the court in Constantinople, had much to say of Bulgarian affairs. The two Bulgarian princes in Byzantine service, the "impious and abominable" brothers Petar and Asen, tempted by ambition beyond their station, instigated a "string of Trojan woes" by raising a rebellion against Emperor Isaac II in 1185. They began in Turnovo, and—deepening the provocation—they called on St. Demetrius to help.

I had had no idea that Demetrius had ever been lured away from Thessalonica, and by the prayers of Slavs, but I would try to find him in Veliko Turnovo.

Turnovo was spread along a main road of the European Middle Ages, which ran a course from the Danube and down across the Thracian Plain and thus to Constantinople. Of medieval Turnovo's churches and towers and fortress walls, stables and smithies, apartments, courtyards and passageways, much is now left to the imagination of the visitor.

I stand, fleetingly, in front of the church dedicated to St. Demetrius of Thessalonica, the city's oldest, one of the earliest examples of the Turnovo school of architecture and painting, and reputed to have picturesque brick decorations on its sculptured exterior. In fact, it's a modern reconstruction of the twelfth-century original, and it is locked, and no amount of imagination can restore it to its medieval majesty, this the church, now weeping in the rain, where Asen and Petar had declared the uprising in 1185.

I spend the first day in a damp mist that rises from the bed of the dramatic gorge of the Yantra River up into the heights of the town. It is Balkan winter with a vengeance: I walk around with my jacket and scarf pulled tight around me against the clammy air. I take coffee and a bun in an unheated café then drift through the softness of the fogged-in streets, making my way along pitched and cobbled streets, turning corners on deserted churches and once-grand, now abandoned houses. To get out of the cold, I loiter in a bookstore. And, with a squeak of delight, I pull from a shelf a slender storybook, *Legends of the Kingdom of Tarnovo*, published in Sofia, in English, and shipped here precisely so that I would find it.

"Once upon a time at the foot of the Balkan Mountains in the central fields of Moesia, there lived two bold and brave boyars, the brothers Peter and Assen." So begins the first of the tales, "Legend of the Renewed Bulgarian Kingdom." "Peter was a wise and peace-loving man and he often turned to God in his prayers. He built a beautiful church on the right bank of the Yantra River. Assen, the younger brother, was strong-minded and energetic, he gathered young men and taught them the art of war." They would need it, for "life under the Greek yoke was becoming harder with every passing day, the people moaned with exhaustion, the number of the disgruntled was steadily increasing." Subsumed within Byzantium, the people were saddled with Greek and Armenian feudal landlords who burdened them with new taxes, forced labour, and extortionate tithes of harvests, fish, and livestock.

Now, in their exhaustion and humiliation, the people of Turnovo in 1185 took heart from the new church built in the name of "Good Martyr Demetrius." For they had heard the rumours circulating in the marketplace that St. Demetrius himself, the Greeks' own Patron in Thessalonica, had also protested the Byzantine "cruelty and perfidiousness." He had left the city, it was said, taking his blessing away with him. It was even rumoured that he was on his way to Turnovo— minstrels with their stringed rebec sang of the astonishment of it all, that "from the blue skies above, Demetrius, the Holy Martyr" had been sent with good news for the Bulgarians.

And there were a few warriors and farmers and monks of uncommon piety who cried out the news that the Great Martyr was in their midst already: there was his icon suddenly placed on the altar of his church in Turnovo, its doors left open to receive him should he visit, and they swore he raised his iconographic hand in blessing. "Then Peter and Assen realized that it was exactly the long-expected sign sent to them by God in order to release the enslaved Bulgarian people."

Pilgrims assembled in Turnovo from the whole region while bells festively rang them in through the great gates, and hymns glorifying the Saint turned in the air over the river that plunged down its gorge through the city. Everyone knelt to pray to St. Demetrius to strengthen their hands and minds to the task of their own liberation, and "the eyes of Thessalonica's wonder-maker glistened in the light of the candles in a benevolent way." If the Slavs could not get to the Thessalonian shore, the Saint would come to them, to the beautiful sanctuary built for him among the Bulgarians.

I step outside and make my way to the Tsarevets Hill citadel. Other visitors disappear from view and reappear as I walk among the excavated foundation stones of a medieval fortress city. On this stony outcrop once stood a royal palace, a patriarchal office, and a multitude of small, cross-domed churches, as well as the citadel. Compared to the mere twenty-five colours of the frescoes and mosaics of Constantinople, those of the palace and churches of Turnovo, including St. Demetrius, boasted thirty-five colours and were embellished by ornamentation carved of pink marble, green serpentine, and Egyptian porphyry. There is nothing of this to see now, and the mist mutes what is already muffled by the passage of time, the reckless abandon of attackers and occupiers, and the negligent carelessness of those whom historical memory has deserted.

But we may view the remains of the so-called Baldwin's Tower, commemorating the devastating victory over the crusading knights of 1205 at the battle of Adrianople by Tsar Kaloyan. The little book of legends of the Kingdom of Turnovo spins a bittersweet tale of the capture and imprisonment of Baldwin, Count of Flanders, and of the illicit love that Kaloyan's wife felt for this knight, a handsome man "very different from Bulgarian men," with his fair hair in heavy locks that covered his broad shoulders, his blue eyes, "proud and sad," a renowned warrior and Kaloyan's "worthy enemy." Baldwin spurns her love, she betrays him to Kaloyan, and "in the next morning, the rumour of the death of Baldwin Flandersky spread all over Tsarevets Hill. This death was wrapped in a shroud of mystery."

Not so mysterious, in fact. Baldwin—called arrogant and insufferable in some histories—met a terrible end in Turnovo, related in agonizing detail by Byzantine Niketas Choniates: captured and put in chains, "he was confined for a long time in Trnovo....Ioannitsa [Kaloyan] seethed with anger against the Latins, and his wrath grew in intensity, nearly driving him to distraction. Removing Baldwin from prison, he gave orders that his legs be summarily chopped off at the knees and his arms at the elbows before being cast headlong into a ravine. For three days Baldwin lay as food for the birds before his life ended miserably."

I walk away from the hill, wondering down which of these wild precipices the wretched knight had been flung, and think of the three days, morning and night, that the people of this town had listened to his moans from behind their shuttered windows.

Professor Yordan Andreev, wrapped up in his big black coat inside the university cafeteria, while a space heater warms the air around our knees and the morning fog hangs mournfully outside the windows, is not very impressed by stories of saints in Bulgaria. Modern Bulgarian identity is not tied to them at all, he argues, not even those of the Wonder-maker, Demetrius, none of whose relics was ever deposited on Bulgarian lands, and whose miraculous icon was taken away from Turnovo and back to Thessalonica in any case, under the arm of a victorious Byzantine emperor.

There is something about all this saintly business that doesn't sit well with the professor, who would rather his students root their modern identity in Bulgarian political history. "We can prove to ourselves that we are Europeans," he declares, combatively, as though a connection between his city's history and the story of St.

Demetrius—the medieval wailing masses, the rumours of miracles, the imagery of martyrdom—calls this into question.

"The mentality of the *medieval* Bulgarian was much inclined to miracles," Andreev concedes. "People expected to witness a miracle at any moment, and if they did, they assigned it to St. Demetrius. For the Bulgarians, he was the creator of miracles. Seven of the *Miracles of St. Demetrius* are directly concerned with Bulgaria and the Bulgarians. The first five of them are connected with the Slav-Bulgarian sieges of Thessalonica in the sixth century. Even in the early Middle Ages this St. Demetrius of Thessalonica was a very popular saint in Bulgarian territories. But the only thing left of him is the memory of him and of his icon and of his support for the rebellion against the Byzantines." He pauses while I write out the translation. "Recently, I have noted that the rebellion of the Asen brothers began on St. Demetrius Day [*Dimitrovdan*], which is a big Bulgarian, even Orthodox, holiday."

I ask: "But why would Bulgarians tell the story of a Greek saint absconded from Thessalonica to join ranks with them?"

"In 1185 Thessalonica—a town guarded by the Saint, defended by him—was conquered by the Normans. The medieval citizens believed that the only plausible reason for their city being conquered is that the Saint had abandoned it. Note that this was considered a calamity for the Byzantine world as a whole," Andreev wags his finger at me, "not just for the Greeks."

The Norman Kingdom of Naples occupied Thessalonica August 24, 1185, after a short siege by land and sea. Betrayed by their own governor, who opened its gates to the enemy, Thessalonians were then subjected to intolerable assaults and insults at the hands of their conquerors. No dwelling was spared looting, no passageway its gangs of thieves and rapists, no hiding place its discovery; no prisoner was shown pity, no plea for life heeded. Citizens fled to the Basilica of St. Demetrius, under whose protection they had flourished; but the Normans had got there first, offering up slaughtered priests as mock sacrifices, hurling icons to the ground, stomping on them or breaking them up as firewood. They ripped the silver off the Saint's tomb. They made use of the *myron*, the fragrant and healing ointment exuded from his bones, to flavour their fish soup and to polish their boots.

"Even more unholy, and terrible for the faithful to hear," wrote Choniates, "was the fact that certain men climbed on top of the holy altar, which even the angels find hard to look upon, and danced thereon, deporting themselves disgracefully as they sang lewd barbarian songs from their homeland. Afterwards, they uncovered their privy parts and let the *membrum virile* pour forth the contents of the bladder, urinating round about the sacred floor..."

The Normans, or "Latins," were "most accursed," "workers of evil deeds," an "alien race," supercilious, boastful, pompous, who now swaggered about as lords of Thessalonica, guffawing at the emaciated and swollen-bellied bodies of the starving Thessalonians, booting helpless beggars into mud puddles. They confiscated property from widows and installed harlots in the houses, bellowed at each other and barked like dogs during church services and "mooned" and broke wind in the face of diners in the dining halls.

No wonder the city was rife with rumour that their Patron Saint and Protector, Demetrius, had abandoned the Thessalonians. Their Bishop Eustathius had had a premonition of this catastrophe. Quoting from Psalms, he had preached to the people of the abandoned city, "Then again we cried aloud, 'Come to save us...' But [St. Demetrius] did not listen to our prayers and removed himself from us." Provoked beyond endurance by their sinfulness and shamefulness, The Great Martyr and Warrior had taken up residence elsewhere.

In Bulgaria, apparently.

When, on the occasion of the consecration of the Church of St. Demetrius in Turnovo in 1185, a large crowd of Bulgarian and Vlach religious ecstatics gathered there, Choniates considers them a gathering of devils and demons, mad people who "rave like lunatics: they would start up and shout and shriek," they "leaped with joy at rebellion." The ecstatics were there to announce that St. Demetrius himself had arrived in their midst to be their accomplice in their struggle for liberation.

"Every social uprising—as with the rebellion of the Bulgarians in Turnovo—has a psychological impetus," Professor Andreev continues. "Or, as we used to say, has an 'ideological inspiration' for the event. And for this uprising, the impetus was the rumour that St.

Demetrius left Thessalonica and had reappeared in the miraculous icon in Turnovo. And inspired the Bulgarians to start their uprising.

"In fact, in the past and even now some Bulgarian historians have believed that the people at that gathering really were mad, were possessed by the devil. There is a Bulgarian saying that, if someone is mad, he is not alone. Who is that other person with him? God."

Professor Andreev, now thoroughly warmed to the topic, has forgotten about me entirely and directs his considerable enthusiasm at the two young students, my translators, who listen like wide-eyed children, mesmerized by the troubadour: his big head, thick mop of grey hair and beard, his gravelly voice mellowing like a good red wine...so here is St. Demetrius, I am thinking, still hanging around in Bulgaria when he gets the chance. He's found a voice at this table over cups of espresso wreathed in wisps of tobacco smoke while the cold seeps in from the erasing mist outside.

For the Byzantines, however, it was a spiritual, even cosmological, catastrophe that God was with the frenzied, leaping, dishevelled, rebellious Bulgarians, and not with the Greeks. The Byzantine order of the universe was off-kilter, Heaven and Earth had gone their separate ways. "None of the high-throned bishops," Choniates laments, "who reaped the highest honours, or the thick-bearded monks, who pulled their woollen hoods down to their noses, pondered God's almost total abandonment of us."

Petar, crowned with the gold-leaved circlet of kings and booted with scarlet buskins, marched off to war, throwing the Byzantines out of the Bulgarian lands between the Balkan Mountains and the Danube. They would never return.

But Greek armies did succeed in taking St. Demetrius back with them. He had a job to do in Thessalonica.

In 1197, after his two brothers, Petar and Asen, had been murdered by treacherous Bulgarian nobles, Kaloyan, Beautiful John, Good John, inherited the kingdom. In 1205, having disposed of Baldwin of Flanders, he moved his armies south and west, through Byzantine territory until, in 1207, he was at the gates of Thessalonica.

"A strong in numbers army beleaguered the beautiful Greek town," *Legends of the Kingdom of Tarnovo* tells me, "the fields were white with tents; sounds from the horses' hooves and rattling arms echoed in the air...Kaloyan's soldiers were immaculate in the art of war, they loved their tsar and were ready for the battle. However, they were confused. There was a rumour in the camp that at nights on the fortress walls stood St. Demetrius, the Patron of the God-preserved city. The Saint was frowning, and he was not benevolent towards the Bulgarian people. He stood there for a long time then went to the temple that carried his name. The tsar heard about that rumour and prayed. If the Saint helped him to conquer the city of Thessalonica, he would not only name a temple after his name but he would also build a beautiful monastery in his honour. But this prayer made St. Demetrius even angrier, he did not want his native town to be destroyed....

"It was getting late in the evening. The tsar came into his tent and lay down to sleep. In his dream, he led the battle. He arranged where exactly the battering rams should be situated. He knew that his army was very good and that Thessalonica would surrender. The sentries were at their posts as usual. It was quiet and peaceful every-where. Suddenly, in the half-lit royal tent there appeared the shadow of a man with a spear in his hand. After that, the tsar's death cry could be heard. The sentries ran into the tent and the only thing they could see was the dying Kaloyan. 'The saint did it,' the soldiers whis-pered. 'Thessalonica's wonder-maker killed the tsar and defended his town.'...

"Not wasting time, they put the body of their brave tsar onto a purple bed and headed for Turnovo."

Kaloyan died on the Feast Day of St. Demetrius, October 26, 1207. The Byzantines would ever after call him, Skyloyannis, after a dog.

Two hundred years later, the Ottoman Turks fell upon the Bulgarians, and captured one town after another, forcing even Emperor Ivan Shishman to deliver his sister, Tamara, to Murad I's harem. In 1393 the Turks laid siege to Turnovo, which fell after many weeks of desperate resistance; its Patriarch, Euthymius, disappeared from sight, a prisoner within his own monastery. An eyewitness, Grigoriy Tzamblak, watched, and then wrote, of how the "barbar-ians," the Turks, raged against the people, swearing to have them chopped to pieces and burnt in fire, unless they gave up their senseless defence of the city. "Oh, holy host of warriors," Tzamblak addressed the doomed men and women of Turnovo, "not one earlier and not one later, but all of you at the same time presented yourselves to your tormentor...the tormentor left your bodies for food for the birds of heaven...they were one hundred and ten in number, the ones whose blood made the church turn scarlet."

ON MY LAST MORNING in Veliko Turnovo I was to have an interview with the local Bishop, but he had left for Sofia and I was offered a monk-deacon instead, an *Ierodiakon*, who serves in the bishopric. And so, whisked inside, through heavy doors and into a dim vestibule, I wait. A door to an adjoining room swings open, a shaft of daylight pierces the gloom, and I find myself in the imposing presence of Br. Petar Gramatikoff, a young man, tall and very broad-shouldered, huge in his cassock and eiderdown vest, who hears me out, his hands up his sleeves, then invites me up a flight of stairs and into a large boardroom. We sit down on wooden chairs. Br. Petar is courteous, but he has not smiled yet. Perhaps it has something to do with the wan midday light, or the looming wall-paintings of Bulgarian and Romanian saints likewise mirthless, or the exigencies of his office. I have never met an *Ierodiakon* before.

I begin by asking about the state of the churches in this historic region—a quite large bishopric of nine regions, almost half of northern Bulgaria.

It is a tragedy, he replies, that ten years after the fall of Communism, "we Orthodox still cannot enter our churches or receive our lands and properties. How can we compete with the new religions? Pentecostals? Adventists?

"The Bulgarian Orthodox Church had no property under the totalitarian regime but at least the government paid for the reconstruction and renovation of churches. But now? The Church is discriminated against and isolated. Sveti Dimitar Church, for example—there where the brothers Asen and Petar called together the noblemen in 1185 to revolt against the Byzantines, and where St. Demetrius had joined them in encouragement—is a museum."

He stops for a minute while I write all this down. He has spoken matter-of-factly, but even in the half-light I can see that he is glowering.

"As for the Saint's Day, October 26, we don't celebrate there *because it is not a church*."

Another pause. We both sit in contemplation of that reconstruction, that museum piece, closed to worshippers, which I had visited for just a minute, standing in the rain and mud. Why would a saint want to visit such a place? I can feel the wrath of Br. Petar, and something of what must be his loneliness.

"Our people have venerated Sveti Dimitar for a very long time. He is one of our treasures. There are about three hundred of our churches that have him as patron, throughout Bulgaria. Canonically he is always represented as the martyr but there is a very popular hagiographic representation that shows him as the mounted warrior-saint."

He rifles through a vest pocket and hands over to me a small paper copy of an icon: St. Demetrius sits on a rearing roan horse, preparing to plunge his spear into the breast of the fallen soldier at his feet, that is, Kaloyan, prince of Bulgaria.

I point to the image. "Is this really Tsar Kaloyan, and is St. Demetrius really his murderer?"

Br. Petar glances skeptically in my direction. "I have heard the version that the man on the ground must be understood only symbolically, or as a vision, that St. Demetrius is not a killer. Humph. And nowadays, here, after the fall of Communism, there are those Bulgarians who see this fallen figure as a Communist!" He is still glowering.

"But this is a kind of heresy, and this image should not be interpreted nationalistically. Kaloyan was a historical figure who was seen historically as the Antichrist by his own soldiers who assassinated him in a coup d'état, at the gates of Thessalonica, assisted by St. Demetrius."

We stare at each other, while I fumble for my question. "Why would Bulgarian soldiers think their own tsar was the Antichrist? He was their captain, their beautiful hero who challenged the perfidious Greeks."

"But this is not about Greeks and Bulgarians."

"*It's not?*"

"I try to explain to all the Bulgarian nationalists who don't like the icon that this image is a good lesson for our politicians not to betray Orthodoxy." He pauses.

"In 1204 Kaloyan was crowned Bulgarian king, yes, but by a *cardinal* in *Rome*. In exchange for an imperial crown, Kaloyan had promised Rome to recognize the spiritual supremacy of the Pope and to place his lands under the jurisdiction of the Holy See. This is what he wrote to Pope Innocent III: 'In the first place we as a beloved son want from *our mother, the Roman Church*, a Tsar's crown and dignity as our old Emperors had them.'" The emphases are all Br. Petar's. "The Pope's envoy, Cardinal Leo, even made the trip to Turnovo in 1204 to anoint Archbishop Vasili *Primas* of the Bulgarian Church and the next day crowned Kaloyan *Rex* with a crown brought from Rome.

"Kaloyan preferred to be made a king by a Catholic pope than an emperor by Orthodox Byzantium. He is speared by St. Demetrius not because he's a Bulgarian but because he is anti-Orthodox."

He stops.

"In 1235," he resumes, "Bulgarians returned to the Greek Church."

...Skyloyannis [Kaloyan the Dog] managed to gaze on Thessaloniki, which was suffering for the sins of its people. But that same evening, dressed in white, St Demetrios, the protector of the city himself, who has on many occasions dispersed the hostile storm and delivered his Mother city, takes the form of the barbarian general, Manastra, and entering Skyloyannis' tent, runs him through with a spear. Be sure to remember this, making the Great Saint the anchor of your faith.

—NIKOS PENTZIKIS, 1998

"AND I HAVE OFTEN ASKED MYSELF," Mme Tapkova-Zaimova had said to me in Sofia, "where did the Bulgarian iconographer get the courage to have his prince speared by St. Demetrius? Why? Because there is an ecumenical—a universal—side to this, and that's the

Church, the faith, which continued down through the centuries on all the icons, even in Bulgaria."

I have been barking up the wrong tree. Kaloyan died not as a Bulgarian but as a scheming schismatic. This is not about a bloodline, about "Greek" Demetrius and "Slavic" barbarians in some sort of ethnic gladiatorial combat; it's about a church. Kaloyan, son of Byzantium, had negotiated with a pope in Rome and had promised to recognize his spiritual authority. For this treachery he would be crowned king, though an emperor, *Basileas*, already sat, God-anointed, on the throne of Constantinople.

Kaloyan would have been called king, *rex*, along with his successors in Bulgaria, had not the Saint intervened, with a spear through the heart.

When I woke up that last morning in Turnovo and looked out the window to the chasm of the Yantra's course through the red-roofed neighbourhood, I could see nothing through the December fog except a naked tree here and there and a spire suddenly exposed by a rift in the cloud. Late in the afternoon, leaving town by bus, I watched the countryside, laid out on both sides of the highway, dissolve into that same fog as though it were being exhaled by the very clods of the black earth itself.

⋮ *Letting Go*

:: *Monemvasia*

IN 1830 the Austrian polemicist and scholar Jakob Philipp
Fallmerayer published an ethnological history of the Peloponnese
(known then as the Morea) that has never been translated into
English but that in its Greek translation set off a storm of protest
among Greek intellectuals and their philhellenic friends that has
never completely died down.

The crux of his argument was that the Greek claim to descent
from the Greeks of antiquity is false. Modern Greeks are Christians
of Slavonic descent: "Not a single drop of real pure Hellenic blood
flows in [their] veins." Their Classical heritage could not possibly
have survived the successive waves of Slav and Albanian invasions
during the sixth and seventh centuries of the Byzantine era. Did not
Emperor Constantine Porphyrogennetos, from the middle of the tenth
century, on an itinerary of the Balkans, remark that "our whole land
has become slavicized," the whole world having been swept by the
barbarian plague? Fallmerayer wrote: "The Greek race in Europe is
completely exterminated. The physical beauty, the sublimity of spirit,
the simplicity of customs, the artistic creativeness...have disappeared
from the Greek continent....And were it not for the ruins, grave-hills
and mausoleums...we would have to say it was an empty vision..."

Now picture the thirteenth-century Byzantine historian, Niketas Choniates, a student and great admirer of Classical Greece, who has arrived in Athens with the enthusiastic plan to sit on the Acropolis in contemplation of its antiquities. Instead he encounters a miserable population of peasants who seem not to have kept the least remembrance of their illustrious ancestry and whose language, he fears, is going to barbarize him, the gentleman from Constantinople.

Over the centuries the situation does not seem to improve. The British cartographer W.M. Leake in *Travels in the Morea*, published the year of Fallmerayer's history of the same region, is a disgruntled traveller scrambling over rock, thorn bush, and stream, in the "semi-barbarous" back-of-beyond of the Ottoman Empire, consoled only by contemplation of "Greece's connection with the Hellenes and the Olympians." (The intervening thousand-year history of the Byzantine Empire is not mentioned.)

The revolutionary project of the liberation of Greece will be a hard sell in enlightened Europe if the oppressed and beleaguered Greeks were to be exposed as mere Slavic riffraff, the debris of a migratory species. In 1912 the French Byzantinist, Alfred Rambaud, surveyed the ethnographic maps of the Balkans. He saw there on the maps no "uniform hue consecrating the triumph of Hellenism" but rather "the strangest hotchpotch of colours."

In the Introduction to his *Medieval Greece*, Nicolas Cheetham remembers that, when his father was appointed British Minister at Athens in 1924, his Classics master at school commiserated with the boy, "with a curl of his clerical lip, on the prospect of my having to consort on my holidays with what he called 'those nasty little Slavs.'"

Slavs captured the cities and took numerous forts and devastated and burned and reduced the people to slavery, and made themselves masters of the whole country.

—JOHN, BISHOP OF EPHESUS, *sixth century*

This "staunchless spring of tribes, this voluminous flux"—as Patrick Leigh Fermor wrote so vividly after he had trekked down to the southern tip of the Peloponnese in the 1950s—"on it went: over the fallen fences of the Roman Empire; past the flat territories of the Avers; across the great rivers and through the Balkan passes and into the dilapidated provinces of the Empire of the East, silently soaking in like liquid across blotting paper." The destruction of the Justinian walls across the isthmus that connected the Peloponnese to the Greek mainland was so complete that they are now unlocateable.

There where the barbarians settled on their territory the Byzantines called Sclavinia. In 581 John of Ephesus called them Slavonians and "an accursed people." The countryside had become a wasteland abandoned by its farmers, turned now into a "Scythian" (Slav) wilderness of pestilence and famine. Bishoprics were uprooted and administrative machinery collapsed. Highways fell into disrepair. When God is angry with humankind, it was said, He sends signs: plagues, earthquakes, floods, shipwrecks, civil wars, enslavement, and barbarians. In 542 a great bubonic plague consumed whole villages and towns; four thousand people in Patras were buried by an earthquake in 561.

Byzantine culture was overwhelmed in the greater part of the southern Balkans. And "when the darkness begins to lift from the peninsula" in the ninth century, the Roman names for places have vanished, replaced by Slavic: Greek replaces Latin as the official language of the state, the Byzantine populations have been reduced to "murmur indignantly and endure."

Yet Byzantium did recover her territory, stationing troops in coastal cities such as Thessalonica, Patras, and Monemvasia, and settling Greek farmers in the Balkans. Then she enserfed the Slavs, pressed them into the army, and evangelized them.

As brutish as it had been, this Slavic incursion had not been a military conquest. Once resettled, Slavs proved to be a rather mild people who soon enough were practising small-scale agriculture and who asked nothing more than to be allowed, as clans of families, to pasture their flocks and cultivate their fields in peace, usually in unpopulated areas such as mountain slopes and valleys. They left shards of ceramics in Argos and Tiryns, fibulae in Laconia, and some soldiers' belt buckles in graves near the walls of Corinth. Their contribution to Greek vocabulary was negligible and to folklore they served up a repertoire of vampires and water sprites.

"Byzantine" was not an ethnicity but a culture, indifferent to its racial antecedents, which were, in fact, complex and derived from an empire spread over vast numbers of peoples. What has been so intolerable to modern Greeks in the notion that there is no such thing as a racially pure Greek? To quote Ruth Kark, a British-Russian-Jewish traveller to Monemvasia in 1995, "the idea of ethnic or genetic homogeneity in societies which have lived through centuries of movements of population, of immigration, emigration and re-migration, let alone invasion and occupation, is bogus and dangerous romantic twaddle."

After all, the barbarians did settle down in Byzantine territories, lived alongside Greeks, and eventually became Hellenized and Christianized, practically indistinguishable from their neighbours. This process of the assimilation of the Slavs into the more powerful and sophisticated culture of the Byzantines has been called the "reconquista."

Slav culture had proved no match for the glittering accomplishments of the Greeks, which lay all around them: their fertile land ploughed and sowed and reaped, their caravans on the way to markets at the crossroads of amber and pelts, silks and spices, their caravels speeding all sails to the wind between the Bosporus and Thessalonica, Syracuse and Alexandria, their frontier guardsmen towering behind gilded shields, their priests moving with ponderous gestures in garments stiff with brocade under domes from which loomed the very face of the Pantocrator himself, the Lord of the Universe.

The Byzantines had won. They had absorbed these pesky barbarians, erased their language and gods, and gave them Greek words and the Liturgy of the great churches of Constantinople. Why were Greeks still so indignant that once upon a time these people had been Slavs?

It is fitting for Greeks to rule barbarians.

—EURIPIDES, *Iphigenia in Aulis*

I RIDE THE BUS down from Sparta, down through mountain passes to the sea and the formidable outcrop of rock that squats off the coast with its back to the Peloponnese and its face to the Sea of Crete: Monemvasia. It was here in 1924 that the renowned Byzantinist

Sir Steven Runciman first set foot on Greek soil, and it was a sorry sight then, the decaying old town straggling at the feet of the precipices of the southern slope. One hundred years earlier, when W.M. Leake arrived, leading his nag down from the mountains and over the bridge, he was lodged in the Turkish governor's house, and he noted the town boasted three hundred houses and exported olive oil to Trieste along with figs, onions, and cheese, although a twelfth-century church had been reduced to its bare walls. In 1948 the British writer and scholar Kevin Andrews arrived by skiff and went climbing to the summit of the island-rock, slapped around by the sea winds, while a solitary woman with her little herd of goats leaped in bloodied bare feet from one rock to another, "screaming at them above the wind."

The (unreliable) medieval chronicles ascribe Monemvasia's foundation in the sixth century to Greeks fleeing their lands, and the cities and villages on the mainland, while Slavs and Avars ransacked them up and down the mountain valleys. Some managed to find refuge on the island of Aegina or to slip out of the port of Gytheion, merchants with their own ships, and off to Sicily. According to the chroniclers, "Others found an inaccessible place by the seashore, built there a strong city which they called Monemvasia because there was only one way for those entering, and settled in it with their own bishop." Until the bedraggled Greeks arrived on this rock, by some accounts, it had never been inhabited. At its peak it had a population of 60,000, controlling the sea lanes from Italy to Constantinople.

I first visited Monemvasia in 1982 when there was already a thriving tourist town on the mainland, a manmade causeway to the rock, and an old town in a state of half-restoration, while the rest of the buildings rested awkwardly on collapsed foundations and the narrow streets between them led to dead ends of rubble and rubbish. But now, almost twenty years on, the old town had been handsomely restored, and there is much to admire in its townhouses, churches, and shops. According to oral tradition, the building housing the Archaeological Museum had begun as the Church of St. Peter in the Byzantine period. It then served as a sixteenth-century mosque, for which there is archaeological and textual evidence, and enjoyed a late-seventeenth-century Venetian renovation. Restored to the new

Greek state in the 1830s, it was turned into a prison, according to travellers' information. At some time in the early twentieth century it had been a coffee shop.

But now it is a museum scrubbed clean of its earlier functions. On the walls I examine glazed plates imported from the ceramic workshops of Asia Minor and polychrome painted bowls of Italian provenance, and a note informing the reader that the Byzantine habit of reusing earlier sculptures as construction material for new buildings should not be held against them: the Roman and Early Christian system of quarrying and trading marble had collapsed. This is the only whiff I get in Monemvasia of that world where the eighth-century pilgrim Willibald, Bishop of Eichstadt, on his way to the Holy Land, docked for a while on the sea route from Sicily and dictated to the nun Huneberc of Heidenheim that he had come "in Sclavinica terra."

But the fact is that Monemvasia itself had never been subdued by the Slavs, and its residents "even to this day...are called 'Hellenes,'" wrote Byzantine Emperor-historian Constantine Porphyrogennetos in the tenth century. "The place where they live is waterless and inaccessible, but bears the olive, whence their comfort is." The Slavs were not so comforted. Once they had made themselves at home on the olive-bearing earth, they were enslaved by the great landowners, including the Church, and produced food for the Malvasians clinging to their rock.

> This landscape is as harsh as silence, it hugs to its breast the scorching stones, clasps in its light the orphaned olive trees and vineyards, clenches its teeth. There is no water. Light only. Roads vanish in light and the shadow of the sheepfold is made of iron.
>
> —YANNIS RITSOS, 1993

The day started with a good omen, a bright rainbow in the eastern sky, rising and sinking in the churning sea and arching over the little settlement, Paleo, on the opposite shore. I have read that Paleo was the last place of Greek settlement before their final flight from the Slavs. Then straightaway they "proceeded with all haste to Monemvasia... for they saw that this peninsula was high and long and cut off from every side and situated well above the sea, rivalling the sky in height and seeming to touch it," as Cardinal Isidore of Kyiv tells us from the fifteenth century. I make my way on the causeway to the old town and feel the satisfaction of the twenty-first century Slav-Canadian, just another peaceful tourist, making her way with impunity into this Greek fortress.

"AT THE BEGINNING of the fifth year of [Emperor] Heraclius [615 CE] the Slavs took Greece [Graeciam] from the Romans." So had pronounced Isidore, Bishop of Seville (as he was then), in *Chronicon*. He was a most learned man of his age, and a Saint. I have lugged his pronouncement around with me like an assigned penance for the historical misdeed of my genetic ancestors: but for the rude intrusion of Slavs into the Balkans, the Greeks would still be basking in their unbroken link with the glorious Classical civilizations of the Mediterranean.

But perhaps the entire Mediterranean world had been forever altered by another force altogether, that of the expansion of the "thalassocratic Arabs," which is to say the sea-ruling ones. Even the islanders of medieval Rhodes, not just the Peloponnesians, had failed to build much in the way of churches and public buildings during the seventh and eighth centuries. In a warm and sunlit café in old Monemvasia, while a wild wind kicks at the windows' shutters and children returning from school are blown about the cobblestoned alleyways, I learn in a disarming footnote in a French book from 1951 that such absences from the material record are "universal symptoms of the decadence of the Mediterranean world beginning from the second half of the seventh century." "From the 7th to the 11th century Islam was incontestably the master of the Mediterranean." The Arabs constructed the ports of Cairo, Alexandria, and Tunis, as Henri Pirenne recounted in his magisterial *A History of Europe*. Against such genius, what havoc could the Slavs have wreaked in their hollowed-out tree trunks that hugged the shores of marshes and swamps, and who avoided the cities, dragging wagons and driving cattle, whose milk they drank and hides they wore?

On the way back to the new town, I have a view from the causeway of the gilded cumulus of cloud gathering over the setting sun, Monemvasia no longer in view around the red escalation of brute rock face. The winter wind whips my coat and scarf as if to rip them away, and the white foam of the heaving sea is sending all boats home.

Approaching my hotel, I hear the bells pealing from the church in the next street. Vespers? I slip inside, and stand at the back along with several women and a couple of men. Two cantors sing at the front of the little nave, an old man leaning on a cane and warbling weakly, and a young man I recognize from the old town in the afternoon, still in his windbreaker and sneakers. I stand, hands at my sides, and try to recognize the Greek for "in the name of the Father and the Son and the Holy Spirit," so that I can make the sign of the cross—*I am Orthodox, see me sign!*—but I remain baffled. The white-bearded priest, big-bellied under his black cassock and gold stole, gestures perfunctorily. Well, he is a civil servant, after all, and wants to be home for dinner.

This is how I become one of those Slavs at the farthest reaches of the Peloponnese: I stand motionless in front of an iconostasis, my hands by my sides, bewildered by the goings-on, and become a Christian. It will be ages and eras before I believe, but I will show up in Orthodox churches because it is my memory of the gods.

Byzantium—her marble palaces, her gilded saints, her peacocks opening up the turquoise feathers of their tails like fans in the empresses' gardens—will be transplanted into the quiescent humus of Slavic souls, who will receive her without resistance. Slavs could not yet follow the Liturgy, nor read the Holy Scriptures, nor name their children after saints. They did not yet have their own alphabet, but when they did, they would write a poetry all their own under the blue domes of Byzantium.

As I ride the bus out of Monemvasia, I think of the long trek of Slavs south, out of their traditional homeland in the Carpathian basin and marshes of east-central Europe to settle here on the gritty, high-lying plateau of the southern Peloponnese. From a window in a café in Yeraki near Sparta, I had looked out across dusty terracotta rooftops and cascades of bougainvillea to the famous vista of the Taygetos range, and thought of its celebrated fastnesses through which Slav invaders of the sixth century had driven the Greeks to the coasts and then settled onto the plains of the Eurotas River and the slopes of the mountains far from the sea.

Behold Taygetus at night while the sky proclaims the sea's blueness and cries are heard from invisible dogs. What do you wait for, Greek, facing the stars?

—N.D. KAROUZOS, 1964

When the morning mists lift from the valley floor, the broad Laconian plain becomes a garden of olive groves and orange orchards, iridescent fruit hanging like baubles in the dark green foliage. The stone-faced Taygetos rises spherically, dominating the Peloponnesian heartland; on Mizithras hill, Prince Guillaume II de Villhardouin built a castle in 1249 to establish Frankish power and lord it over the Peloponnese and the region's insubordinate Greeks and Slavic tribes. The Greeks had honoured Apollo here, Artemis, and their mother Leto, and on the peak of Taygetos, the second-century traveller Pausanias tells us, "they call it a sanctuary of the Sun, and there among other victims they sacrifice horses to the Sun."

But as Christians, on these same stone slabs of Taygetos in the late-Byzantine city, Mistra, they built churches and monasteries, including the thirteenth-century Metropolis Church dedicated to St. Demetrius, its lovely honeyed hue of masonry in warm interplay with the red terracotta tiles of the apses. Inside, the dramatic scenes of the martyrdom of St. Demetrius are plastered in vibrant blues and reds and golds, all over the walls. Demetrius is enthroned in prison, guarded by rigid Roman soldiers under the elemental geometries of the medieval city of Thessalonica. He dies seated between the red columns of a red-and-green-domed portico as the soldiers, half crouching, impassively thrust their long spears sideways into his body. The tips of their weapons protrude through the stiff drapery of his immaculate white chlamys while the Saint holds up his hands in surrender and tilts his haloed head toward the soldiers with an expression of the gravest melancholy.

Local villagers (Slavs? Greeks?) light their beeswax tapers and stand together, the same prayer on their lips: *The world has found in you a great champion in time of peril, as you emerged the victor in routing the barbarians. Holy one, great Martyr Demetrius, invoke Christ God for us, that He may grant us His great mercy.*

I note on my map a village called Sklavouna way down south on one of the fingers of the Peloponnese. I look mildly at the vista, wondering idly if there were still somewhere embedded in the mental DNA of these villagers an iota of a memory of their first homeland. The men in the tavernas, playing backgammon and watching the soccer game on television, the women in the gardens planting dill, may they be some sort of relatives of mine? Did we stand together once, outside the walls of Thessalonica, impatiently battering on the gates while St. Demetrius strode the walls? We didn't yet recognize him, or we thought he was a horseman like all the others we had seen, ploughing up the dust of the steppes with sword and chariot wheel. But he was an Eros who aimed his spear at us all, and we would die of love, there in Macedonia.

⸬ *Lord, have Mercy*

:: *Aegina*

MY OLD FRIEND, the poet Katerina Anghelaki Rooke, spends whatever time she can at her Aegina island home. She and her husband Rodney are blanketed by the warmth of their kitchen on the blustery winter day that I pop by to see them before I return to Canada. This big, pink house is connected with the family of the writer, Nikos Kazantzakis, for Katerina is his godchild, and the cluttered interior feels as though the house has become the depository of generations' worth of memorabilia. But the kitchen is simplicity itself: soup, barrelled wine, BBC radio news, and island gossip. Her friend, the architect, Andreas, is in town, she announces; formerly an artist and architect, he is now a full-time icon-painter. Would I like to see him?

I remember Andreas from a visit some ten years earlier as a handsome man with a scarf tossed dashingly around his neck and with architect's blueprints casually rolled up under his arm. We sat at a harbour café while he talked to me about how Orthodox churches are built, how the architect always makes a deliberate mistake in the construction so as not to be guilty of the sin of professional pride.

Katerina gets on the phone to Andreas; he'll pick me up and drive me over to his studio to talk about painting Demetrius's icon. In his car, bouncing over the stone-strewn track to his house, he tells me he painted or "wrote" this icon for a priest, and he has represented Demetrius, prostrate, to the left of the enthroned Mother of God with St. Gennadius, the early medieval patriarch of Constantinople, to the right. An unusual representation: no horse, no Thessalonica, no barbarians at the walls, no Bulgarian Antichrist.

Andreas lives in a fine house with a panoramic view over the stony fields and out to the sea. A small white loaf of a chapel with a curved blue roof is set in the winter garden, which blooms with red and pink geraniums. In his kitchen, tucked into a corner of the counter, an oil lamp burns in front of an icon of the Mother of God. It is the room's only illumination.

By the time we are seated in his studio to catch the last light of the afternoon—the flawless sheen of gold from the icons on the walls and easels is the last light to leave—he has already asked whether my parents were religious and what sort of people I've been talking to on my travels and what is the *real* reason for my interest in St. Demetrius. "Let's speak personally," he offers. To bring out my note-book and ask for an interview would be to miss the point, his point anyway, and a kind of profanity, and so I sit and listen.

For it is he who does the speaking, disquisitions on the difference between Catholicism and Orthodoxy, for instance: "Everything that *we* believe is life, they believe is death, and everything *they* believe is life, we believe is death!" On the utter nothingness of modern human beings: "Because of the Fall, we are wretched zeros, we are torn souls shattered by Western civilization." On the meaning of the Incarnation, the meaning of the Holy Trinity, his profound regret, even anguish, that he spent so much of his life captured by Western ideas before he returned to the Orthodox Church. He chides me for my "humanism," interrogates my feeble knowledge of the teach-ings of the Church Fathers, the Nicene Creed, the Jesus Prayer ("How is it said in Russian?" I have no idea but I come up with *Gospodi Pomiluij*, Lord have mercy, which he accepts), and the Church Slavonic rendering of the Greek word *Logos* (I have no idea but I try *slovo*, literally, word). He wants to know just what sort of church is the Ukrainian Orthodox Church of Canada, is surprised it is not within the Moscow Patriarchate, asks me when my Saint's Day is. "*Myrna* isn't a Saint," I explain. "It's just the name my mother liked." What's my baptismal name? I have no idea. "Ask your mother."

But it seems he has my best interests at heart. "Whenever I meet someone baptized in the Orthodox Church—and believe me, even though you were a baby and remember nothing, it is very important—I feel an affinity."

In the middle of what Katerina will call "this religious falderol" he stops mid-sentence, looks keenly at me in the gathering gloom, and says with almost deadpan matter-of-factness, "You know, you don't have to struggle alone with this. Christ said, 'You can do nothing without me.' You should have a guide." I do not cringe or wince; in fact, I am aware that my heart aches to hear it.

"You should go to the priest of your church, you should tell him everything; even if he doesn't understand or tells you something that doesn't seem sensible, it doesn't matter." (Help! I don't have a church, I don't have a priest!) "As a priest he has received the grace of God. And, another thing: do not try to approach God directly. Go through the saints and the Mother of God. And you are not going to get there by means of an intellectual or literary 'project.' And another thing: you do not need to be in special places—churches and crypts and Byzantine ruins—to receive God's grace yourself. It can find you anywhere. Even in the church in Edmonton. And who's to say that the old, illiterate peasant woman sitting next to you in church doesn't have more of it than you?"

When I return, shaken, to Katerina's kitchen and describe the conversation, she sums it up: "Ha, the 'Andreas Experience'"! Then, subdued, she adds: "We are all preparing ourselves for the last act."

Two years later she will send me a new poem, *Safe*; it reads, in part: "Be calm; the sky's now permanent night won't be lit again by fugitive visions. Your hair won't be tangled in the wild weeds....Terror arrives with its thick body and will now be the day's single genuine emotion."

:: *According to the chronicles*

IN 907, *with a vast army from the tribes of Great Scythia, Prince Oleh*
sallied forth from Kyiv by horse and by ship to Constantinople, to seize
it for himself. But, when he found the entrance from the Bosporus to the
Golden Horn—that vital channel below the eastern sea walls—blocked by
a massive chain, he commanded his warriors to fashion wheels. These they
attached to the ships, and when the wind blew favourable, they spread the
sails and bore down upon the city from the open fields. "When the Greeks
beheld this, they were afraid," and offered to pay tribute, and sent out to
Oleh vessels of food and wine, which he refused, knowing it was poisoned.
The Greeks were frightened again, and exclaimed, "This is not Oleh but St.
Demetrius, whom God has sent upon us!"

:: *November 8, St. Demetrius Day, Old Calendar*

THE ROADWAY to the Jaroslaw Church of St. Demetrius from
Edmonton weaves through a desolate countryside under a low,
slate sky: witness the lifeless fields, the bony limbs of leafless
trees, the light layering of snow on the frozen furrows, the tumble-
down barns and farmhouses, because yet another generation of

Ukrainian-Canadians has grown up in the city and the working farms lie farther and farther apart.

My mother and I enter the nondescript church and stand at the back and look around. There are perhaps thirty worshippers, all elderly, the women gamely singing the service with their thin and quivering soprano voices, the *diak* (cantor) occasionally overriding them with a stentorian bark. This parish had originally been Russo-Orthodox with a priest from San Francisco, but the iconostasis and the framed religious pictures hanging here and there on the walls seem Roman Catholic to me—the over-production of crucifixion scenes, the too-amiable expressions on the faces of the archangels and the sugary loveliness of the Mother of God. In the right-hand corner of the front wall within his own elaborate frame hangs a painting of St. Demetrius as a teenage warrior—big, wide-open eyes in a cherubic face—astride a stony landscape with unspecific crenellated fortress walls on the horizon.

Fr. Palamarchuk, young, stout, florid, has arrived at his sermon: "What is it we learn about human nature from the life of St. Demetrius? Here was a guy born with a silver spoon in his mouth: that kind of kid usually doesn't amount to anything these days! But here we have a young man born into a rich but modest family, his father the governor of Thessalonica and region, and a Christian. A quiet Christian (just as today *real* Christians are going inward, saving their souls, holding onto what we valued fifty, sixty years ago). Here we have a young man who gave up his life at twenty-eight years of age but who had already lived a lifetime. His mother taught him never to brag, though. He finished school, took his father's position in the city, and made a big name for himself far past Thessalonica, right up to the Roman emperor, who decided to see what was going on in Salonica."

This is a very odd text, I am thinking, less the Life of a Saint than a chatty obituary by a family friend, but then I begin to hear something new and creative at work—the retelling of St. Demetrius's life for us here and now, humbly assembled in the Alberta countryside, as though this protean Saint had evolved a new identity for our needs and purposes. At the end of the service, Fr. Palamarchuk sings a *Panakhyda* (memorial service) for the dead of the Second World War;

the small altar in the nave has been set with a crucifix pricked with red poppies and a stack of three braided breads pierced by a beeswax candle. Among the ornate words of the Ukrainian Liturgy, we hear the names of the dead: Fred, Harry, Steve, Steve, Harry, Mike, Frank, Fred...dead these sixty years, and I suppose their mothers who bore them and then sent them off to die are now in their own graves.

I have a view through the narrow, stained-glass panel on the north side of the church out onto the stubbled field with its protective grove of spruce and the sheltered graves of the little cemetery. This is St. Demetrius Day, and he is not on the battlements of a Byzantine city but loping across the frozen furrows of a western Canadian quarter-section, the souls of the dead trailing behind him, their good shepherd, while we, teetering at the edge of our own afterlife, warm inside the little church with the big dome, watch the earth open up and receive its inheritance.

PART TWO

Demetrius in Byzantium

⋮ *Interlude*

ONE HOT JULY AFTERNOON in Saskatchewan's Qu'Appelle Valley, the air so stilled from heat that even the flies could not be bothered lifting themselves off the windowpanes, I sat with my friend, Trevor Herriot, also a writer, who had bought this land we were viewing from the cabin porch, a sere and undulating landscape shaped by the meandering ribbon of water in the valley bottom. His children ran in and out of the house, not caring about the heat, and played whoop-up games around the canvas tipi on the slope below us. Inside the cabin, Trevor's wife, Karen, who home-schooled these children—books lay all about, and binoculars, and insect specimens, and desiccated birds' nests—prepared us all lunch.

When you've grown up on the North Saskatchewan, as I had, the Qu'Appelle River seems more of a stream, merely a tributary to the surge of water bound for the oceans, but its impact on the land has been dramatic: it has eroded the soft, treeless, prairie soils into deep and serpentine coulees into which the prairie suddenly collapses and drops you down from the horizon. It has also had a dramatic impact on Trevor, who has walked this terrain his whole life, eyes to the ground looking for burrowing owls and tipi rings, then, head back, scanning the skies for the land's last song birds, and, perhaps, for the skies' avenging angels. After a long lapse, he was once again a practising Roman Catholic, and in a public struggle, in his books, with a spirit divided against itself: the man of culture and civilization, the householder on these very fields, and the wild man, more forest than farm, venerating Earth, not ploughing and cropping her. We had become friends as writers. I didn't know people of his (younger) generation, let alone mine, who still went to church in all sincerity, but then I didn't know many writers who prayed for spiritual wholeness along with literary finesse. I paid him close, if askance, attention.

We were talking about ambivalence and anxiety, that peculiar state of people who have experienced themselves all their lives as rational beings (we two, for example), only to be sabotaged, blind-sided, shaken, upended, by what Trevor called "a longing for the holy," which arrives seemingly out of the clear blue heaven, but which also, if you think about it, makes perfect sense. I had told him something of my travels with St. Demetrius—what I was calling my investigation into a "deep, personal cultural grammar," its twists and turns, its blind alleys, its tears and sighs from an unexamined heart—and now I was listening to my friend with mounting agitation, for I guessed where this was heading.

The "sense" to be made of ambivalence and anxiety, he said, was that not everything could be known by the exercise of logic and judgement, a modesty lost to us since the Enlightenment. Considering all the materials I had gathered in my "Demetrius project," did I not feel, he asked, the urge to go beyond the narrative and intellectual limits of history, ethnology, and politics? Did I not want to push the boundaries of what I already knew from intellectual experience, a push from my religious heritage, not to mention from a certain Saint of Byzantium? We may understand saints as our intercessors with God, he said, and here was one who was tapping me on the shoulder. God may or may not be out there, but we certainly aren't going to find out one way or another by the application of our reasoning alone. We are likelier to find Him through the slippages offered by uncertainty and ambivalence, what Trevor called the "anxious threshold experience" of travelling between rationality and faith, doubt and spiritual longing.

A few months earlier, away from home, I had picked up the copy of the Gideon Bible, discreetly shelved in the hotel cupboard drawer, and let it fall open. I was exquisitely aware that not so long before I would have made jokes about the "Gideons" and about Bible Belts, but here I was, reading the Holy Bible, an exercise, I told myself, in random thought association. The book had fallen open at James 3:6. *And the tongue is a fire, the very world of iniquity; the tongue is set among our members as that which defiles the entire body, and sets on fire the course of our life, and is set on fire by hell.*

I had not even known that there was a text by St. James, but it was still a shock, that harsh Biblical language of judgement, yet so vivid and stirring. I had "left the church" precisely in order to go out into the world of ideas and argument, my tongue on fire: how could I agree that such fiery speech could ever defile the entire body of the community?

If I had to choose, between the iniquity of the spiritual "tongue" and the clamour of the social "body," I knew which I would choose. As the German philosopher Theodor Adorno wrote: "The illusory importance and autonomy of private life conceals the fact that private life drags on only as an appendage of the social process." All through the decades of my intellectual maturation and beyond, even as the idealized models collapsed—the Left into a dustbin of history, feminism into post-feminism, the "peace dividend" into perpetual war—I believed passionately in the possibility of human solidarity.

When political scientist, Peter C. Emberley, in *Divine Hunger: Canadians on Spiritual Walkabout*, investigated the phenomenon of so many of the "60s" generation searching for "spiritual" meaning in their middle age, he made this observation: that our youthful commitment to social and political change and to the communities we lived in had been, in part, tools of consciousness—love and solidarity, hope and compassion—through which "the divine" could now speak. Like secular ideals of revolutionary change, Christian morality, for example, has always expressed faith in the possibility of change, renewal, amelioration of the human condition.

Decades after our engagement by the great movements for liberation and justice, some of us return to churches and temples or at least to spiritual rites and rituals not as gestures of private despair at the collapse of political and social projects but as an acknowledgement of the "return of the repressed" desire for some kind of collective hope in transcendent ideals in a sickened world. Even that veteran of the German Left, philosopher Jurgen Habermas, in his *Time of Transitions*, argued that, at the foundation of the modern structures of consciousness in the West, lies the culture of Christianity. "Egalitarian universalism, from which sprang the ideas of freedom and social solidarity, of an autonomous conduct of life and emancipation, of the individual morality of conscience, human rights, and democracy, is the direct heir to the Judaic ethic of justice and the Christian ethic of love....To this day, there is no alternative to it....We continue to nourish ourselves from this source. Everything else is postmodern chatter." It was true that, since my return from Greece, I had taken to clipping and posting wise or lyrical quotations from writers who seem to have anticipated my quandary: whether a spiritual seeker must abandon her intellectual capacities. I recognized the challenge from earlier in my life, back among the hippies and the politicos, the stoned vs. the revolutionary path to freedom, or, among the feminists, smashing the patriarchy vs. swooning with the moon goddess: choose one or the other. The paths cannot be straddled. But now I read of Richard E. Byrd, polar explorer, who spent the winter at the South Pole in a tiny cabin on the ice. Even in that desperate circumstance, he believed that his despair ("man's despair") was groundless, once he allowed his feeling that a "beneficent intelligence pervaded the whole" of creation to "transcend" his rational thoughts and enter his heart. It was that "transcend" which hooked me, not being sure about the beneficent intelligence.

An Orthodox priest-scientist I once spoke with, Archbishop Lazar Puhalo, and to whom I admitted my stumbling efforts to understand Christian "realities," such as mystery, grace, and revelation, retorted that modern physics, for example, is an experimental science, not a purely rational one, "which brings it close to the workings of Orthodox theology." As a scholar of quantum physics himself, he had never had difficulty with the idea of energy endlessly forming and reforming in clusters of matter, deforming and forming again. Resurrection? Transfiguration? Christianity stands charged by Nietzschians as opposed to the heroic ideals of Classical philosophy, embracing morality over sensuality, pity over heroism, guilt over joy, the lure of the hereafter over *joie de vivre*. Yet, as the Romanian Orthodox theologian Fr. Dumitru Staniloae wrote of the Feast of the Resurrection, overcoming the sorrow of death is this "explosion of cosmic joy at the triumph of life." It is not the Judeo-Christian God but Nietzsche who is dead. I plucked William James's *The Varieties of Religious Experience* from the shelf, the ninety-five-cent paperback I'd had in my library since 1967 and had never read. He saw great utility in religion's teaching that happiness is increased by the "surrender and sacrifice" of the self, "and if it be the only agency that can accomplish this result, its vital importance as a human faculty stands vindicated beyond dispute." I wondered if this claim for the importance of the transcendence of the self related to my own attachment to the ideals of collectivity and solidarity, and I was a little startled when he went on to describe science itself as a "sect," an isolated conceptual system framed by our own minds. "But why in the name of common sense need we assume that only one such system of ideas can be true?" I had no idea that an experimental psychologist writing at the turn of the twentieth century would appeal to "common sense" as a vindication of the view that "religion and science, each verified in its own way from hour to hour and from life to life, would be co-eternal." This sounds almost theological, almost Orthodox. *Still the Father and the Son and the Holy Spirit have one divinity, equal glory, and coeternal majesty.* And that "rational consciousness" is but one form of consciousness. But James would know: in his review of literature about experiences of religious conversion, for example, reading these as a series of case studies, he locates the "root of the matter" in the experience of yielding one's imperfect, egoistic self to a "new life."

And so I went to visit a new friend of mine, an Anglican priest in Edmonton, Fr. Don Aellen. (This is how I thought of him, following High Churchiness: Father and Priest. I did not yet appreciate how profoundly the Protestant Reformation had split the One, Holy, Universal and Apostolic Church, and that his own parishioners called him simply "Don.") We began our visits with duelling Bibles, as it were. I had just begun to read the Orthodox Study Bible, in preparation for a second trip to St. Demetrius Basilica in Thessalonica, and I would read out the Orthodox commentaries to this Revised Standard

Edition while he would contrapuntally read from his. Now, after reading William James, I wanted to know more about the Christian idea of the "self." "What is the 'self' beyond its private life?" I asked. "Is it fully encompassed by the historical, the political, the socio-logical? If not, what are the documentations of this larger self?"

Fr. Don fairly jumped out of his chair and went straight to his Bible and read from Romans 8:26. That St. Paul might be a source of wisdom and consolation was rather a shock to me, who had thought of him only as a misogynist typical of patriarchal religions who believed that women should be silent in church, among other prohibitions. But I listened. "Likewise the Spirit also helps in our weaknesses. For we do not know what we should pray for as we ought, but the Spirit Himself makes intercession for us with groanings which cannot be uttered." I confessed, feeling stupid and unlettered in this Christian language, that I didn't really get it.

"Self-understanding is seeing ourselves as God sees us," Fr. Don patiently interpreted. "Part of our fallenness as humans is to see ourselves only as self-created," —I was all ears—"and not in His image. The self is in fact embedded in God's knowledge. This is the source of our internal coherence." The "fallenness" made me squirm (it seemed the sort of thing a Protestant would say), but I felt a little leap of my spirit. Something was expanding within me at the idea that my "self" might be the creation of some transcendent energy beyond economic, historical, cultural, and gendered necessity.

This would have to be, in some sense, a "secret self," as Peter Emberley has written, for the news that I was becoming seriously interested in the tradition of worship in the Orthodox Church, which prided itself on its roots in Christian antiquity, would, I feared, shock friends and family. Wouldn't they wonder how I could reconcile my social and political values with the doctrines of a patriarchal insti-tution dead set against, for instance, same-sex marriage, abortion, and premarital sex (although it tends not to make a fuss)? Would I really submit to the discipline of Orthodox spiritual practices? Great Lent, for instance, forty days before Easter, not eating meat, and pros-trating myself before icons? Isn't there some more "reasonable" cult I could join, mother-goddess worship, for instance? Could I not be accused of seeking just another but more exotic version of post-political self-fulfillment?

As I rose to leave, Fr. Don detained me: "Christian truth develops along a progressive line between the self at one end and God at the other with Christ halfway between. Where would you put yourself on this line?" I experienced a couple of seconds of familiar anxiety: just as I had always wanted to give the "right" answer to political questions put by political activists, I wanted now to give the "right" answer to this man of God so that he wouldn't regret the time he had spent with me. But I answered truthfully: I could see myself moving to the idea of the Divine, with the help of saints and the Church Fathers, but Jesus, well, I could not truthfully say I was moving to Him. I felt apologetic about this, but for the moment I felt only a kind of giddiness, thrown off-balance by something "unutterable."

"Are spirit and mind really at such cross-purposes?" I asked Fr. Don on a subsequent visit, thinking of what happens in the act of creativity, that mysterious arrival out of nowhere of a thought or image you did not know you were thinking or seeing. I asked him, "May we not discern here in the creative moment the collaboration of the spirit and the mind?" He whipped out St. Paul again: Romans 12:1-2.

"And do not be conformed to this world but be transformed by the renewing of your mind, that you may prove what is that good and acceptable and perfect will of God."

Mind, yes, but mind renewed, transformed into the highest faculty of human nature—the eyes of the heart, "the eyes of your understanding" (Paul to the Ephesians), as though we could turn our gaze inward straight to our knowing the will of God. "Jesus cannot conceive of a mind and spirit that are not in relationship," Fr. Don said, animatedly, and not for the last time was I both bemused by and envious of his intimacy with the Word, not to mention the Living God. He added that he could see that I had been called to just such a "renewed mind," and certainly not to the suppression or abandonment of my intellect. "Keep reading the Bible!"

Keep reading the Bible for one's intellect? In its introductory pages, the *Orthodox Study Bible* asserts that "theological knowledge is first of all personal and experiential and then thought out and verbalized." But this is not the end of it, for that would be blind faith, a form of super-stition. No, "revelation" arrives and our intellect is illumined. All my conscious life I had assumed—indeed, experienced—the revelation that "arrives" *after* the illumination of my intellect. Now I was being invited to reverse this way of thinking, or at least sidestep it, and to consider that here perhaps is where the heart is, at the epicentre of mind and spirit. It was not going to be easy, this unlearning. St. Paul again: "I do not lie; my conscience joins with the holy Spirit in bearing me witness that I have great sorrow and constant anguish in my heart" (Romans 9:1).

And I read Tom Hayden again, whose (politically and socially) visionary manifesto, *Port Huron Statement*, had "converted" me in 1966 to the New Left project; thirty years later, he writes of the "lost gospel of the earth," an environmentalist's manifesto to be sure, but not only. When we recognize that the plenipotentiaries of Earth have "smothered" our souls, then "being spiritual" is no longer a choice, for we *are* spiritual beings. Our humanity is fully realized in the connection with "living creation," that eternal object of our yearning: something bigger than ourselves. "Illumine our hearts," Orthodox Christians pray before the reading of the Gospel begins. The triumph of Christian thought in the first four centuries, writes Orthodox theologian Vladimir Lossky, was not "the rationalization of Christianity but the Christianization of reason." "I believe," we begin, and perhaps from the believing proceeds a new understanding of who and where we are, and not the other way around, as my lonely, rational self had always assumed.

Years earlier, I had printed out a phrase from an essay by poet Don McKay: "Home," he writes, "is the action of the inner life finding outer form; it is the settling of self into the world." I thought about this for some time, as it had moved me, drawn me to itself, demanding my concentration on it. I thought about what the poet meant about himself, given his poetic theme of the human process of representa-tion of the self and the "other" as an act of appropriation, "rendering of the other as one's interior." For me, though, I realized that the process was exactly the reverse: my outer life—my life as a student, a citizen, and a writer well-settled in the world—was now struggling to find its way home to an interior form, rendering all that "otherness" as a passage to the somnolent spirit within, and there opening "the eyes of the heart."

I had stood in that great seventh-century Basilica dedicated to Thessalonica's Patron, Demetrius, surrounded by his beautiful images. Had I found inner form in the icon of a Byzantine Saint? I was startled by the possibility.

I had been struggling for a "self" that is neither reducible to some private psychodrama nor dismissible by an ironic, despairing flourish of postmodernism. I was admitting to myself, icon by icon, that my "self" is embedded in the matrix of spirit, as well as in history, politics, culture. And even as I began to thresh about for a spiritual vocabulary for my desires, I knew that "salvation," like "liberation" and "revolution," is not undertaken alone but in the company of others. In some places they call that a church.

And so I resolved to return to Demetrius's home, his Basilica in Thessalonica, to be there with all the others on his Feast Day, October 26. The "outer forms" of his life would be there, the icons, banners, mosaics, hymns, prayers, lamentations, but perhaps, by our standing attentively within their sound and light, St. Demetrius would find within us all his inner form.

IN DECEMBER 2000, my companion on the bus ride from Belgrade, Ana, was a graduate student of English, willing to accompany me on that wet and blustery day along the Pannonian plain to Sremska Mitrovica, once the Roman town of Sirmium, where the retired director of Srem Museum, Petar Milosevic, had agreed to an interview. He was, I had learned from people in Belgrade, someone with a point of view all his own on the cult of Demetrius.

It was a tedious trip; I did not know that our destination lay at the frontier with Croatia from which endless columns of Serbian refugees had tried and would try to cross the border to their "motherland," whose men would be turned back and whose women and children would be stranded, weeping from hunger. Ana told me this, as the bus wound through the city, but it was Sirmium, the oldest city in Yugoslavia, a city lying in the rubble beneath the modern city of sorrows, that I was interested in.

We met the professor outside the museum. In spite of the presence of a cheerful café in the town where they served cappuccino amid plants and bamboo furniture, Professor Milosevic led us toward the Ambassador Hotel, one of those Tito-era masterpieces of cement and brown carpeting. We were the only customers in the vast restaurant, and we drank, with its after-flavour of kitchen slop, the worst cup of Turkish coffee of my life.

"We are talking about the old cultures that existed here before the Romans," he began, emphasizing the antiquity of the town. "We know about the Pannonians that lived here some three thousand years ago. Those are the Neolithic cultures, the cultures of the early Bronze Age and Late Bronze Age, by which time the Celtic people appeared in the region. That happened approximately during the fourth century BC."

The ancient history alone spans a period of some six centuries, and excavations have brought to light a section of city walls, public buildings (a bathhouse, several warehouses, a hippodrome), villas and apartment complexes (insulae), an urban church, and several chapels outside the ramparts, probably erected in cemeteries. The Eastern Church venerates Epenetus and Andronicus, as first bishops of Sirmium and disciples of St. Paul.

Professor Milosevic had participated in some of the archaeological digs himself, as I learned later from publications, though oddly he didn't mention them to me. For example, his colleague, the archaeologist Vladislav Popovic, credited him with "successful investigations of the road," meaning the public highway by which emperors, augusti, barbarians, and whole armies came and went, and grateful populations greeted their suzerains with lights and flowers and good wishes, shouting "Augustus!" and "Lord!" as they escorted them to the palace.

From the very beginning it has been the Romans' mission to teach good sense to those who lack it, and not to be thought to lack it ourselves. Shall we hand over Sirmium to barbarians?

—BYZANTINE EMPEROR JUSTIN II, C. 570 CE

Sirmium, located strategically on the Danubian frontier with the barbarians, including the Slavs, became, after 568, the immediate objective of the supreme ruler of the tribal Avars, the ruthless Khagan Bayan. "They crossed the Danube and fell upon the country folk, who were busy with their harvest and had no thought of an enemy," we are told in a lively account by Menander Protector, a late-sixth-century historian and palace guardsman from Constantinople. Most of the country folk were killed, taken by surprise and slaughtered without mercy, or carried off together with their livestock, victims of "peoples addicted to rapine and brigandage...and gloating over the ashes of burnt farms and the sufferings of the murdered inhabitants." But neither is he impressed by the Roman defences, in the shape of the military commander.

"The praetorium prefect Probus, who was quite unused to the horrors of war and was then at Sirmium, was so overcome by this novel and melancholy experience that he could hardly raise his eyes from the ground and was long in doubt what to do. He had a team of swift horses got ready, and decided to fly the following night, but then thought better of it and stayed where he was....So he mastered his fears and roused himself by a strong effort to meet the crisis." He cleared out the moats, which were choked with rubbish, raised the greater part of the neglected and decayed walls, and erected high towers with battlements from materials that had been meant for the construction of the theatre. Then he waited for Khagan Bayan.

According to Menander's account, the Avar Khagan assembled a fleet of enormous ships on the Danube and manned them with soldiers and oarsmen, "who rowed not in rhythm but in a barbarously uncoordinated manner," and sent the vessels down the river while he with the whole of his army marched to lay siege to Sirmium.

Emperor Tiberius in Constantinople was outraged. "I should rather betroth to him one of my two daughters than willingly surrender the city of Sirmium. Even if he should take it by force, I, while awaiting the retribution of God whom he has so insulted, shall never consent to abandon any part of the Roman state."

For the first three years of the cruel siege, he was true to his word. The Avars blockaded the river and all supplies destined for the city. Losing all hope of Roman rescue, the people of Sirmium, barricaded within their walls, began to starve and turned to "unlawful food." When Tiberius learned of this, he decided that it was pointless to surrender the citizens, already ground down by suffering and misery, along with the city, and so ordered the commander to end the siege by surrendering his command to the Avars, "on the condition that the inhabitants of the place be allowed to leave en masse, taking with them none of their possessions beyond their lives and one cloak each."

We can imagine them, haggard and emaciated, their flesh withered on their bones, as they shuffle out the city gates, such a pitiable sight that even their conquerors, the Avars, moved to a compassion "worthy of Christians," pressed food upon the refugees. Some died immediately from sudden overeating, for the wretches had had only cats to eat.

Almost nothing remains of the agony of Sirmium except a pitiful inscription on a brick in ungrammatical Greek: "Lord Christ, help the city and smite the Avars and watch over the Romans and the writer. Amen."

A new settlement of craftsmen and merchants, Mitrovica, rose in the twelfth century at the same place, named for the old Sirmium Church of St. Demetrius; in the thirteenth century, after the devastation of Tatar invasions, a monastery of St. Demetrius, the residence of a tenacious group of Greek and Slavic monks under the jurisdiction of a Catholic bishop, gave the settlement yet another name, *Civitas Sancti Demetrii*. The City of Saint Demetrius.

"Why have you come to Sirmium?" Professor Milosevic asked rhetorically. "Because here is where the real St. Demetrius, Great Martyr and Miracle-worker, lived and died."

Galerius, who had conducted the bloody campaigns against the Christians in the eastern empire, died here a few days after halting the persecutions. Professor Milosevic worked on excavations of the city's Christian necropoli, the interred buried with their faces toward the Resurrectional east. But the team failed to identify, at the centre of the antique city, a basilica with transept and three naves built on a thick layer of ash as the Basilica of St. Demetrius, the "all-holy church" built by the prefect of Illyricum, Leontius, to house the martyr's cloak, "drenched in the saint's blood," as the Passion of St. Demetrius has it.

This must be what he showed us on the way to the hotel—the forlorn site of a semi-excavated Byzantine church's foundations, stones of the apse of a basilica under murky glass extended from the floor of a sad little shopping centre. Christian historiography contains some data referring to the building of a temple dedicated to the Sun god by Diocletian in Sirmium, but no one seems to be looking for this.

Milosevic continued: "But in the beginning of the fourth century, Emperor Diocletian began a persecution of Christians. This persecution reached its peak in 304 when the co-ruler of Diocletian, Maximianus—who was born in Sirmium!—arrested and persecuted the entire Christian hierarchy in Sirmium starting with the arrest of the first Bishop Irenaeus and his deacon, Demetrius. That's where the history of Demetrius begins."

On April 1, 304, Bishop Irenaeus and Deacon Demetrius were executed at Sirmium on the orders of Probus, the governor of Pannonia.

Of Irenaeus the scholars have written, of his beauty, his family happiness, his brilliant career. When he was arrested, his relations and his own children begged him to do the empire's bidding and sacrifice even just a few incense grains to the emperor. "Sacrifice, or I will put you to the torture!" cried Probus. Even the mob called out to him: "Have pity on your own youth!" It made no difference to Irenaeus.

"I rejoice in that, for I will take part in the Passion of my Savior," he replied; then, as Paul Allard, historian of the Diocletian persecutions, relates:

> The governor ordered him beaten. "I've been taught since childhood to adore my God, I adore him now, he supports me in my trials, it's to him that I sacrifice. I cannot adore your man-made gods."..."Don't you have a wife?" "I have none." "A son?" "I have none." "Parents?" "None." "And who then were those people weeping in front of you the other day?" "My Lord Jesus Christ said, 'He who loves his father, or his mother, or his wife, or his son, or his brothers more than me is not worthy of me.'"

Milosevic added: "They led first Irenaeus and then Demetrius to a bridge over the Sava River where they cut off their heads and threw their bodies in the river."

The martyrs' memory lingered on in the works of Roman chroniclers and the written lives of Christian martyrs. In Sremska Mitrovica in the 1950s, a French archaeological dig uncovered a headstone inscribed with Irenaeus's name, indicating the site of a church devoted to him. It was Vladislav Popovic, who had joined in the excavations of Roman Sirmium, who wrote, emotionally, that "Sirmium had an exceptionally large number of martyrs or Christ's witnesses during the persecution during the first decade of the fourth century. Each square foot of its ground was drenched with the blood of the faithful....Sremska Mitrovica is a holy place indeed." In 1904 French historian of the early Church, Jacques Zeiller, travelled to Sremska Mitrovica where he saw only a small part of a funerary chapel with fragments of frescoes and mosaics intact. Thirty years earlier, however, vestiges of a "simple, cross-shaped church" were still visible. "It is quite likely that this construction was the sanctuary of St. Demetrius," he concluded, perhaps over-confidently. "We have the tomb of St. Anastasia," Milosevic confirmed. "We also have the tomb of another Greek, Sinerote. Leontius who was sent from Thessalonica as governor of Sirmium erected the Church of St. Demetrius here. However, we have not been allowed to dig around the Church of St. Demetrius even though we wanted to look for the headstone with his name on it."

It must have been driving him mad to think of how his time was running out if he wanted to get back to the excavations. The funds stopped in 1957, but the excavations were the only means he had of proving his speculations. If he could have kept on digging, Milosevic was absolutely convinced, "as a man of science," he would have found what he was looking for, the inscription saying something like: *Here lies buried Demetrius of Sirmium, martyred Christian.* "Maybe time will solve the question once we find the inscription, since for me the inscription is Number One. That's my goal. That's science."

Science: that St. Demetrius the Great Martyr known throughout the Orthodox world as "of Thessaloniki," *Solunski*, is a fraud, a mere legend. The real, historical Demetrius is this one who was martyred in Sirmium/Sremska Mitrovica; his cult originated here and then migrated hundreds of years later to Thessalonica, where the Greeks made up a cock-and-bull story about his being a Thessalonian, and forcibly adopted him.

After an hour's interview, Milosevic checked his watch, abruptly announced he had to leave us, but not before throwing out one last time that tantalizing and forlorn hope of a scientist of lost causes.

"We have researched Sirmium since 1950 and we have managed to establish some new discourses, scientific discourses, and to get rid of mythology. Maybe there was a Demetrius from Thessalonica but he does not have anything to do with the one from Sirmium. It is more likely that Demetrius from Sirmium has to do a lot with Demetrius from Thessalonica than the other way around. Only time will tell. When we find the inscriptions all will be clear." And with that he left us, treading the shabby brown carpet with considerable dignity.

Professor Milosevic has never published a book—the papers he showed me, thick in a cardboard folder, were written in German by his friend, the late archaeologist, Vladislav Popovic—and he speaks only Serbian. Had he ever been to an international conference? Had he ever left this town?

"He's still alive?" exclaimed Dr. Ljubomir Maksimovic, Byzantinist in Belgrade, who'd last seen him twenty years earlier. Since then, nothing had been heard from or of him. I considered my interview with the local "mad professor" a scoop. Years later, in an entry on Sirmium in Wikipedia, there he is, cited as a source for further reading: Petar Milošević, *Arheologija i istorija Sirmijuma*, Novi Sad, 2001.

IN A LOCAL LEGEND from Sremska Mitrovica, Professor Milosevic had recounted, Deacon Demetrius was martyred at the bridge on the Sava together with five virgins, pious women who lived quiet, ascetic lives in their own homes. "No one knows their names. Only God knows. They were beheaded first. Then, it was the turn of St. Demetrius. He turned to the citizens of Sirmium and said, 'I will be back.'"

IN THE BASILICA dedicated to St. Demetrius in Thessalonica, before the same icons I had come to know, in the same soft, honeyed smoke of incense, the saintly brothers Cyril and Methodius of ninth-century Thessalonica had also come to pray to their Guardian. Of high-ranking family and educated, in Constantinople the imperial capital, in astronomy, geometry, music, and rhetoric, and eventually placed in important monasteries, Cyril and Methodius likely had no inkling that they would be called to a more strenuous mission: to leave their cells and go out among the Slavs as ambassadors of Byzantine spirituality, Scriptures in hand.

It is told that in 862, Rastislav, prince of (Slavic) Moravia, sent messengers to Byzantine Emperor Michael III, saying, "Our nation is baptised, and yet we have no teacher to direct and instruct us and interpret the sacred scriptures. We understand neither Greek nor Latin. Some teach us one thing and some another. Furthermore, we do not understand written characters nor their meaning. Therefore send us teachers who can make known to us the words of the scriptures and their sense." Michael heard them out, then sent for Cyril the Philosopher [a.k.a. Constantine] and had him listen to the matter, "for you [and Methodius] are both Thessalonians and all Thessalonians speak pure Slavic."

Certainly, Cyril had heard all about the history of the Slavs, in the Homilies thundered against them in the Basilica of St. Demetrius—they had arrived in the Balkans in the sixth century and settled, after much violence against the city, in the Thessalonica hinterland—in the cautionary texts inscribed in the mosaics, and in the account of Demetrius's miracles (assembled as a single text in the seventh century). And it is generally agreed that he and his brother were familiar with the Slavic speech of Macedonia, perhaps were even born to a Slavic mother. As he and his brother Methodius walked about the city and its marketplaces, they would have spoken with Slavic-speaking peasants selling their produce from the Macedonian countryside. Each morning, when the great gates in the city walls opened—the Golden Gate, the Letaea Gate, and the Cassandria Gate—groups of Slavs would enter the city and pursue their affairs there, including buying and selling among the Greeks in verbal exchanges of pidgin tongues.

And [Michael] said: "Philosopher, I know that you are weary, but it is necessary that you go there. For no one can attend to this matter like you."

And the Philosopher answered: "Though I am weary and sick in body, I shall go gladly, if they have a script for their language."

Then the Emperor said to him: "My grandfather and my father, and many others have sought this but did not find it. How then can I find it?"

And the Philosopher answered: "Who can write a language on water and acquire for himself a heretic's name?"

And together with his uncle, Bardas, the Emperor answered him again: "If you wish, God may give you this as He gives to everyone that asks without doubt, and opens to them that knock."

The Philosopher went and, following his old habit, gave himself up to prayer together with his other associates. Hearing the prayer of His servants, God soon appeared to him. And immediately Constantine composed letters and began to write the language of the Gospel, that is: "In the beginning was the Word, and the Word was with God, and the Word was God," and so forth.

What Cyril/Constantine composed was the Glagolitic script, from Slav, *glagol*, "word," as though the very strokes of the letters could speak. Scholars have come forward to claim its origins in Georgian, Hebrew-Samaritan, Syriac, and even Byzantine alchemical symbols. But to the biographer of Cyril it was God-given. And at its arrival from his prayer, "the Emperor rejoiced, and together with his counsellors glorified God."

So, Cyril gathered Methodius and other monks, and together with them set off in the spring of 863 for the court of Rastislav.

Once they were in Moravia, the missionaries taught their flock Matins and the Hours, Vespers, and the Compline, and the Liturgy in Slavonic—the Life of Methodius recounts how he and Cyril placed their translations under the patronage of St. Demetrius—and "the ears of the deaf were unstopped, the words of the Scripture were heard, and the tongue of stammerers spoke clearly. And God rejoiced over this, while the devil was shamed."

This, at least, is how the Byzantine world saw matters.

The cultural, and spiritual, history of the Serbian, Montenegrin, Macedonian, Bulgarian, Ukrainian, Belarusian, and Russian Slavs begins with this act of literacy inside the Byzantine world. It was founded by the brothers who "taught" the Slavs and initiated them into the cultural currency that would constitute the central part of their own identity. The thoughtful and elegant Metropolitan of the Ukrainian Orthodox Church of Canada, Ilarion, writing in the 1950s, exulted in the Great Commission of Jesus Christ to his disciples—"Go therefore and make disciples of all the nations"—as an instruction to "inculturate" God in the nations, just as God had "bent the heavens" and became incarnate in Christ.

So Greeks and Slavs alike rejoice in the richness and beauty of the spiritual tradition they have inherited from the early Church. The so-called Cyrillo-Methodian tradition testifies to its homeland not in Greekness and Slavness but in a Christianity "churched" in Constantinople, the Queen of Cities and the New Jerusalem, dedicated to the "all-holy, most chaste, Mother of God, the eternal virgin Mary," as the Hymn to the Theotokos praises her. Did not the Apostle St. Paul himself say, "In offering my prayer to God, I had rather speak five words that all the brethren will understand than ten thousand which are incomprehensible?"

In a bookshop in Sofia, I will find yellowing greeting cards—*Happy Saints Cyril and Methodius Day!*—designed with Cyrillic typefaces and images of the venerable brothers. They are white-bearded holy men assembled at a table holding their riches: the Gospel, a globe, and a banner of the alphabet.

The brothers were forced to defend their work before synods and symposia in Rome. Cyril's reply has been recorded by his biographer in Slavonic, although it is certain he addressed the Roman clergy in Greek. With this masterful stroke, to all future generations of Slavic Christians this little treasure of spiritual and moral compassion, this gesture to the Slavs of recognition of their dignity before the face of God, was given. Cyril said: "But does the rain not fall equally upon all people, does the sun not shine for all, and do we not all breathe the air in equal measure?...Tell me, do you not render God powerless, that He is incapable of granting this?...For David cries out, saying, 'O sing unto the Lord, all the earth: sing unto the Lord a new song.'"

And so the Slavs came into Byzantium, singing.

:: *Sofia, Bulgaria*

MORAVIA WAS NOT LONG within the Byzantine orbit—after the deaths of Cyril and Methodius it reverted to the authority of the German Catholic bishops—but Bulgaria was, and so I have come again to Sofia, this time not in quest of national, ethnic, or tribal heroes and anti-heroes, not to lay claim to bloodlines among intermingled peoples, but to understand how my people, broadly understood to be Slavs, became citizens of that other mother country known as the Orthodox Church.

At Vespers at Sveti Sedmochistensi (The Seven-numbered Ones, including Saints Cyril and Methodius), I have sought shelter from this miserable night, my shoes squishing water into the carpeting.

The church was built in 1528, I presume as a mosque, by commission from Suleiman the Magnificent, and it's said to be some kind of miracle how the enormous dome rests directly on the four walls-in-square. I like its gloomy atmosphere very much and feel cozy within the shadows and the feeble light of the oil lamps and beeswax tapers on fire, listening to the soft shuffle of the elderly in their winter boots who make the round of the icons. They look poor, their coats thin and damp, so they are here, too, to warm up.

The apse is decorated with the image of the Mother of God Praying—not the Western posture of palms pressed together and eyes rolled back into her head but of the arms opened wide and a serene gaze straight into the viewer—a daughter of Eve, humanity's gift to God, writes Bishop Kallistos Ware in his wise book about the Orthodox Church, because she like us was born a human being. I also like the frescoes that depict Cyril and Methodius, and the scene of the Bulgarian Tsar Boris, who accepted Christianity for himself and all his subjects in 864 (a century earlier than the subjects of Volodymyr of Kyiv), here enthroned and dressed like a Byzantine emperor, receiving the Cyrillic alphabet on behalf of his people. There it is, written on the two pages of a book opened as an offering, almost like a Gospel. Those letters! I have only a faint memory of learning to read and write them in Ukrainian Saturday School in the church basement, but it's as though I recapitulated the entire historical experience of the Slavs' entry into literacy by my own hard struggle of learning how to shape the Щ and the Ж.

Although as Cyrillic the alphabet was named for Cyril, it was not Cyril and Methodius themselves who had devised these venerated letters, but their Bulgarian followers, Clement and Naum. When the Cyril-Methodian mission in Moravia collapsed, and after Methodius's death in 885, the new Moravian prince, Svetopolk, expelled Methodius's disciples and even auctioned some of the younger ones on the Venetian slave markets. But three, with Clement in the lead, made their way to the Danube, beyond which lay the Bulgarian lands. On a makeshift raft they crossed over to the frontier-post of Belgrade, whose governor promptly dispatched them to Bulgarian Tsar Boris, who sent them onward to Ohrid. In excellent living and working conditions in the Bulgarian kingdom, they set to work to educate and indoctrinate a Slavo-Byzantine-Christian elite.

Boris himself struggled mightily to understand the rules of the new cultural order into which he had been baptized in 864 in a village near Bulgaria's border with Byzantium. In a correspondence with Pope Nicholas in Rome about the implications of Christian conversion, he wondered plaintively, among 105 other questions, whether he may still pray for the souls of his pagan ancestors.

> *Must women cover their heads in church? Is it really necessary, as the Greeks [Constantinople] insist, to wear a belt when receiving the eucharist? May men wear their turbans in church? Is it true, as the Greeks claim, that no one should take a bath on a Wednesday or a Friday? May a Christian eat meat slaughtered by a pagan? Or by a eunuch? Is it necessary to abandon the ritual in accordance with which the khan is accustomed to eat at table all by himself? Is it permissible to mark a table with the sign of the cross? Is hunting allowed in Lent? Can we continue to swear oaths on a sword? What is the correct posture for the hands at prayer? How should suicides be buried?*

Here is another scene in the apse of the Seven-numbered Ones: the scriptors at the monastery of Titca in Preslav, skinny young monks and acolytes in knee-length tunics working under the direction of the grey-beard, St. Clement, a Slav himself and taskmaster of this prodigious labour of bringing the Slavs into Christianity and into their own letters at the same miraculous moment.

Some days later, in Mother of God Church in Plovdiv, in Liberation Square, I look at a tall fresco painted between windows that shows Cyril and Methodius, looking more like Byzantine hermits than priests, offer the alphabet. It is rolled out on a scroll, a revelation to the marvelling people, who are here represented as elders with their chins propped thoughtfully on their hands, shepherds in rough capes, warriors in round iron helmets with pointy tops, a peasant family in thick layers of embroidered clothing, the woman's hand resting encouragingly on the back of her child, leading him forward to the scroll. In the far background, a Byzantine church.

*Listen now, all Slav peoples, listen to the words coming from God, which feed
human souls, words that heal our hearts and minds.*

—CONSTANTINE OF PRESLAV, *Prologue to the Slavonic Scriptures*

THE SLAVS OF THE BALKANS, the first beneficiaries of the Cyrillic
alphabet, have produced proud, even insolent, descriptions of its
importance to them. In the Afterword to an anthology of medieval
and Renaissance Serbian poetry, I read that Cyrillic letters, unlike the
historically dead-ended Glagolitic, possess "Christian stylisation" in
their soft, curved, rounded "harmonic shapes," in which the pagan
Slavs, having proved insusceptible to Latin letters, were finally able
to express their baptized Christian spirit. In the late ninth century,
a Bulgarian monk writing anonymously as Khrabr ("brave") argued
that, while the pagan Greeks needed several stages to devise their
alphabet, "the Slavic letters are holier and more respectable" because
they were devised all at once "by a saint." By the end of the twelfth
century, a Serbian revision of Old Slavonic had emerged, and one of
its treasures is the Miroslav Gospel: "I, sinful Grigorije," its scribe
intones, "unworthy to be called Scribe, have set this gospel in gold…"

The Byzantines, perhaps ambivalent about their cultural acqui-
sition of these "new people," promptly set about to Hellenize those
close to imperial territory, such as the Bulgarians, even though, as
historian Dimitri Obolensky writes, all three men, Cyril, Methodius
and Clement, "spanned the two worlds" of the Slavs and Byzantines,
"working for the day when this Graeco-Slav culture would become
the common heritage of the peoples of Eastern Europe."

At lunch with a friend in Sofia I learn of the recent uproar in
Bulgarian intellectual and political circles provoked by an Austrian
Byzantinist, recipient of a Bulgarian state prize, who deplored the
fact that, as a consequence of accepting a Slavonic script instead of
sticking to Greek, the Slavs had forever placed themselves "outside
Europe." My friend, a Byzantinist at the Institute of History, shakes
his head. The Byzantines thought of their culture as a universal
expression of civilization—an improvement even on the Late Roman,
which was not Christian—and scorned as well as pitied the barbarians who lived outside it, including low-ranking Slavic nations. The

entrée to their culture was through Orthodox Christianity and its texts and rituals. Even St. Cyril, who was to devote so much prayer to the labour of alphabets and translations for the Slavs, argued in an Arabic court that "all the arts come from us," meaning the Byzantines.

When the first large-scale Slav invasions overran the Balkans in the late sixth century, the Byzantine Emperor Justinian was ruler of lands from beyond the upper Tigris River, across the western slopes of the Caucasus and the Crimea, along the Danube and Alps, to a foothold in Spain. Byzantium dominated North Africa, much of Egypt, Palestine, and Syria. (Meanwhile, remnants of Western Christian culture clung to the walls of damp Irish monasteries.) "In the ninth and tenth centuries, which were decisive for the Byzantinization of the Slavs," writes Byzantinist Ihor Ševčenko, "the empire's capital at Constantinople was, with the possible exception of Baghdad and Cairo, the most brilliant cultural centre of the world as not only the Slavs but also western Europe knew it." Churchmen were diplomats, scholars, and even politicians, the educated elite read and wrote commentaries on Plato and Euclid, emperors commissioned encyclopaedias, the public demanded ever newer and stylized Lives of the Saints. The church of Hagia Sophia was the largest building in the known world, and the ceremonial of its Liturgies, feasts, processions, and vigils, including the elaborate choreography of the court's participation, dazzled visitors. Mosaics, church organs, silk, cutlery, theological speculations: all arrived from Byzantium to the West; if they impressed Venetians, one can imagine the amazement of the Slavs. Who would not want to be a Byzantine?

Yet the Byzantines sponsored the development of literacy among the Slavs based not on their own Greek language but on that of the Slavs themselves, a Slavonic literary and ecclesiastical language that went hand-in-hand with their Christianizing mission. The Greeks did not assimilate the Serbs and Bulgarians and Rus, Ševčenko argues, they Byzantinized them, and at the summit of medieval Byzantine values stood the Liturgy.

So the Slavs got on with the primary task of learning to read the basic bibliography of early Christian texts—Gospels, Psalter, Epistles, Homilies, Classical histories, some natural science and geography—

a classic "learning curve," having to catch up with the works of Basil the Great (fourth century), John Chrysostom (fifth century), and Gregory the Theologian (sixth century), from whom they also gleaned some ancient physics and astronomy. Tsar Symeon of Bulgaria commissioned a veritable encyclopaedia of theoretical knowledge, which was quickly transmitted to Rus where it shows up as an illuminated manuscript from 1073 in the library of Sviatoslav of Kyiv.

Canadian historian of Eastern European history, John-Paul Himka, conceded (in an interview in December 2006) that, while it's true that Byzantium gave Rus an entire culture, with law, mathematics, a certain degree of sciences, but mainly religion, "yet there are problems with the way that the Slavs accepted and took over the Byzantine heritage. It's well captured in the words of a Polish Jesuit in 1577, Piotr Skarga, a leading Polish champion of the Counter-Reformation, when he was talking to the Rus in a book urging them to join the Catholic faith, to reunite the Churches. He said: 'The Greeks, O, Rus, have deceived you. They gave you their faith but not their language.'

"And his point was that Rus and the other Slavs only had access to that which had been translated into Slavonic. They were able very quickly to master this language because it was very close to the native languages they spoke and in that sense I think of it as a fire made of straw and kindling which blazes immediately but it had no real depth because they didn't know Greek, they didn't know Latin. They only knew that which had been translated, primarily in the ninth century, and then some translations for a few centuries thereafter. And then the translations from Greek just stopped."

Nevertheless, for all the limitations of translation, Old Slavonic did become medieval Europe's third international language after Greek and Latin, thanks to the influx of the Slav nations into Christianity.

In 1762 the Bulgarian monk Fr. Paisii of Hilendar Monastery on Mount Athos in Greece, without benefit of archives or documents, and plagued by prolonged headaches and stomach ulcers, nevertheless became Bulgaria's first historian of a national history when he wrote the slender account, *History of the Slav-Bulgarians, their kings and saints and all Bulgarian deeds and events*. (For this feat of national consciousness, the Bulgarian Orthodox Church gives Paisii his very own day of homage, on June 19.) Paisii urged his compatriots to bask in the reflected glory of their ancestors, "the most famous of all Slav peoples...the first to call themselves tsars, the first to have a patriarch, the first to become converted into the Christian faith." Bulgarians need not hang their heads in cultural shame before the Byzantines. "I have written for you to know and remember that our Bulgarian kings, patriarchs and prelates had their annals and codices....They had knowledge of everything and of the life-stories of many Bulgarian saints and of religious service." Pity that they had not bothered to write any of it down.

The truth is that the Slavonic lexicon was massively augmented by Greek borrowings not just for ecclesiastical usage but in everyday life as well. There are some 1,400 such borrowings in Bulgarian. The Slavs may not yet have been beneficiaries of the very latest erudition from the salons and scriptoria of Constantinople and Thessalonica, but they did get words for *onion*, *cabbage*, and *fried eggs*.

:: *Down in the archives*

ELISSAVETA MOUSAKOVA, who can read Glagolitic, is an art historian who is head of the Manuscript Department of the National Library of Sofia, fittingly named for Saints Cyril and Methodius. She works mainly with Bulgarian and Slavonic illuminated manuscripts. Arm in arm, we clatter down the marble steps to the library's Stygian depths for a cup of diabolical coffee, which we drink wreathed in Bulgarian cigarette smoke. I am here to ask her about old languages. ("Glagolitic is my favourite script," she has offered. "It's very round, it's very interesting.") The oldest manuscript in her collection comes from the eleventh century, discovered during restoration of a country church but so dirty as to be illegible. Then the National Library's restorers got to work.

"It's a very simple illumination, but legible—the very oldest Slavonic, that is Old Bulgarian, version we have of the Acts of the Apostles."

Curiously, the library's materials that relate to that first Bulgarian state are in Latin, and they concern Boris I's acceptance of Christianity on behalf of the Bulgars and then also the missions of Cyril and Methodius. But there are many interesting Slavonic manuscripts that feature inscriptions in their margins, "for example, notes about troops coming and destroying a village…"

Eta drifts off for a minute. "I was thinking about a Greek manuscript in the Vatican library. There is a very interesting Slavonic inscription in it, and it is one of the rarest juridical documents— a contract between a woman and a priest. The woman is evidently a very poor woman, for she sold her child to this priest for a piece of land, some corn, and a piece of fabric. That's what's been written on the pages of this Greek gospel. It is a very luxurious manuscript, with high-quality parchment and illumination, probably written in Constantinople. How it came into Slavonic hands, we don't know."

> Cyril dreamed that God said: "Cyril, go to the lands of the Slavs, called Bulgarians, for God has elected you to convert them to the faith and to give them a law."
>
> —THE THESSALONIAN LEGEND

The legend was first reported at the end of the twelfth century, and in it the city of Thessalonica is the place chosen by Providence for the Slav peoples' reception of the word of God. Whether the brothers thought of themselves as Greeks, or half-Greeks, or Byzantines, or Romans for that matter, it is undeniable that they were patriots and lovers of Thessalonica, their birthplace. At least we know that much about Methodius, who wrote a canon to St. Demetrius shortly before his death in 885. Remarkably, he wrote it in Slavic, or Old Slavonic, not in Greek, in accordance with the rules of Byzantine hymnography to be sure, as though there could be no offence in addressing the shining warrior of Thessalonica's battlements in Slavonic speech: "Come, let us praise Demetrius!"

> Come, let us praise Demetrius.
> [Demetrius,] preserve those who
> sing thy praises from thine own native home

now extolling thee,

we all celebrate thy most sacred memory.

— CANON TO ST. DEMETRIUS OF THESSALONICA

Harassed by clerical enemies, Methodius languished in a Moravian monastery until his death, and it is something of the melancholic Thessalonian far from home, deprived of the consolation of the Patron Saint and the radiance of his presence within his sanctuaries, and wearied by strangers, that I hear in Methodius's plaintive hymn: *Hearken, O glorious one, to us who are poor and belong to you, and pity us, for we are parted and far away from your radiant temple. And our hearts burn within us, and we desire, O holy one, to be in your church and, one day, to worship within it through your prayers...*

He died, in 885, without ever having returned home.

The original text, written in the ninth century, has not survived, but copies have, and they keep coming to light. In 1986, for example, the Slavicist Konstantinos Nichoritis worked on a copy up to then completely unknown. He figured the handwriting dated from the thirteenth century, but what struck him was the repetition of the refrain he had nowhere encountered in Greek: "Demetrius, preserve those who sing thy praises from thine own native home." It was an original text of Slavic literature, apparently part of an entire Liturgy dedicated to St. Demetrius, and one of the earliest, written in this version in what is now known as Middle Bulgarian. Nichoritis studied it in the National Library of Sofia.

I ask Elissaveta if I might look at the document, too. And so, as I sit expectantly in a reading room, it is delivered to me from the archives of medieval Bulgarian manuscripts, within a slim cardboard file folder, laid on the table like an unearthed artefact of a lost library. The only condition of my examination is that I not use a ballpoint pen to make my notes but the pencil provided me. And so I begin, writing down the file's name: *Minei Praznichen* [*The Festal Menaion*, a liturgical book of special hymns for the feast day of Orthodox saints].

But what am I looking at?

I gingerly open the cardboard sleeve enclosing the parchment pages that have been bound to the spine with delicate loops of string.

Was the string also thirteenth century? I have never in my sheltered Canadian life been so intimately in contact with something remotely so old—my fingertips are brushing the surface of the rigid lamb-skin, or is it goat?—that I think I should scarcely be breathing in its vicinity. Nor should I have been allowed to let it rest in the sunshine coming though the high, uncurtained windows of Reading Room Number One. But no one seems concerned that I am lifting these ancient pages with my naked fingers with only my shoulders to block out the sun.

The pages are badly stained, but where they are clear I find—thanks to the leftovers of my schooling forty years earlier in Church Slavonic, a single semester at the University of Washington—I can actually read what is written here. The letters are carefully penned in black ink with some red letters scattered about and between the lines. If St. Demetrius is inscribed here somewhere, I am not finding him. Is he under the creases? Vanished with the torn-away corners? I plod on, and here and there recognize the words for Jesus Christ, the verbs *khvalite* and *sluzhiti*, to praise and to serve, the adverb *mnogo*, many or much, the nouns *smrt* and *liubov*, death and love. I am uncommonly pleased with myself. Then suddenly I am reading the words for Wise Demetrius, the Miracle-worker, for Thessalonica, city gates, barbar-ians, for victory and glory, and I know I have found him.

> *The hoarding of books causes the spiritual starvation of an entire people. If you think and care about the salvation of your brothers, why do you not give them books that they too might copy and read the words of God? Do you realize what calamity we are facing through the unknowing and the unreading of books? Is it not evident that all evil emanates from the fact that we do not read books?*
>
> —PRESBYTER KOZMA, *tenth-century Bulgarian priest*

In the Cathedral Church of the Holy Trinity in Saskatoon, there hangs the iconic representation of the Baptism of Ukraine. Saint and Prince Volodymyr, high-cheeked and moustachioed, supervises the rite. His people throng waist-deep in the river while priests lean over from the riverbank, blessing the waters, and soldiers stand in disciplined ranks before them. Here then are all the social orders. From Volodymyr's hand spills a scroll: *God Almighty who created heaven and earth, look now upon these new people, and grant, Lord, that they acknowledge you the true God as the Christian nations have done.*

There's one in every Eastern-rite Ukrainian church I've been in, in vestibule, nave, or basement: a depiction of the Christian baptism of Rus in the waters of the Pochaino River, tributary to the mighty Dnipro, in 988. The entire population of Kyiv has been assembled on the river's shore and some are already knee deep in the stream while Prince Volodymyr, dressed as a Byzantine knight in long white tunic and bejewelled belts, sternly directs them into the water.

Then Volodymyr sent the children of the noble families to school, to learn to read Greek and Slavonic, fulfilling the prophecy of Isaiah: *In that day shall the deaf hear the words of a book, and the tongue of the dumb shall be clearly heard.* A century later, a prince of Rus spoke six languages, others founded schools, including the first for girls and one for translators, and another opened a public library in the cathedral of Kyiv.

"WHEN THE PEOPLE were baptized, they returned each to his own abode. Vladimir, rejoicing that he and his subjects knew God himself, looked up to heaven and said: 'O God, who hast created heaven and earth, look down, I beseech thee, on this thy new people, and grant them, O Lord, to know thee as the true God, even as the other Christian nations have known thee.'" The Bulgarian khan Boris had converted in 865, the Serbs a few years later, successfully having petitioned Emperor Basil I that "they be placed under the humane yoke" of Byzantine authority.

This momentous event is completely ignored by its agents, the Byzantines. "This extraordinary success in converting Rus to Christianity under Prince Volodymyr in the 10th century is not once mentioned in any Byzantine source," says Cambridge historian Simon Franklin, in an interview. "It is not reflected, hinted at, described, or praised." For the dignitaries in Constantinople, in their stately ambulation between imperial palace and Hagia Sophia, stiff in gold-threaded brocade, ceremonially genuflecting to Christ enthroned in golden tesserae above the imperial doorway, it didn't happen. "Not that they deny it, they just don't mention it." But to the Slavs baptism was viewed as some kind of miracle, for it inducted them into a community of faith that Greeks now shared with Slavs as sisters and brothers, reborn into full humanity.

:: *Of monks and monasteries*

BACHKOVO MONASTERY, dedicated to the Mother of God in 1083, was once a potent community, now enfeebled. During the month of my visit alone, three more monks had died with none incoming to replace them. So laments my host, Br. Simeon, as we speed along the road from Plovdiv, chauffeured by a poet commandeered for the day from Plovdiv's writers' society. The monastery, a huge complex, remains a popular weekend excursion destination, however, and as we arrive the grounds are already filled with families admiring the old buildings. They light candles and reverence the icons in the churches, and fill up bottles with water spouting from a mountain spring. I admire yolk-yellow persimmons that still hang on the leafless tree, and I watch a queue of visitors offer donations to a monk: they press crumpled bills into his outstretched hand, and he then "passes" them on in the form of prayers he whispers into the ear of a tethered ewe, who is contentedly munching her hay off to one side. Br. Simeon chuckles all day, remembering this scene. Every inch the monk in his black cassock belted around his heavy hips, his hair tucked under his soft black conical cap, he behaves with a minimum of devotional gestures inside the churches, unlike the pious who light fistfuls of beeswax tapers and fall to their knees before the miraculous icon of the Virgin, wiping it with their fingers. "They're told by the priests that the more expensive candles will get their prayers to Heaven faster. Magic. Bah!"

We are admitted into the sixteenth-century refectory, whose frescoes include a remarkable series of ancient Greek philosophers: Plato, Aristotle, Diogenes, Plotinus, and Socrates, right up there on the barrel-vaulted walls with the Prophets and Church Fathers. "Socrates was a pre-Christian Christian," says Br. Simeon, solemnly, adding that in the porch of the Nativity of Christ Church in the village of Arbanasi near Turnovo the iconographer has even given the philosophers haloes, as though, to the newly converted Slavs, these sages of the Ancient World were part of their spiritual history. As indeed they were to the first Christian communities among the Greeks as well. "Greek philosophy purifies the soul," wrote Clement of Alexandria (150–215 CE) "and prepares it to receive the faith on which truth constructs knowledge." Simeon points out the marble refectory table that was constructed of barely legible tombstones of the dead brothers who had lived and died here generations earlier: "So the dead and the living break bread together."

We drive on to another monastery, Saints Cosma and Damian, little visited except for the annual patron saints' day, high up in the mountains south of Plovdiv near the Kuklen village area: we leave the Plovdiv-Asenovgrad road to drive across a broad plain toward the mountains. The monastery is up there. A vast and decrepit metal works sprawls for a kilometre along the highway, still belching emissions out of its two stupendous stacks. I thought such a relict enterprise would have been abandoned in the transition-from-Communism, but, no, it is still smelting gold, zinc, and copper. The toxins pour in torrents out of the stacks and out onto the surrounding fields, including vineyards, and then I remember glimpsing a score of farmwomen, stout and thickly padded against the wind, digging potatoes as we rolled past. This enterprise is apparently in the ownership of shareholders in London who pay farmers to keep gathering crops although they assure Bulgarians the produce is not for sale: the soil is too contaminated. A make-work project, then? Root vegetables to absorb the soil's toxins? Wages for useless fields?

We leave paved road and drive along cobblestoned track, which peters out into dirt rutted and boggy from melted snow. Fine for a donkey or one of those Roma wagons with high axles. We creep up and pass a flatbed coming down, loaded with logs. "Forest mafia," says Simeon. The hills are still government land, elsewhere confiscated from the churches, but "someone" is reaping a mighty profit from logging them. (Haven't these governments heard of stumpage fees? I guess the point is there's no control.)

Finally, we are at the monastery, an imposing white-plastered and timbered complex with second-story galleries, an orchard, a pile of sawn logs, a cypress planted in 1936, several fountains spewing healing water, a new church built under the inspiration of a now-vanished Mother Superior, a twelfth-century church named for Saints Cosma and Damian, the healers, a pride of cats, and two residents, Fr. Ivan, a priest whose wife and children live in Kuklen, and Br. Ioan, formerly a carpenter, "like Jesus of Nazareth," who worked for the railway, now a monk these last two weeks. They have emerged onto their porch to welcome us.

Fr. Ivan is about seventy years old, white-haired under his cap, with a pink, lined face of expressive sweetness. He single-handedly restored this monastery, with donations from "businessmen" in the region. Br. Ioan, who does not mention family, is short and square, perhaps sixty, with a knobby nose and a broad mouth often pulled even wider in a generous smile.

The monastery is famous "ever since the reign of Tsar Ivan Alexander mainly for the literary school there, its cultural influence and the waters of the holy spring, curative for mental disorders." The brochure explains that the monastery was "devastated" by Christians turned Muslim but was reconstructed with subsidies "of the patriotic people from the Plovdiv region" and became a cultural centre—a school for "grammarians, calligraphers and transcribers." We are invited to visit the church. Of note are frescoes in the narthex applied by Greek priests overtop the Bulgarian ones, according to Br. Simeon, but the brochure assures me that the "harmony of the soft muted colouring, the classic purity of the image [of Archangel Michael] and the refinement of its graceful construction bring it close to the best paragons of Bulgarian art of painting from the Middle Ages." Here also, set into the thick wall of the narthex, is the iron chain-and-collar used on the poor deranged who came up to the monastery to be healed.

We are welcomed into their kitchen. Fr. Ivan renovated it—it is cleanly painted, with not a single icon or crucifix or any other bric-a-brac on the walls. Only a string of dried red peppers hangs by a deeply recessed window. There is an electric oven the size of a microwave, a small stack of dishes in the sink, an iron-cast, potbellied stove burning olive tree branches on which sits a red kettle boiling the water for our tea. The tea is dried herbs and flowers gathered from the neighbouring meadow by Br. Ioan. He pours it into plastic cups. It is a fragrant, surprisingly pungent, yellow liqueur. I am happy that I can offer my bag of smoked almonds. They are poured onto a plate and placed in the middle of the little table. There is a kitten underfoot. It is a scene of poignant domesticity, two aging men living intimately in their perch on the Rhodope Mountains, no sounds other than Nature's own, no company except for the procession of the icon of Saints Cosmas and Damian on their Feast Day when villagers come to the church. Otherwise they are left alone by the world. Well, not quite: they have a 4-wheel-drive Russian Jeep (Italian engine) donated by Orthodox faithful in Russia. On our way down from the monastery we will be passed by Fr. Ivan bouncing along while we creep and slither on the frost-slicked mud.

On our way out, Br. Simeon draws my attention to a particular tombstone, upright against the church wall. It is a Muslim grave, the resting place of Mehmet Kehaya, an early-nineteenth-century Ottoman administrator in these parts and the richest sheepholder in the district. He had successfully petitioned the sultan in far-off Istanbul for a charter, or *firman,* to protect this Orthodox church from conversion into a mosque, and so, one day when the Janissaries (special Ottoman troops) inevitably came to rout the Christian monks, Mehmet was able to brandish the charter and turn the soldiers away. For his courage and solidarity with them, the Orthodox honour him with this burial place alongside their church. And to this day, the village of Kuklen—according to Simeon, who is visibly moved by the telling—still celebrates all the holy days of its residents: Orthodox, Catholic, and Muslim. "Compare this with how Christians have treated mosques, for example in Bosnia," he says, with a savage mournfulness. The rest of the Balkan world seems to have come unglued from this belief in the essential holiness of other people. "During all the Ottoman centuries, the Orthodox monopoly of candle-production—the main source of income—was protected. Not even the Bulgarian Communist Party dared end it. But this *post*-Communist order...." The government has yet to restore Church lands and properties. The Protestant sects are meanwhile freely proselytizing.

This is how Simeon wants to live: in peace with all the people on Bulgarian lands touched by God. Instead, he is caught up in the world of the Bulgarian Orthodox Church, which is making him angry and bitter only a year into his monastic vocation. He explains that an ecumenical initiative inside Bulgaria has ground to a halt because the Orthodox Church refuses to cooperate; it doesn't want to loosen its grip on privilege or have its corruption exposed. Important meetings of the Synod dwindle out into one-day "meetings" that are taken up entirely by a Liturgy and a banquet. Simeon speaks, looking at me sideways, from one eye, in the Sportna Sreshta Bar of Old Plovdiv, drinking rakia, smoking feverishly, a hulking, tense, male mass in his camel hair coat, the cassock discarded. I tease him about monastic abstinence, to which he responds that "it doesn't matter what goes in your mouth, but what comes out, and anyway I don't eat meat," and he pours out more wine for both of us, while I think of Jovinian, a fourth-century monk from Rome, who gave up ascetic practices as spiritually meaningless. Eat, drink, and be merry with your family and friends, by all means, he preached, but do remember to offer God a prayer of thanks for these gifts. He was declared a heretic and sentenced to the lash.

Simeon's cell in the monastery has been entered and his furnishings rearranged in his absence. "They were probably hoping to find money secretly stashed in my mattress....I have no 'brothers' there." Nor does he find much consolation among the rest of us, whom he calls the neo-pagans of postmodern Orthodoxy, "Christmas Christians" who only "perform" belief with no content, people who don't even pay attention to the words of the Lord's Prayer. Or humanists, who believe that the human is already godly, whereas "the Christian opens a space inside himself for God." I'm a humanist; does he mean me? I surprise myself with the thought that I do not want to be a disappointment to this monk.

Simeon and I stroll along Plovdiv's pedestrian street, passing several groups of young Muslim women in head scarves who are returning from Koranic lessons at the mosque, with its minaret brilliantly lit. It was originally a church and then, ever after, a mosque. Simeon has no problem with this. But he is disgusted by the church-turned-mosque-turned-discotheque. As a student on summer archaeological digs in Plovdiv, excavating Christian-era streets, he had been heartbroken to find Roman-era statuary—"the head of a beautiful young girl!"—used for paving stones. Plovdiv was Trimontium to the Romans. The Roman theatre is still in use. Christianity has been here almost as long—two thousand years—and there are Greek inscriptions on tombstones in the old cemeteries. A St. Demetrius church was given over to White Russian émigrés after the Bolshevik Revolution; they eventually dispersed and now the church has no parish, and is locked up. "St. Demetrius takes care of all of us anyway, who pray to him," Simeon says cheerfully, swinging his arms, adding that Plovdiv, as Philippopolis, had also been the site of a breakaway council of bishops in 343 and thereafter a place of exile for Manichean heretics of the Byzantine era, who survived long enough, away from the spies and diplomats of the court in Constantinople, to convert to Islam, in some cases, and to "Jesuit Catholicism" in others— a perilous enterprise, for the Catholic spokesman of the Plovdiv converts, when he arrived in Constantinople to argue formally before the bishops, was torn apart by an Orthodox mob.

Constantine the Great himself commissioned the building of the church in which the council of 343 took place, the largest basilica in the Balkans. But only its southern portion can be excavated, for the Catholic church now sits on top of its northern walls, and "gorgeous mosaics" lie undisturbed beneath the rubble and sand of the site— until such time, of course, when the bulldozers move in and convert the "useless" scrubland to a business centre, an initiative of the city council. Twenty years ago Simeon worked on this dig, too, and there it rests, a few marble blocks, stumps of column, a trench around a portion of exposed brick wall. Yet the Basilica had been such an important structure that the city altered the lay-out of the old Roman streets in order to link the Basilica with the Bishop's residence, itself reputedly used for the very first *agape* meals of the fledgling Christian community in the third century. The first converts were undoubtedly Jews, baptized by one of the seventy priests consecrated after Pentecost and sent out from Jerusalem, and they would have been more receptive than the Greeks and Romans here; "Jews already had scripture, psalms, prophets."

This is Br. Simeon's first learning, I muse, the underground church of the late Roman world at its Balkan extremities, whose communicants took care of each other because the rest of the world was murderous and succour uncertain. And he tells me of a dear friend of his, an elderly priest in a village church, instructed by his Bishop to support himself by selling candles. "At Christmas Eve service there were three people present, himself, the cleaning lady, and Jesus Christ." The old man is dead now, worn down by poverty. Br. Simeon raises bits of money for the Roma children in the local orphanage— for new clothes for the first day of school; it's important—whose photographs he stops to show me, pulling them out of his notebook. As I comment on the attractiveness of the children, a tiny and wizened old woman makes a beeline for Br. Simeon across the square; she is collecting donations for the Bulgarian Red Cross—she holds up her ID—and Simeon gives her a few coins, and they chat. She says: "When I was a young woman, I had a beautiful voice, and I sang in a choir that went to the homes of the rich people to ask them for money for the poor people. Now I'm a poor old woman myself, and I'm still asking rich people for money."

I leave Br. Simeon with a heavy heart, thinking of all his troubles. But he's put his trust in God. "He has helped in unbelievably bad times before. And He will again." We kiss three times on the cheek, exchange e-mail addresses. "It's no accident that you are following St. Demetrius," he adds. "This is a message that you are supposed to bring to the Orthodox: we are not separate nations in the Church, we are Orthodox together. It is more important to me that you are Orthodox than that you are Slav and can read Cyrillic."

This comes out in a passionate outburst at the door of an Internet café, and then he vanishes within, leaving me to consider the possibility, so new to me but part of Br. Simeon's old soul, that my "country" is a church.

I return to the Sportna Bar the next afternoon for a solitary meal. An entertainer sings along with his keyboard. I warm up with rakia and French fries sprinkled with cheese. Couples drift in and sit holding hands, three elderly male friends all in a row tip out glasses from glass carafes, three young, laughing women and their grey-haired, pony-tailed companion sip coffees and brandy and pore over a copy of *National Geographic* together. Perhaps they are planning an escape.

I look up at the wooden ceiling, and along the walls at the boxing memorabilia (a local hero?) and dark oil paintings of Paris. This restaurant is an extension of the guesthouse where I am accommodated. A house built by a rich Greek, Panchidis, it then became the residence of the Slaveikov family, who ran a school and whose son, Petko, became a celebrated writer, in spite of the fact that as a child he crippled himself with a fall into the Maritsa River. Br. Simeon was pretty pleased with himself for having scored me this accommodation—I am the only resident—but the truth is that I hover in this restaurant in order not to have to return to my room, alone in the dark, creaky hallway, to an unheated room and a bath with no hot water. I try to be cheered by the fact that the building has been proclaimed a monument of culture: "The guests have the unique possibility to feel the atmosphere of the Bulgarian National Revival architecture in combination with the cosiness and conveniences of the present day," the pamphlet wheezes. It is a handsome, rearing house from the outside, with ranks of tall and narrow windows, but in the cold and the dark it is creepy.

Now two kids have come in, in blue jean jackets and woollen caps, she with a great tumble of curls spilling out. They greet the waitresses and join them at their table. Things are heating up. The crooner is singing "Michelle," which I interrupt with a request for Macedonian songs. My wish is his command; but, whatever it is he's playing, he's singing it like a waltz. Do Macedonians waltz?

I return my attention to the photocopied essay that I've been dragging about in my knapsack, "The Byzantine Holy Man in the Twelfth

Century," by Paul Magdalino. He refers to a letter-writer, Tzetzes, who is admonishing his runaway slave, Demetrios Gobinos, who seems to have started up a new life as a sausage-maker, of all things, in Philippopolis/Plovdiv. He can't understand why Demetrios doesn't return to Constantinople where, by the simple expedient of donning a monastic habit, "every disgusting and thrice-accursed wretch like you has only to...hang bells from his penis or wrap fetters or chains round his feet, or a rope or chain around his neck...immediately the city of Constantinople showers him with honours, and the rogue is publicly feted as a saint above the apostles..."

It had been a dark grey day today with a nasty little wind that blew up the hill into the old city. There were very few of us in the streets even in the afternoon, but I was determined to trek along them all, looking for historical plaques. Just outside the walls of St. Nedelia Church I found one that explained that the bodies of local citizens including children are buried within the churchyard, in a padlocked, whitewashed, and windowless ossuary, having been slaughtered by Turks in 1832.

What a bloodied ground. A thousand years earlier, Prince Sviatoslav of Rus, who had routed Bulgarian armies and captured fortresses, swooped down with his army of 60,000 on Plovdiv and impaled 20,000 of its residents. He rounded off his Balkan campaign by chopping off the heads of three hundred notables of Silistra on the Danube. Sviatoslav got his comeuppance, however, at the hands of the Pechenegs, killed by their prince, Kuria, who sawed off his head and made of his skull a cup, overlaid with gold.

"Now a special song for the nice lady." I look up and grin back at the singer. "Are you lonesome tonight?"

A stone's throw from the Roman theatre I viewed the sculpture of a music professor holding his violin on his knee with a suggestion of defiance: this is in memory of the students of the Music and Fine Arts Faculty, purged by the Communists. On the side of a crumbling house where no one gives a damn anymore: "Here lived the first Communist activist of the Georgian language."

Another plaque in a large square, fixed to a stone wall: "Here were killed the 37 martyrs of Trimontium in 304." I studied this plaque for some time and took photographs, for 304 was the year of the martyrdom of St. Demetrius, in that rich and important Greek city, Thessalonica, on the far side of the Rhodope Mountains on the Aegean Sea, far from the notice of these ones dying in the Roman province of Moesia. They were unknown to each other, yet they had been scooped up together in a narrative that would eventually triumph over the pagan magistrates who had sent them to their deaths. They didn't know that, but I do.

181

⋮ *The Byzantine Saint*

:: *Skopje, Macedonia*

IN SKOPJE, my friend, Ljubica, and I walk through the soft, muffling
fog along the Vardar River to our meeting with Academician Dr.
Cveta Grozdanov, art historian, in his office at Cyril and Methodius
University. Ljubica has cautioned me that the professor finds my
profession, that of "fulltime writer," too exotic for his tastes. Also,
he is a very busy man. But he turns out to be all charm. He wants to
order coffee for us, and when we request cappuccino, he chortles, and
calls us *cappuccinisti*.

Of what importance, I want to know, is the veneration of St.
Demetrius among the Macedonians?

"There is no church in Macedonia without its image of St.
Demetrius. His icon is present in every home as a family icon along
with that of Matka Bozha [Mother of God], though smaller. He brings
health. The Slavic faithful made the pilgrimage to the tomb of St.
Demetrius in Thessalonica to collect his *myron* [oil exuded from
relics]—for healing—in small lead or silver bottles inscribed with his
image. Such objects have been excavated on the island in Lake Prispa
along with Greek and Albanian artefacts."

The telephone rings but he ignores it. "In the list of martyrs,
Demetrius takes second place to St. George but, because Thessalonica

is so close to us"—no border ran between Greeks and Slavs in
Byzantium— "it is not unusual that in Macedonia St. Demetrius has
pride of place. In any church where the frescoes have been preserved
St. Demetrius is always there."

And he is there in various aspects, Grozdanov explains: in a
patrician's cloak of Imperial Rome, carrying a cross as a sign of
his martyrdom; then, while Byzantium was waging war with the
Persians, he is represented as a military saint in military attire; and
in the fourteenth century he began to be presented as a contemporary nobleman, *vasileus,* in the Heavenly Court in charge of the
Earthly court. Jesus is the emperor, and is accompanied by St. George
as a kind of *despot,* then by St. Demetrius as a grand duke, then by
St. Theodore and St. Procopius, warrior-saints already in Paradise
because, as soldiers, they have spilled their blood for Christ.

He advises me to visit St. Mark's Monastery at once, just outside
of town.

In the good old days, the monastery had considerable wealth in
estates and cattle, subsidizing the accumulation of icons, manuscripts,
books, and relics. Much has been stolen since, and much has ended
up in libraries, public and private, in Serbia, Bulgaria, Austria, and
Russia. Nevertheless, in Professor Grozdanov's opinion, it remains
"one of the very best Balkan churches" with its fourteenth-century
fresco series of the Passion of Demetrius.

And so on a warm and sunny Sunday afternoon I wander around
Markov Manastir with Ljubica, damp leaves of apple trees rotting
underfoot from the gnarled orchard gone wild, rotting apples
squishing against my boot. I walk around the monastery church.
"Hamzi Pasha added the porch in the 1830s," a small plaque informs
us, but in fact the monastery retained its original medieval structure and form through all the Ottoman centuries. The brick and stone
facades are richly ornamented with zigzag lines, chessboard patterns,
rays, and crosses. On a marble inscription above the southern
entrance personalities of the medieval court come alive: "This divine
temple of the holy Christ's Martyr, the victorious and miracle-worker
Demetrius, has been renovated by the cordiality and the favour of
the faithful king Volkashin and the faithful queen Elena and their

very much beloved daughters and sons, the faithful king Marko and Andreash, Ivanish and Dimitar, in the year 1377 and this monastery was begun to be built in 1345 during the days of faithful tsar Stephan and the Christ-loving king Volkashin and was completed during the days of King Marko."

The iconographic program inside, with "tremendously important" and "highly unique" features, is closed to us. I have recourse only to an old guidebook to Yugoslav cultural treasures: "The common features of the paintings are a tendency to lively movement, vigorous expression and deformed physiognomies," it asserts, tantalizingly, "but it's too dark inside to see anything."

But in a fresco over the church door in bright, almost harsh sunlight, St. Demetrius, seated on a pretty white horse with a startlingly blue eye, announces this is *his* church. Battle mace upheld in his right hand, a gold circlet around his brow, his armour and weapons borne by a sextet of red-robed angels diving down from Heaven: Demetrius at least stands in the light.

VOICE OF THE SAINT from the frescoes:

They shut me in a monastery in a church
I was shut in isolation
that neither rain should wash me nor wine nor the fruit of the bounteous sun
under these hills
They bound me to the wall to the back of the lime
with the colours of the hill with the odour of chestnuts
They bound me young and made me a saint
and I loved the vines and eyes of the village girls
at the grape harvest at the fair at the Slava
And now you have come in excitement in surprise
charmed that I am hanging here surrounded by envious old men
And I would like to descend from these walls
following the nightingale that pecks under the arcade
the lapping of the waters the tendrils of the vines
because desire still gnaws at me and time eats me

—MATEJA MATEVSKI, *"Sveti Trifun"*

LJUBICA'S DAUGHTER, SLAVICA, and I climb steadily out of the gloopy murk of fog squashing Skopje this morning and reach the delicious little eleventh-century church of St. Panteleimon in the now-Albanian village of Nerezi. Since my last visit in the bone-rattling rainstorm of a winter evening in 1997, this little compound, formerly a monastery, has become a popular tourist destination, with its vast, glass-enclosed patio piled up with tables and chairs commanding the best view. Slavica hates the glassed-in idea: flies, drawn from the manure heaps in the village's barnyards, splat themselves messily in front of diners. But it is clear and crisp and brilliant with sunshine up here, the flies are long dead, and Slavica, who is a professional artist, shows off the church's celebrated fresco of the Lamentation of the Mother of God.·I am pleased to find a pretty good fresco of St. Demetrius as a warrior-saint. "He guards the church," explains Goce, the church guide, who then swiftly abandons us for the company of visitors who draw him into the cozy taverna, originally a lodging house for pilgrims, which is where we see him, holding forth over glasses of rakia, when we, too, come in for coffee.

I've known Slavica since she was an art student. I know that she was hoping to do graduate studies in the U.S., but neither she nor her parents can afford to support her there. Now she's hoping to make her living as an artist, or at least as a freelance, and will not be easily persuaded the idea is lunatic. For the moment she is my guide.

In 1164 in this village nestled on the slopes of Vodno Mountain a monastery church was built with funds from prince Alexius of Constantinople, grandson of Emperor Alexius Comnenus and nephew to the celebrated biographer Anna Comnena, and dedicated to the Holy and Praised Martyr Panteleimon ("all-merciful") of Nicomedia. Panteleimon's father was an idolater but his mother was a Christian, and so he, too, was duly baptized into the faith. His *Life* tells us that, though he practised the profession of physician, healing every manner of illness, his skill was really more a gift of the grace of God than of the medicines he carried about in the open-lidded carved box with which he is always represented. That is how I instantly recognize him, in his own exquisite marble niche in the nave, his slender body draped in white, his right hand pointing gracefully to the box he holds, just below his heart, in his left hand; and by the leonine mop of curly hair swirling about his youthful head, which he lost to the executioner in 305. He is the sweetest Saint.

No sooner had the masons completed their work than the *zographs* began theirs, the fresco-painting that has brought such renown and veneration (and local patriotism) to its five-domed Byzantine loveliness. Figures in fresco—pigment applied to wet lime-plaster— demand spontaneity of gesture from the painter, quickly, before the plaster sets. Perhaps this explains their liveliness. Aneta Serafimova, art historian in Skopje, has called it "the most significant Slavic-Byzantine shrine of the century," and she finds, in the profound drama of its most-celebrated wall-paintings of "The Deposition from the Cross" and "The Lamentation of Christ," that "delving into Antiquity," which informed the spirit of the Comnenian age of Byzantium, the dynasty of the Comneni rulers, 1081–1185, as extolled by a princess herself:

> I, Anna [Comnena], daughter of the Emperor Alexius and the Empress Irene, born and bred in the Purple, not without some acquaintance with litera- ture—having devoted the most earnest study to the Greek language, in fact, and being not unpractised in Rhetoric and having read thoroughly the treatises of Aristotle and the dialogues of Plato, and having fortified my mind with the Quadrivium of sciences [geometry, arithmetic, astronomy and music]...

And so, continues Serafimova, the artist-monks, unknown to us now, in the same spirit gestured grandiloquently across the stone surfaces in a glorification of "humankind." The usually lugubrious expressions of Mary and the saints are here emboldened by the drama of their grief, the mother collapsed alongside her son's insen- sible body, one arm cradling his head and the other clasped around his waist, in a mournful echo of the embrace of the Theotokos who once held God as an infant on her lap, her regal face now almost desperate, knotted by disbelieving sorrow. Even the angels are weeping. The historians say that here is a wholly new interest in the expression of individuals' feelings, an approach that will eventually dominate in the art of Renaissance Italy. I remembered that array of art books of icons spread out on the library table of St. Peter's Monastery library in Saskatchewan, and their display of saints across the ages and peoples: by contrast with the saintly face, in radiant repose, the saintly body seemed inert or even absent altogether. When represented as a warrior-saint, Demetrius, for example, is an often awkward assemblage of torso and disproportionate limbs; when represented in flowing martyr's robes, his body disappears into all the drapery, with the toes of his shoes sticking out. And what is the matter with post-Byzantine painting? The iconographer of a large seventeenth-century panel of St. Demetrius in the icon collection of Thessalonica's Museum of Byzantine Culture had painted the Saint's left foot backwards through the stirrup as though the bottom half of his body had been assembled separately from the top half.

Now I am to understand that this is his "Heavenly" body. "It must not be a real body," said Ana Serafimova, whose handsome little book, *Medieval Painting in Macedonia*, I've tucked into my purse for easy reference. We were chatting in her home, a small apartment decorated simply with tasteful *objets* scattered on shelves; she looked like a bit of a Byzantine fresco herself, with thick kohl around her dark-browed eyes and a bright pink streak across the lids, a long thin nose and plump red mouth. "That's what makes iconography Byzantine and not Renaissance. The body is destroyed at death. *Psyche* is important, the resurrection of the soul." Of course from the Western point of view these "Heavenly bodies" look simply deformed and rigid, but Westerners miss the point entirely. "Beauty resides in our thoughts and meditations, not in the flesh."

The painters, of Ohrid for example, came probably from Constantinople and Thessalonica, and worked with local masters in the period (ninth century) of Saints Clement and Naum, the educators of the Slavs. The Church of St. Clement, restored in the 1960s to something like its original brilliance from under six centuries of dirt, triumphantly displays the Balkan genius for representing suffering humanity even in the Prophets and Saints, who swirl around the church's interior like a choir of mourners writhing in deepest grief. Only Christ and the Mother of God are serene. "So it wasn't important where you came from as a painter; but whether you knew how to paint Christologically." Some painters even came from the monasteries of the Adriatic coast, heavily influenced by Western styles. And they kept on coming, even after the establishment of Ottoman rule on Byzantine territory in 1395, when, according to Serafimova, the preservation of Christian spirituality was a priority of greater import than ethnic or political issues, especially when you consider that St. Sophia in Ohrid, that "largest surviving unit of painting in Europe," had become a mosque. There was no question of loyalty to a state, only to a church, and to its aesthetic traditions and spiritual archives.

The Turks were everywhere victorious over the Christian powers of southeastern Europe, the Bulgarian capital falling in 1393, the Serbian principalities in 1371 and 1395. Thessalonica, the prize that stood between the Ottomans and Constantinople, fell in 1387. The great frequency of the Passion Cycle in the art of this era can be seen as a direct reflection of the political reality, Serafimova suggested. "They insist on painting scenes of the agony of Christ, and of the suicide of Judas, which had not been depicted in the Byzantine period. Also very important is the emphasis on the days of the church calendar marking the martyrdom of all the saints, focussing, not on their whole life but on their cruel end."

I see her point when, the next day, just a few streets away, in the office of her colleague, Victoria Korobar, at the Museum of Macedonia, I peer through a magnifying glass at a black and white photograph of a seventeenth-century icon of the Life and Passion of St. Demetrius, which remains in the museum crypt unpublished, uncatalogued, and never displayed.

Twenty years ago Victoria was herself interested in the cult of St. Demetrius—but when I ask her what led to her interest she waves aside the question, saying she is "embarrassed"—and opens an old paper file of her long-ago research to show me its contents: some photocopies, some handwritten bibliographical references, a page or two of Macedonian translation, and most particularly this photograph. I squint at the little scenes, several of them destroyed, which narrate the story. Demetrius's birth (Victoria points out the cradle, the diapers), his education (there is a seated teacher figure), baptism,

Galerius on a throne in Thessalonica, probably Nestor on a horse in the arena, a wrestling match (the struggle with Lyaeus), Demetrius's execution, and the miracles on the ramparts of Thessalonica.

When we were arranging to meet, Victoria told me that her office was located "by the mosque," but as I zigzagged in the direction of the only mosque I was familiar with, I discovered to my dismay, through fruitless plodding up and down and around, that I was surrounded by mosques and minarets. This is in part a Muslim city.

Victoria's Demetrius icon belongs to the post-Byzantine era of the Ottoman Empire, of Orthodoxy orphaned within a Muslim world and obsessed with its subordination. It was this tortured body of the man who was still among the living that rested at the centre of popular veneration, not the Resurrected luminosity of the Martyr beyond all earthly care. Where earlier the believer appealed to the presence of the *Heavenly* authority contained in the portrait, or image, now it was the Saint's life-cycle mired in history that seemed powerful to the supplicant.

:: *Ohrid, Macedonia*

Give me wings and I will don them;
I will fly to our own shores,
Go once more to our own places;
Go to Ohrid and to Struga.
There the sunrise warms the soul

— KONSTANTINE MILADINOV, *"Longing for the South"*

I TAKE A 9 AM BUS from Skopje, with the city in such a dense fog I cannot make out the lights of the bus station, only the wan yellow street lamps as I pass under them, and bundled figures hurrying by, momentarily visible before they vanish into the enveloping murk. The murk does not lift until suddenly, as we career through the beautiful hills on our way down to Ohrid—monumental treasury of the Byzantine—the sky opens up to a cheerful sun.

Sonja, a friend of a friend, and I sit outside at a café and admire the splendid vista of the lake trimmed by purple hills and red-tiled villages. Then, to change our point of view, we trudge uphill toward the wreckage of the walls of poor stricken Samuil, tsar of the First Bulgarian Kingdom (997–1014 CE), who had dreamed of riding in triumph through the golden gates of Thessalonica. The Byzantines had once trembled at the thought of him, "invincible in power and unsurpassed in strength." Instead, according to legend, just before he died heartbroken, Samuil, commander of a defeated army blinded by the Byzantines, gathered up the mutilated eyes of his soldiers and buried them in a gold casket in Lake Ohrid: we see the water shimmering below us, tossing gilded waves. We stop at the chapel-sized Church of St. Demetrius. An unremarkable icon fastened to the outside wall shows the warrior-saint on a white horse straddling the supplicating figure of Kaloyan, that other Slav who would be denied Thessalonica. Already the shadows are long on the grass as we move back out through the walls and to a dimming view of the rooftops and churches of the city, all the light now gathering over the placid lake, a warm gold puddle from which a huge flock of ducks suddenly rises in silent unbroken flight out to sea.

In a souvenir shop, I buy a small wooden icon of St. Clement from the stacks of hosts of saints on view. With one hand he blesses us, with the other he supports a jewelled Gospel. And then I buy a little palm-sized icon of St. Naum; they go together, Clement and Naum. While the one laboured in Macedonian territory, the other founded schools of Old Slavonic literature elsewhere in Bulgaria, in Pliska and near Preslav, under the patronage of Bulgarian Tsars Boris and Symeon. "And no one had seen him idle either," wrote his biographer, Theophylactus, in the twelfth century. "He was teaching the children, showing the letters to some, explaining the written text to others, and instructing them how to write by holding their hands."

Though he did not spill his blood, Clement of Ohrid is in Paradise among the saints. A Thessalonian of Slavic descent, he was sent by his Bishop in 866 to Ohrid on the so-called Macedonian Sea to baptize pagans, celebrate the Liturgy with them in the Slavonic tongue, and discern among them those with a priestly calling. "The rain of divine understanding came down upon my people," he rejoiced. But two hundred years later, Bishop Theophylactus, sent out from the scintillating imperial city, Constantinople, to serve in the See of Ohrid, went joylessly about his task; he compared his charges to swine possessed of demons and himself to an eagle, forced to live with frogs in the mud. Clearly, in his mind, their Christian baptism had not lifted them from the Slavonic muck. "By saying that you have thoroughly become a barbarian among the Bulgarians," he wrote to a Greek friend similarly posted to the Bulgarian lands, "you, dearest, say what I dream (in my sleep). Because, think of it, how much I have drunk from the cup of vulgarity, being so far away from the countries of wisdom and how much I have drunk from the lack of culture." To console himself while the incessant winds from the south blew around his house, he composed iambic verses.

Clement laboured in Ohrid for thirty years, and it is impossible not to be witness, even now a millennium later, to the beauty of his undertaking when you visit Ohrid and walk from one Byzantine church to another, each a harmonious enclosure of Orthodox cosmology, as though retracing the comings and goings of a generation of black-robed celibates who hurried to the scriptorium there to bend over their parchment scrolls with exactly the same stoop of reverence as they had at prayer.

As we say goodbye at the bus station in Ohrid, Sonja gives me a card of St. Demetrius, with the Tropar of October 26 printed on the reverse. *Saint Demetrius, invoke Christ God for us, that He may grant us His great mercy.* Now I have three saints on my night table. To me Demetrius is the saddest Saint, slump-shouldered and barely holding his Martyr's spear upright in his child-like hand, dark bags under his eyes that are looking off to the side, as though he has caught sight of his approaching executioners and there is no more fight in him. We know Clement by his high, swollen brow, his long white beard that comes to a sharp point halfway down his breast, and by his episcopal robes. Naum has a full head of brown hair and the same long and pointy beard, but he wears the coarse garment of a monk. They look slightly away from me, as though averting their eyes, caught by something wonderful outside the frame that arrests them still. They neither frown nor smile, they are simply sobre and steady, having been translated direct from their monasteries to weightless Paradise, as their iconographer knew, and we guess.

:: *Monks of Macedonia in their monastery on the hill*

A WALK IN THE PRE-DAWN DARK to the Skopje bus station takes me over the stone bridge where the peddlers have assembled to sell wind-up toys, men's socks, and lottery tickets. They have set up their little tables (their diminutive cups of coffee, their paper cones of roasted chickpeas) under the phantom corpses of the men of Karposh's Rebellion who raised a revolt against the Ottomans in 1689, were defeated, captured, and then impaled on stakes mounted on this same bridge. They took days to die.

Arambasha Karposh had raised a revolt, captured a Turkish stronghold and held it briefly, then succumbed to the ferocious assault of detachments of Ottomans and Crimean Tatar mercenaries under the command of Khan Selim Giray. Giray had Karposh brought to Skopje and to the stone bridge. After a long agony impaled on a Tatar lance, his body was hurled into the Vardar below.

Near the bazaar, in a wee, dark shop, I buy packets of roasted almonds and pistachios carefully measured out on brass pans by two wordless Albanian men, I guess father and son, gesturing with great delicacy as they tip the pans into small paper bags and slowly fold and crease them shut.

It is raining fitfully, the city is once again sentenced to terminal dreariness as the slick mud overtakes all the surfaces, the world seems clogged and soggy and full of rubbish, and it does not improve until we're well southwest and climbing into mountains and everything sits quietly and cleanly under a sprinkle of snow.

I climb off the bus at the foot of the monastery of Sveti Jovan Bigorski (dedicated to St. John the Baptist). A young monkish-looking man strides toward me under an umbrella. From Skopje I had telephoned the abbot and explained my interest in Orthodox monasteries. "Ukraina?" the monk asks, and I have to let him know I am just a Ukrainian-Canadian, which he seems to accept as he swings my knapsack over his shoulder, and we climb together to the monastery along the flank of Mount Bistra. I follow him to a large, square room, whitewashed and trimmed in brown, made comfortable by swaths of Turkish carpets, large sofas and chairs, big potted plants, icons, jugs, and what look like Turkish *objets d'art* arranged on all the tables and shelves, articles whose use is no longer obvious. The windows in the belvedere look out onto the shingled roof of the building opposite, and everything is glistening with rain. The monk withdraws.

The monk returns, bearing a little plate of cubes of Turkish delight dusty with sugar and a glass of cold water, and I've barely tucked into these when I am summoned to "dinner." It is ten o'clock in the morning, the monks have been up since four o'clock, they must be starving. I join a dozen people in a small, warm kitchen and my chair is indicated. All the women sit at one end of the table—a cook, a solemn young woman in cheerless clothing (I guess she is on a retreat), and a very thin, anxious-looking mother with two young boys, perhaps relatives of a monk, who are the only ones at table to break the deep silence into which we subside to eat our cabbage pie. We eat with our fingers, there is not even the sound of clinking cutlery. At each squeak and squall of the children, all male heads swivel and stare, not unkindly but in a fixed, unblinking gaze, as though uncomprehending the source of such sounds. So that is our meal: cabbage pie, ketchup, olives, water.

I am invited to make a tour of the place, which has truly been reborn from the demise of Yugoslav Communism, "by the grace of God," as Br. Bartolomei puts it. He introduces himself and Br. Dositej; they are round-faced and boundlessly pleasant, even cheerful, with black beards sprouting uncertainly on their cheeks. *Sweet*. I peer into the nineteenth-century church chapel, the dining hall (a replica of one at Mount Athos), an old bread oven, the impressive several stories of the *konak*, or Turkish-style residences: white plaster, lots of dark wood carved into porches and banisters, the belvederes. The church has recovered its miraculous icon of St. John the Baptist, which had been found more or less intact at the bottom of a well. Water gushes out of the mountainside through three iron spouts; most likely it has healing properties and would be one of the attractions of the place. There's a stone tablet: *Brothers, Christians, drink this sweet and cold water to refresh your thirsty soul and remember Neophit the monk from the village of Vevchani, Ohrid, as he renovated it in 1877. The end. God be praised!*

A few paces away stands a little square stone structure that houses the skulls of the community's dead, lined up in an orderly fashion on shelves. Br. Mikhail is in charge of this strange, cold, hard, little room. A Czech, soft and blond, he converted to Orthodoxy after a trip to Bulgaria. On a chance visit to an Orthodox church, Mikhail knew, as soon as he had entered it, "I was closer to God than I'd ever been." As I watch, he refills the oil lamps, lights wads of incense, censes us and the skulls, pronounces the Lord's Prayer in Macedonian, and then explains that the skulls were recovered from the monastery when it was rebuilt and then preserved just in case one of them should turn out to be miracle-performing and exude *myron* one of these days or years. (It was first built in 1021, according to its own chronicle.) "Don't be afraid," he says as I stare back at the gaping-eyed departed. This monastery and its district were once a centre of transcription and icon-writing and wood-carving for the churches, and perhaps I am looking at Prior Arsenie from the village of Galichnik, Prior Mitrofan from Lazaropole and his successor Archimandrite Partenie Zografski, the painter.

There used to be eighty men here, now there are five. On the Saint's Day in September, a thousand people come for dinner. Mikhail says that most believers, when they visit, bring something for the community's good. Cooking oil is popular. "We have barrels of it now." "What else do you need?" "Not much. We're vegetarians and we don't eat much anyway. Bread and water if we have to."

I return to the profound quiet of the reception room, aware only of the muffled murmur of the Radika River far below in the valley, while cloud and fog sink and rise and sink again over the mountain peaks hugging us all around. The Muslims of the villages hanging on the opposite slope of the valley are hurrying home to have dinner before sundown. It is Ramadan for them, while on this side a monk bangs rhythmically on a wood plank, the *semantrion*, with a mallet outside the church doors to remind his community that Vespers will be sung in fifteen minutes. They have been banging away like this ever since the Turks forbade the use of bells—for the sound of bells attracted evil spirits and drove angels away—but also as a reminder of Noah's banging and nailing of boards to build his boat when God so commanded. It's true that the rain is not letting up at Sveti Jovan.

:: *Belgrade, Serbia*

MY FRIEND ILEANA CURA was horrified to learn I had arrived in Belgrade by bus. "My dear," she said, stroking my sleeve with her long red fingernails, "you should always arrive *elegantly*."

Belgrade herself has become more elegant in the most unexpected places. Dom Omladine, for example, the home of the Belgrade Youth Association, where once international peace activists piled off the Peace Buses in front of the building for a rally against the Yugoslav wars of the 1990s, young people are doing a brisk business in pirated CDs. Where once we stood shoulder to shoulder, in a smoky room shabbily furnished, remembering the political bravura of the intoxicating June Days of 1968, the walls have been removed, the ceiling is strung with paper lanterns and track lights, and young Belgrade sips espresso at shiny round silvery tables on smart little steel chairs. And the staircase where I had found purchase to sit, crouched, in the throng, trying to make sense of the impassioned discussion about student revolution, is now a sleek black staircase to a bilijar [billiard] klub.

I take the #26 bus on its interminable route down to the far end of Kalemegdan, the old fortress hill now a vast urban park. I have decided simply to walk systematically up and down all the streets in Stari Grad, or the old city. I did this walk years ago and remember how startled I was to come across a working mosque, all the shoes lined up on the carpet outside the main door. I see it again now, hemmed in by new apartment construction. I also see airy new cafés next to the neighbourhood *gostiljna* [cheap and cheerful eatery], renovated neo-classical buildings in pink and yellow, vestiges of sculpted reliefs on devastated facades, a little theatre, passages leading into courtyards with their inner apartments with Turkish loggias, and a few insalubrious Yugo-blocks. Belgrade's eternal mishmash.

The next day I am back on the bus to Kalemegdan Park, where the bell of the Ruzica Church, shrine of the birth of the Holy Mother of God, peals joyously as I approach. I cross its cobbled courtyard to another little church, St. Petka, whose cult has been honoured in Serbia since 1398.

A year earlier I had been too shy to walk in. Now I see that the ceramic mosaics, which cover entirely the barrel vault of the interior, catch the morning light through the windows so that everything sparkles within, especially the icons, around which the people shuffle, genuflect, and lay their kisses. Pure white cloths cover pristine blue enamel pails filled with blessed water, and a little hand-lettered sign begs us to take only one litre per person of this holy water, please! A young priest stands at his post at one of the icons, and I listen to his voice intone, over and over and over again, what must have been a prayer of repentance as he drapes his stole, the brocaded *epitrakhil*, over the heads of those kneeling to make a confession.

This is enormously homely, all this matter-of-fact coming and going, the splash of the blessed water, the plastic bottles stuffed into shopping bags, the crowded shelves of icons, the fussing children, the women venerating a very large icon of St. Petka, their hands spread wide over the pane as though to embrace her.

I return from the churches at noon to visit 69 Medakoviceva Street, the apartment building that is a virtual village of women, and am hailed over by my friend Kaja and old Semka, neighbour Zdenka, her daughter Nada the medical student, to join them at a little round table in the front courtyard. It is a lovely day, warm and sunny. It's noon. Out come the bottle of *loza* [grape brandy], cigarettes, and pot of Turkish coffee. There's a conversation about the inadequacy of men. How women in families have to do all the work, have to care for others all their lives long. This is all said with considerable humour, but we all understand the truth of it. I pass around the bottle of blessed water I have taken away from St. Petka's blue pail, and my friends sip from it as though from a communion cup, which I suppose it is.

NONE OF THE SCHOLARS I had hoped to interview in Nis are in
town or returning messages. This frees up time for a course of beauty
treatments that my host, Professor Vesna Lopicic, insists I undertake.
Appalled by my overgrown haircut, she escorts me to her hairdresser's, shoves a pile of hairdressing magazines at me, inviting me to
pick a style, consults authoritatively with the hairdresser, and breezes
out. Two hours later she returns and pronounces the new cut and
colour a complete success. Heartened, I agree to her next command, a
facial treatment. The mistress of the establishment—a loudly cheerful
middle-aged woman with big blond hair and a cigarette in a long
black holder she waves theatrically over cups of Turkish coffee—
turns me over to the care of a young beautician-machinist who grinds
my face with a kind of sanding machine, pokes my cheeks with
needles and electrodes, and slaps on applications of masks and mois-
turizers while my eyebrows are waxed and my hands submerged in
a molten wax bath then tied into flannel mitts. Between procedures I
am sent out into an adjoining bathroom and instructed to hose down
my face with a length of rubber hose attached to bathtub faucets
for this purpose. All around me buzzes the subculture of this little
neighbourhood salon: Madame treating all her clients as long-lost
daughters and nephews (a row of teenage boys submits to acne treatments), husbands looking in on their wives and staying for a coffee
and cigarette, the steady stream of chatter among the beauticians,
working on us clients laid out helplessly on small beds and exposed
to general view. I stagger out while all present wave goodbye. "So
beautiful!" they cry.

Next, Vesna and I take a coffee break in Caffe Galeria, surrounded
by icons. It seems the café owner is a collector. Unsure of the artistic
value of what he had purchased, he engaged an expert from the
Institute for the Protection of Cultural Monuments in Nis to evaluate
the pictures and then produced a catalogue, which we examine,
looking for Demetrius. He's here, *Sveti Muchenik Dimitrije*, Holy
Martyr Demetrius, in eighteenth-century guise: the stylized waves
of his hair now a coiffure, his Byzantine hands curled effeminately

around the cross and spear of his martyrdom, his expression not so much imperturbable as placid, set with a pretty mouth. We read that the artist was Djordje Zografski, "a great painter from southern Serbia," responsible also for iconostases and fresco details. "The portrait of St. Demetrius represents a nice example of idealized painting." We protest together that it is deplorable.

The "expert from the Institute for the Protection of Cultural Monuments" is unnamed. Perhaps it's Misha Rakotsija, art historian with the institute, a specialist in medieval Byzantium, with whom Vesna has secured an interview for me. He receives us in his office amid the usual alpine topography of a scholar's books and papers in piles on the floor. Was I aware that here in Nis Emperor Claudius "Gothicus" II repelled a Gothic invasion of the Balkans in 269? No, I was not, but I am interested. I mention that I'm aware that Nis had its beginnings in the Roman Naissus, that it was Constantine the Great's birthplace, and that I've been taken to see the excavations at Mediana not far from town, a cluster of late-Roman villas that formed an imperial residence. The monumental floor mosaic is particularly impressive. Congratulations to the Institute for the Protection of Cultural Monuments! He regards me glumly: Seven second-century tombs with their early Christian frescoes have been lost—"crumbled away like dust"—when a city road was stupidly widened.

Naissus/Nis was a *martyropolis*, along with Constantinople, Antioch, Rome, and Thessalonica, the site of a repository of relics. It is to be regretted that no specific martyr has yet been found to be associated with Nis, but back in the eleventh century the relics of St. Prokop, martyred in Asia Minor in 303, were kept here until 1386. "The people of Nis don't know that. In the eleventh century the Hungarian army arrived at his church in Nis, severed one of his hands and took it to Sirmium/Mitrovica, to the church of St. Demetrius. A hundred years later Byzantine Emperor Manuel Comnenus took his hand and brought it back to Nis." It's a small world: Demetrius, the persecutions of 303–304, Sirmium, the severed hands of another military saint, all rolled up in Nis, where an emperor liked to take a holiday now and then, and left behind charming palaces to adorn it.

Well, then, on to the subject of my enquiry: Serbian frescoes.

"There are no *Serbian* frescoes. It is all Byzantine," Rakotsija replies. "We are part of that world." This is a key point: Byzantium's holistic cultural space. "We Serbs are part of that world—Greek in art, Roman in law, Christian in faith—which was preserved for the West right through to the Renaissance." He takes justifiable pride in this cultural ancestry, but, as an art historian of the Byzantine achievement, Professor Rakotsija is acutely aware of how his field of research is still marginalized if not outright pushed over the edge into a black hole by the "phobia" of Western scholars about the Byzanto-Balkan world.

"Western Europe still denies its heritage in Byzantium. Next year in Brussels a new museum of European culture and civilization will open that begins the story with Charlemagne," he tells us, voice rising. "Charlemagne! Even the protests of Greece's Minister of Culture did not prevail. 'Might is right.'" And so some eight hundred years of European civilization at the eastern end of the Mediterranean disappear—its inhabitants presumably living phantom lives until Europe finds them while wandering around on a Crusade.

I mutter my sympathies, mentioning that I was baptized and raised in the Orthodox Church. He nods approvingly. "Orthodoxy is a single thing. *Serbian* Orthodoxy, for example, doesn't exist." Yes, but, in the process of "inculturation" of the Gospel message in specific languages, rituals, holidays ("Go therefore and make disciples of all the nations..." Matthew 28:19)...? "Orthodoxy is always beyond nationality. Faith is very often identified with nationality because of history, but that is wrong, and it has done harm to the Serbian people. Ethnic specificities are *peculiarities* not divisions among people. Orthodox peoples in the Balkans have never quarrelled; it was always politics that divided them."

As I rise to leave, Rakotsija offers the information that his family's Patron Saint's Day [*Slava*] is that of St. Demetrius and that his daughter, "a gift of God," was born on *Mitrovdan*. From this domestic datum he launches one last volley: "The Greeks have appropriated Demetrius. Their story is a legend. Who is he and where did he come from? He's a *historical* personality. And science believes he originated in Sirmium and that his relics were transported from Sirmium to Thessalonica." Now I am wondering if he and Professor Milosevic of Sremska

Mitrovica represent a kind of consensus against the Greeks. "The St. Demetrius Church has been found in Mitrovica and he was martyred there, this has all been published."

It is true that the immensely powerful Greek city, Thessalonica, with its cult of St. Demetrius that drew pilgrims from the entire Christian world, *had nothing to produce* when an emperor himself asked to see the relics. Medieval cities competed fiercely to be the sites of martyrs' and saints' relics—those "special dead" whose very corpses and spilled blood remained powerful enough to heal inexhaustibly—and that early Christians had bribed Roman soldiers to look the other way when they came to take away the bodies of their dead, so they might repose in *martyria* and work their miraculous powers for the faithful from beyond the grave.

In one of the versions of the Passion of Demetrius, his friend Lupus gathers up the earth soaked with the martyr's blood and bears it away for the community. He also takes away the Saint's ring, after dipping it in his holy blood. I note the absence of any mention of his body. And I remember Professor Milosevic's rather smug little note of triumph when he had told me the same.

:: *Monks of Montenegro in their monastery on the hill*

Oasis in the desert of contemporary civilisation. The Monastery of Cetinje offers welcome to pilgrims by the grace of the Holy Relics and hospitality of the monks, by fragrance of the oldness and joy of the Age to come, Kingdom of Heaven.

—MONASTERY OF CETINJE BROCHURE, Montenegro

"A STONE UPON STONE," writes the monastery brochure. "Perhaps it is the easiest way to describe the Monastery of Cetinje" in Montenegro. The text continues in a bewildering sort of English to describe the "anti-city" glories of this fifteenth-century rock pile—hewn it seems block by block from the surrounding mountains. (There is no other terrain.) There are fragrant mornings rising from the monastery meadow, birdsong and bells, and the resounding *thunk* of the wooden mallet hammered against the wooden plank, the *semantrion*, wielded by a monk to arouse his brothers to prayer. "In the monastery the monks tangibly feel the Mystery of Resurrection.... Being immersed in this mystery monk and every human can sense even in the rustling of the leaves and chirruping of the birds that the death is conquered."

This Holy Community of the Nativity of the Mother of God is under the eternal protection of the Theotokos herself. Yet, the original building, a domed basilica, has in fact vanished—some say it ascended to Heaven—after its total destruction by that "earthly evil," Ottoman pasha, Suleiman, in 1692. Only some Renaissance capitals remain, supporting the new, ugly, arcades of cemented stone.

Once more I arrive and depart from a monastery in pounding rain. "It's always like this," says Fr. Jovan, greeting our group cheerfully from under a big umbrella. "The Black Mountain [Montenegro] does have a kind of inner brightness. This must be the reason there's not much sunshine on the outside!" Fr. Jovan once cut quite a figure in Podgorica's literary life, an habitué of the capital's cafés. He is still youthful, tall, and slender, with a raggedy brown beard, a knitted skullcap pulled down to his eyebrows, and a gaze of unsettling intensity. In the hour we have for this visit, we are whisked around without time even for the customary cup of coffee: our host is so proud of his monastery and wants to show us everything.

The monastery boasts a chapel that holds the tombs of several members of the Petrovic dynasty, founded by Danilo Petrovic Njegos in the early eighteenth century. He served as both king and supreme prelate of the Church, thereby setting a pattern, Montenegrin men of God and armed to the teeth. Here is the tomb of St. Peter Petrovic, a protector, who on his deathbed in 1830 addressed the Montenegrin chieftains with his last words on the Montenegrin subject: "Good-bye free Mountains and let your glory never fade!" St. Basil of Ostrog was briefly deacon here in Cetinje, and he, too, promises his protection. It was here he performed his first miracle—what a world to have lived in!—when an unborn child spoke loudly from its mother's womb to pronounce Basil's innocence before his detractors.

The little chapel alongside the tombs holds precious relics in two jewelled caskets under glass. Through small glass windows we peer at a piece of the Cross, and the left hand of St. John the Baptist, which looks leathery but beautifully formed in spite of missing two fingers. (Had they been chopped off and sent to various destinations wishing relics of their own?) From the expression of joy on his face, I understand that Fr. Jovan is a believer in the power and authenticity of these relics and that he is inviting us to be exalted along with him. "We who venerate them will have our souls watered with life-giving piety," he says, "just as this hand baptized Christ with the water of the Jordan River." So I, too, bend over the glass case and leave a kiss on the window.

We rush upstairs, to what had been the cell of St. Peter. It still contains his bed, a fire on the little hearth, and his rifle propped up under the narrow window looking out over the threatened countryside. "He was a leader of men in the army as well as a monk," Jovan explains.

Speech of Petar I Petrovich delivered to Montenegrins in July 1796 before departure in battle against Mahmud-pasha Busatlija on Martinici:
Gentle knights and dear brothers! We are Montenegrins, the people who are willing to fight for its freedom till last drop of blood and sacrifices our dearest life on the boundary of our immortal ancestors: but we do not allow damned enemy of Christianity to pass alive in our free and lovable mountains which our great-grandfathers, our grandfathers, our fathers and we ourselves justly flowed by blood!

Then the library, where several grand bookcases are installed, holding a great jumble of books in no particular order or catalogue, and to which nothing new has been added for ages. Still, from Fr. Jovan's pleasure at showing this display, I can see this was meant to be a place for research, for he hints at precious volumes long obscured from the inquiring eye. Did I not know that in 1494, a mere twenty-five years after the death of Gutenberg, the son of the monastery's founder, Djurad Crnojevic, hauled a printing press, the first in the Balkans, from Venice to Obod, a mere stone's throw from here? It printed religious texts in Cyrillic letters—even the Turks, knowing treasure when they saw it, let the press carry on.

Finally, we are at the monastery's museum and its mainly liturgical items of Russian silverware and the vestments of various bishops. No matter the era or epoch, they always wear the white and gold vestments for Easter and Divine Liturgy, blue for the feast days of the Mother of God, green for the Holy Trinity, red for the martyrs. I write this all down, with enthusiasm for my own education.

There has been no sign of monks—though we have smelled their lunch cooking—but as we emerge from the museum a young nun, hovering at the door, grabs Fr. Jovan's hand and kisses it with devotion, then returns to her previous pose, slightly bent at the waist and tilted sideways to the door frame. She is an Orthodox novice from Germany, formerly an actress. Fr. Jovan hurries us on and out to our waiting car. I glance back at the nun: she is still hovering by the museum door, hands held in front of her chest in a clasp of entreaty. There is no other sign of life.

I think I understand the attraction of these Orthodox refuges, sombre and shadowy compared to the Baroque brilliance—their marble and gold, sculpture and painting—of Catholic shrines. I remember the peace that descended on me when, years earlier, I entered the Studenica Monastery in southern Serbia, its sole extravagance the phalanxes of sputtering beeswax candles blazing in the shady narthex. We passed through the main gate and suddenly the noisy little world just behind us in the road—young men on motor scooters, a wedding party—was extinguished, and we entered another acoustic world. It was late afternoon. The splash of water at the fountain, the birds in the convent garden, and, inside the cool, dark nave, the bell-like voices of three nuns singing the serene responses of the Liturgy to the young priest lit up in the dusty shafts of light so that he glittered in his vestments. The saints in the frescoes, their limbs weightless, were so ethereal they disappeared into the gloom under the dome, needing no illumination outside the gold field of their spirit.

"Orthodoxy is not a 'national religion' of peoples." In fact, in Orthodoxy, "nationalism is forbidden." So said Dr. Savo Lausovic, of the Philosophy Faculty at Niksic University, Montenegro. My little tour of Montenegro has ended here, in the jammed dining room of a hotel in a town I had not heard of until the day before yesterday, amid the din of boisterous revellers and shattering wine glasses. The hotel is hosting a convention of high-school teachers. The professor raises his voice. "The universality of Orthodox culture is rooted in the very beginnings of Christianity when the Church Fathers were developing Christian doctrine. It is a mortal sin to believe in an ethnic church." Not so long ago, this assertion would have startled me, but I am here to learn this other way of thinking about "my" church. "We may speak of 'liturgical unity' among the Orthodox peoples, the still-living contact we all have with our Byzantine past." He pauses, takes a swig, gives me a look. "How can you say you are an Orthodox without being a believer? What are you: an Orthodox-Communist?"

But Professor Lausovic does acknowledge that the Serbs entered this new community, near the end of the ninth century, with their own identity. "The pagan story was reinterpreted in a new referential framework for the Serbs. The rituals and customs of the pagans were respected. Let's say, they were redirected. The contract was reinterpreted and the new content poured into it. For example, the *Slava*, which is unique to Serbs."

I drink the schnapps far too fast, and now I lean over the plates of roasted peppers and sheep's cheese, trying to hear what the translator is rendering of Professor Lausovic's pronouncements and write them down, all the while carrying on eating and drinking, my obligation as a guest, after all. Come to think of it, this was a lot like a Slava, the eating and drinking and noise, although of course a very serious purpose underlines the Slava. I remembered the celebratory singing and dancing at the Slava in Nis, the table set with a deep blue cloth and red napkins, the forty-some little dishes of food and the cornucopia of winter fruits and the beeswax spire of candle whose flame blessed it all, all in the name of the family's Patron Saint, Michael Archangel.

"Byzantium wanted to attract pagans," the professor concludes, but didn't want to be too radical. These new Slav nations were not at the geographical borders of Byzantium, couldn't be directly assimilated, and couldn't be given a completely new content." Unlike those other

Slavs who were inside the borders of empire, and who became culturally and spiritually Greek. "Pity," I offer, downing another glass of wine.

In this Demetrius cult we see syncretism at work, animalistic elements, totemism, magic, pantheism. And that's the answer to how Slavs absorbed Byzantine elements into their cultures.

—PETAR VLAHOVIC, *ethnologist, Belgrade*

I remembered what the political anthropologist, Ivan Colovic, had written, about the use and abuse of the words "spiritual" and "spirituality" in Serbia: "Everything that is not entertainment, money or the West may now be spiritual," he wrote mordantly. "The expression 'Serbian spiritual space,' has [become] one of the ways of designating territory that the Serbs consider their own." So, back in Belgrade, I ask Fr. Vladimir of Sveta Petka Church and the School of Theology about his being a Serb as well as a priest. Once again we are in the hushed board room across the polished table, he swathed in his black cassock, a silver pectoral cross glinting between its folds. Orthodoxy acknowledges the secular necessity of warfare, he begins, but it is a sin and must be confessed. As a priest during the wars of the 1990s, he was not a pacifist, so it became a question of how to be "human" in a war. "It was very, very difficult. But there need never have been a war; there should have been negotiations, whenever and wherever needed." Although he is clearly unhappy about "the last fifteen years" and how the regime's purposes degraded the message and mission of the Church, he always believed in the spiritual unity of the "Serbian lands," as they say here.

Can he imagine a "Serbian people" who are united within a spiritual and cultural patrimony but not within political borders? "Yes, and that will be Europe."

He labours to help people to overcome the merely patriotic reason for going to church. "This kind of church-going was popular at first, after Communism, but then nationalists stopped coming to church because it wasn't interesting or exploitable after awhile. But as a priest I must welcome whoever comes into the church. During the old regime, I was told I was 'good' for having received the 'opposition' in my church; but I am a priest for the whole church."

The whole church. But, I insist, is that "wholeness" only Serbian? Where does the Serbian Orthodox person end and the simply Orthodox person begin?

Something barely articulated from my own early experience within the Ukrainian Orthodox Church of Canada has been bothering me, a vague sense of having been trapped inside a specific ethnic spirituality that ministered to the "Ukrainian" person but neglected to nurture her relationship to the Orthodox "Commonwealth" around the world. For Fr. Vladimir, the distinction is false, and it is in this conversation that I again hear the word "inculturation," and I listen with mounting interest.

"Just as the idea of 'Heavenly Serbia'—that Serbs are a special kind of people, better than others—is one of the most manipulated and evil-used ideas, the opposite extreme is when Christians say your nation doesn't matter, only being Orthodox is important.

"Becoming a Christian is a radical act but it does not erase every-thing. This human being we are here—this 'who' that we are now—is not the last truth of ourselves. There is a higher self. But first we are accepted as who we are. And so it is with nations. Christ's point is that in the Heavenly Kingdom the personality is still saved and that which it is built on—family, ethnos, sex, and nature—is transfigured and saved in *me*.

"Inculturation is based on the idea of Christ's Incarnation. God takes human flesh, the Gospel takes the soul and flesh of a people. The Gospel message of Christ is embodied in a specific culture. In the same way as through the Incarnation God takes on human flesh, in inculturation the Gospel takes the soul and flesh of a culture or 'ethnos.' Every culture is able to receive and give its own flesh to the Gospel."

Fr. Vladimir speaks with the unapologetic, unabashed clarity of his faith, using the language of a Christian as though it were everyday speech. I am touched by a kind of melancholy I am beginning to recognize as a regret, a sorrow, a longing for something I didn't even know I regretted or longed for—sharing an act of faith-speech with him. As he speaks of the spiritual shortcomings of his parishioners, especially their veneration of the saints, I recognize myself, with the little paper disc of St. Demetrius tucked into my wallet, the small wooden panel of St. Clement in my suitcase. "If I were to be your spiritual teacher," I hear him say, "I would start with who you are."

:: *Sofia, Bulgaria*

ALL THESE BELIEVERS! I am sitting in the trendy Art Club Museum Café and staring at a menu propped up against the salt shaker: "Lenten Menu"—the Orthodox are always on a fast—translated for the godless as "vegetarian."

Take my friend, Ivan Biliarsky, the young Byzantinist at the Academy of Sciences. In a third conversation here, I learn that, as an act of rebellion against his family of two generations of Communists, he began going by himself to church as a youth and was baptized into the Bulgarian Orthodox Church at twenty. He's a *practising* Christian. He's recently been to Mount Athos, accompanying a cousin, several years younger, who much earlier had converted to a Protestant sect. The boy's parents had been Communist Party apparatchiks, not just ordinary members. At first they were horrified by the idea of harbouring a Christian, but they in turn had converted to Orthodoxy in 1989. Now they were horrified by the *Protestant* in their midst. The poor boy, not knowing where to turn, decided to visit Mount Athos, looking for a spiritual guide.

Ivan and his cousin went to see Fr. Raphael, a Russian monk on the Holy Mountain. A tiny man with a crafty expression and a messy beard, he put Ivan off immediately. But after their talk together, "I could see this was a real Father Zosima from Dostoevsky." What had impressed him so much? He told the young men to pray the Jesus Prayer but to be careful: "It is dangerous for unprepared people to concentrate the prayer in the heart. They must concentrate their prayer on their hands and throat."

I had earlier met Dr. Biliarsky in his other office in the Institute of History. Stray dogs patrolled the entrance. Biliarsky apologized for the place, situated on a campus of seemingly derelict wasteland that reminded me of the edges of prairie towns. Under insipid lighting, the corridors led to his woebegone office, which he was sharing with fourteen other scholars in weekly rotation. A desktop computer occupied one desk, several piles of journals another, and carelessly stacked leather-bound books monopolized the bit of bookcase shelving. Little plastic cups holding the desiccated silt of Turkish coffee were lined up on the windowsill as though for a target practice. I imagined a bored professor with a sling shot. The room's only enlivening décor was a poster of medieval art curling at the corners. The entire effect was deeply dispiriting.

But Biliarsky was cheerful, animated, prepared for all my questions about Demetrius in Byzantium, which he answered in fluent if idiosyncratic French. In 1984 he graduated from the Law Faculty and from the Department of the History of Culture (anthropology and ethnology) at the University of St. Clement of Ohrid in Sofia—his father is a lawyer, his mother a writer of children's literature—the same year as the official persecution of Bulgaria's Turkish minority began. "A very bad, very aggravated atmosphere prevailed, even among the intellectuals."

Turkish families were arbitrarily assigned Bulgarian names, pseudo-scientific theories were paraded "confirming" the Bulgarian origin of Turks in Bulgaria—historians, folklorists, and ethnographers were mobilized—the use of the Turkish language in public was outlawed, and the Turkish Philology Department (language and literature) at Sofia University was shut down. During this so-called "regenerative process," 350,000 Bulgarian citizens streamed into Turkey where their mosques, at least, would not be turned into rubbish dumps, their dead could be washed, and their faithful make the pilgrimage to Mecca, without reprisal.

The post-Communist governments have restored all minority rights to what's left of the Turkish minority, which gives Biliarsky great satisfaction—the Islamic high school in his hometown of Shumen was reopened—but now there is social danger in the deepening hostility toward the Roma people, as well as what he calls Bulgaria's "moral crisis," even more severe than the crisis of "market reconstruction."

In contrast to the shredded social fabric of the secular state, Ivan has entered the world, the community, of the Byzantine *Oikoumene*, that universal church, that universal faith, which has continued down all the Bulgarian ages in spite of what its fractious, ambitious, and ruthless tsars, generals, kommandants, and commissars have plotted against it. Take that Bulgarian prince, Kaloyan, who perished on Demetrius's sword at the pitiless stone face of the walls and gates of Thessalonica. "Generally, Bulgarian historiography argues for a kind of nationalization of the cult of St. Demetrius. I argue differently: that it's not a question of Bulgarians, Greeks, Byzantines, but of *Christians* who created a structure that was not a national state but a sacral one—a state of ecclesiastical character." Compared to the ecumenicity of Orthodoxy, the secular values of nationalism have been appallingly parochial, obsessed by the "uniqueness" of linguistic and national identitites. "The Byzantine Empire's grand achievement in the ninth and tenth centuries was the spiritual conquest of the Slavic world and the creation of the community known as the Byzantine Commonwealth. (I prefer the term *Orthodox* community.) And this is the heritage that must be defended and not cut up along national lines of demarcation."

As with almost every person I've interviewed in the Balkan states, Biliarsky sees in the "terrible" wars in former Yugoslavia the nationalist genii let out of the bottle to create nation-states in an orgy of bloodletting. Byzantium, the *Oikoumene*, was not like that. "The Byzantine state remained an ecumenical empire, universal, in the sense of an empire with claims to being an empire that covered the entire Christian world, just as the old Pax Romana was based on universal citizenship." (*Civis romanus sum!* suddenly springs into my brain from high-school Latin. *I am a Roman citizen!* said the Goth in a toga.)

From Thessalonica the Byzantines spread the cult of Demetrius throughout the Greek-speaking and then Slavic world—one or another emperor made the effort to re-establish him in Constantinople, as well, removing liturgical reference to *Thessalonica* and substituting *Oikoumene*, as in "You, Demetrius, are the person who fights for us in the *Oikoumene*"—and, once attached to or absorbed into the Christian

Commonwealth, the Bulgarians, as all Orthodox peoples of Eastern Europe, embraced the Great Martyr as "the saint of the known world." All saints of all peoples within that *Oikoumene* were Orthodox saints, period.

Bulgarians painted their new heroes over all available surfaces as soon as their churches were built: the military saints, Theodore, George, and Demetrius in Bachkovo and Boiana and Dragalevci, barely distinguishable one from another except for the twist of a moustache or the cut of a beard, seated on horses not thrones and reminding all who gazed at them that these venerable images had been commissioned by princes and army officers, flattering themselves in their reflected glory.

"Christianity was always open to the barbarians as part of human salvation," Biliarsky concludes. "After St. Paul, Christianity is accessible to all of humanity. It was the empire that made of Christianity a world civilization. Jesus's life was lived in the empire and he sacralized the empire the same way he sacralized flesh. This is how the empire is sacralized." And peoples with it: in the words of a prayer in the Vespers Liturgy of the Orthodox Church, *Lord, save Your people and bless Your inheritance.* "Who are these 'people'?" I ask him. "They are all the Christians, everywhere. It's a liturgical expression." *Free us from our enemies,* the prayer goes on, *for You are our God and we are Your people, and we are all the work of Thy hands.*

Byzantium as a world civilization I understand, with its basilicas, palaces, and libraries; as an imperial project of armies, tax collectors, and bishops, it is familiar from other empires; but as a metaphysical space hallowed by divinity, well, that has never occurred to me as an idea. It has never occurred to me that, in accepting Christianity for the people of Rus, my titular sovereign Volodymyr the Great swept the Ukrainians not just into literacy and monotheism but into *God's plan.*

> *Once, when He descended and confounded the tongues, the Most High divided the nations; and when He divided the tongues of fire, He called all men into unity; and with one accord we glorify the All-Holy Spirit.*
> —KONDAK OF THE HOLY PENTECOST *[Descent of the Holy Spirit]*

I REMEMBER A READING from a long-ago university course, *The Primary Chronicle*. It was an important literary text that appeared within fifty years of the baptism of Rus, when eleventh-century Kyiv, said to be one of the most brilliant cities of Europe, adorned with churches, schools, hospitals, and libraries, nevertheless praised the miracle of Pentecost by which the Slavs had come to share in the *spiritual* rebirth of the peoples.

Fr. Petar in Veliko Turnovo told me much the same, and I wrote it down without reflection: "Inculturation is an apostolic message, a gift of the Pentecost, and it is there at the beginning. Read Acts, about the first gathering of believers after Christ's Crucifixion. 'And they were all filled with the Holy Spirit and began to speak with other tongues, as the Spirit gave them utterance.'"

I look more keenly now at the icons of the Pentecost, of that gathering of the disciples, the first assembly that would become the Church, upon whom the Holy Spirit descends in the form of a little tongue-like flame. It is fifty days after Passover and the Crucifixion of Christ, and the disciples are seated in a room, in a circle, with dignified demeanour if a little perplexed, for suddenly they "began to speak with other tongues, as the Spirit gave them utterance." But the story does not end in that room. The multitudes of Jerusalem heard their sounds, "and were confused, because everyone heard them speak in his own language...'And how is it that we hear, each in our own language in which we were born?'" In Acts, there follows a list of the peoples whose languages were given utterance: Partians and Medes and Elamites, those dwelling in Mesopotamia, Judea and Cappadocia, Pontus and Asia, and many more besides, hearing the disciples "speaking in our own tongues the wonderful works of God." That Ukrainians would also eventually hear of the wonderful works of God in their own tongue was a gift of Pentecost.

But this was also a gift of Byzantium, whose "Greekness" was not ethnic or racial but intellectual and spiritual, and claimable by all kinds of people who understood themselves to be Byzantine, if not Greek. Slavs could never be Greeks, but they could be Byzantines.

⋮ *The Guardian Saint*

:: *Thessalonica*

IN THESSALONICA, in late October, I have secured an interview with Very Reverend Demetrius Vakaros, General Vicar of the Holy See, Holy Metropolis of Thessaloniki, and a priest of the Basilica of St. Demetrius. He is also the author of a small book about the life of St. Demetrius that I have seen in all the very numerous religious bookstores in the city. I have come to speak with him because I have timed this visit to Thessalonica for the celebration of Demetrius's Feast Day on October 26, the climactic point of the year's liturgies in his Basilica, and I want to know what to expect.

Fr. Vakaros sits, bald-pated with a string of a ponytail down his neck, with his plump, smooth hands folded on top of his desk, a rather stern expression on his face at my entrance. I wonder if I have offended him by not kissing his hand, but I think only other priests do that. Anyway, he hasn't held it out. Maybe women offend him? The only ones in evidence in the building are the charladies and aged petitioners I passed on my way down the hallways. I express gratitude for this appointment at such a busy time of year. "How much time do we have for this visit?" I ask. "It's not in my hands," he answers, leaning back from the desk, his hands locked across his roly-poly belly, and then he rolls his eyes back, with a bit of a twinkle, and looks off in the direction of Heaven.

Vakaros once studied in Michigan and speaks in English (but uses the Greek words for Thessalonica and Demetrius). I ask him to explain to me how St. Demetrius is still, 1,700 years after his death, the protector of Thessalonica? "First of all," he begins, "St. Dimitrios was born in Thessaloniki and he was a general; in the military he had the office of general. And a general not just of Thessaloniki but of the whole Greece. Thus say the sources. He is a protector of the city not only now but from the beginning. From his death day he protected this city always. And the miracle is very large in number. There is written books and books and books about the miracles of St. Dimitrios. Now the history of his life is clear in the sources, not any doubt about he was born in Thessaloniki, he was the general officer in the military, he die in Thessaloniki. In the martyrdom place."

Here in Thessalonica, Father Demetrius reminds me, Demetrius is known as *Megalomartis*, the Great Martyr, and *mirovlitis*, he whose relics exude perfume. "And also as protector of the city," he adds. "In Greek it is *Megalomartis Agios Dimitrios o Mirovlitis*." There is in fact a legend that Thessalonians would rub themselves all over with the *myron*, the miraculous myrrh shed by his relics, before joining battle with the Bulgarians.

As in the Middle Ages, so now: thousands of faithful converge upon Thessalonica for the Feast Day of Demetrius on October 26.

"They come with faith, with love. And in my estimation, because I have spoken as a preacher of St. Dimitrios Church—twenty-three years now I am preacher right there, also there's a radio and TV broadcast around the world—people believe in St. Dimitrios, in his miracles, in his personality, and many of them they speak of miracles that happened to their personal life, and they come here and give us a description or write it down or speak to us about what happened to them with St. Dimitrios.

"Yes. Now all evidence is put down in my books: early in the beginning, when flow the myrrh of St. Dimitrios," (he disappears into Greek here, then out again) "it's local, the adoration. But because the people who come here outside of Greece, take back with them holy *myron*, it is spread the name outside, in the universal. And the hymn [about Demetrius] change in that time." (He recites in Greek.) "Not only for Saloniki, you see, but the universal, for the *Oikoumene*. From that point, that moment, the universality of St. Dimitrios is spread around the world, from the miracle, the *myron* and little by little his Feast Day is adored around the world."

In Sofia, Ivan Biliarsky had used the same word, *Oikoumene*: how in Constantinople they had praised the Demetrius not of Thessalonica but of the inhabited Earth.

But what about that other story the Bulgarians tell? How Demetrius—Dimitar—in fact once abandoned Thessalonica to go join the Bulgarians in Turnovo?

"No, no!" He strikes the desk top, and I jump. "They have spread in Bulgaria an error. They have *miracles* of St. Dimitrios in Bulgaria but they don't have *him*. He never left. He is a protector of this city not only now but from the beginning. From his death day he protected this city always. He says, 'I never go out of Thessaloniki. I never leave Thessaloniki.' There's a hymn that says: *O patris mou Thessaloniki*. Never is he going to leave."

In a late-sixth-century miracle attributed to Demetrius, the Saint categorically refuses to leave the city even under an Avaro-Slav siege, even when ordered to do so by two angels, God's own messengers. "What life can there be for me if my citizens are destroyed?" he asks rhetorically in defence of his insubordination. "If they must perish, I shall perish also." Well, now that Fr. Vakaros thinks about it, there was one time he did leave. Fed up with the Thessalonians' general bad behaviour, St. Demetrius one day saddled up his horse and rode out the gates, heading southwest, perhaps to Athens. On the road, he met up with another patron saint, Achilles, the Bishop of the ancient See of Larisa, whom he recognized by his long white beard and episcopal seal around his neck. Achilles was also heading south. The two stopped to chat. "St. Achillios says, 'I'm going to leave the city of Larisa because the believers are so bad sinners and I don't want to stay with them anymore.' And St. Dimitrios says to him, 'Also I have the same problem with the Thessalonians.'" They walked along in silence for a few minutes, each thinking of the mess he'd left behind. "'But is it good to leave them without the power of God?' Dimitrios ask." After all, they are patron saints, and they have a job to do. Demetrius and Achilles sighed, they shrugged, and they turned around and headed back home.

But if Demetrius is always in Thessalonica, I ask, is he is able to hear prayers from Canada, say?

"We call him here: 'St. Dimitrios, please protect us.' You call him in Canada. In a few seconds he's right there." Here Vakaros picks up a round paper weight from a pile of papers on his desk and whirls his index finger around it in all directions. "All the saints have their *aikiniton*. They move at the same time in the same moment from east to west, from north to south, yes. They will be there in Canada in two minutes. Saints can do that. They have this power from God."

Months later I will read in a footnote by the venerable Arnold Toynbee that the fourth-century Bishop of Larisa was the "second lease of glorious life" of Homer's Achilleios, last seen by Odysseus as the old man striding away on foot in the meadow, wild with immortal lilies of Elysium, in the abode of the dead.

Next, I visit Professor Anthony-Emil Tachiaos, historian of Byzantine–Slav relations and author of several texts (available in English translation) on the brothers Cyril and Methodius and their reception in the Slavic world. I'm lugging one such richly illustrated volume with me, purchased in a large religious bookstore, hoping the author will autograph it. He receives me with enthusiasm in his splendid apartment full of large furniture and tall bookshelves, and with a grand view to the floodlit Byzantine ramparts of the old city. He has cherished colleagues in Belgrade and Skopje and Sofia and is pleased to hear I have already met some of them.

"Byzantine Salonica," he murmurs, pointing to the cyclopean walls of the medieval acropolis—until 1869 the city had been completely enclosed within them—then turns back to his two guests. Besides me, he is entertaining Valentin, a graduate student from Russia, who is doing comparative textual analysis of Russian and Greek liturgies, and for a few moments we all chatter in Russian, but I cannot keep up and let them do the talking while I have a good look at them. Tachiaos, whenever he takes his glasses off, looks alarmingly pouchy and purple about the eyes, but once the glasses are in place again he is a booming-voiced, white-moustachioed scion of a substantial Thessalonian family that lost its fortune in the 1950s. This domestic "necessity" produced this scholar of Byzantine-Slav relations and of the missions of the Thessalonian monks, Cyril and Methodius, this member of several academies, including the Bulgarian Academy of Sciences. Valentin shifts his eyes away from any contact with my glances, as though he were a monk under interdiction, the way he sips almost surreptitiously from his teacup, and moves minute portions at a time of Mme Tachiaos's cheese pie onto his fork. In any case, he soon puts down the plate and takes his leave.

I've come, I explain, with my question about Demetrius of Thessalonica: is it true what Reverend Father Vakaros said, that the Saint has never ever left this city?

Tachiaos replies: "First of all I should tell you that these narratives, these legends, are very interesting when taken as such, as expressions of feelings and aspirations of the peoples of the nations. They are really very beautiful and very interesting. They cannot be used as historical sources, though; they just witness the feelings of a nation but they cannot be taken as a source of information.

"So, this story of a saint leaving a place and coming to another place is a commonplace motif in medieval literature, be it Slavonic or Greek or Latin or whatever. We just take all these narratives as tokens of a certain epoch. You say that St. Demetrius left Thessaloniki and went to Turnovo. Others say that Cyril and Methodius left Salonica and became Bulgarians. You see, we have such legends and fairytales. It's very common.

"But we should not think of nationalities, we should not think of nations the way we do after the French Revolution. And we shouldn't make retrospective extensions of our present-day views to the past. This is incorrect. You cannot teach history if you have such presuppositions, such prejudices. It's impossible."

As an historian of Slav-Byzantine relations, Anthony-Emil Tachiaos has of course the long view. As far as *Byzantine* Macedonia was concerned, the Slavs had been assimilated into Byzantine culture leaving scarcely a whiff of their Slavic particularity behind them in their passage to the superior identity. There is the charming fact of a certain Perbundus, seventh-century chieftain of a Slavic tribe in Macedonia, who lived in Thessalonica, dressed as a Byzantine of substance and spoke fluent Greek.

"The Byzantine literature, the Byzantine cultural outcome was far superior to that of the Slavs," he asserts. "Why should the Byzantines learn Slav languages at the time when the Slavs themselves were still receiving from Byzantium?" Confidentially, he adds: "Greek fear of Slavs? Ha! Slavs could not even pronounce Greek words. The Slav could never say *Thessaloniki*. Th, th: unpronounceable to the Slav."

The problem of Slav and Greek relations arose again in the context of the Ottoman Empire and a world coming apart at the seams, when nationalists of all stripes challenged what had been satisfactorily resolved as Hellenization: whatever your origins, if you speak Greek and are Orthodox Christian, you are a Hellene, you are a citizen of the republic of Greek culture. But the nationalists saw it otherwise, asserting that "if you speak Slavic, you are a Bulgarian. You must be a Bulgarian. 'No, I'm a Greek.' 'You can't be Greek; you speak Bulgarian, you must be a Bulgarian.' We have so many Greeks living in Greece who, when they came from Asia Minor, were speaking Turkish. My father was a tradesman and a representative of foreign firms and had a vast activity, and he was speaking Turkish. As a tradesman he would not have survived without speaking Turkish. When I was a young lad, I was going to his store, helping there during the summer vacation, and I had to learn Turkish to a certain extent—here in Thessaloniki."

"So he had a Turkish-speaking clientele?"

"Oh, sure! He had colleagues, tradesmen as well, who had come from Asia Minor who were speaking better Turkish than Greek."

"But if I can ask you to think, independent of contemporary politics, about this 'cultural zone' in the Balkans where the Slavs and Greeks have encountered each other, can we think of this as a particular cultural achievement?"

"Look, we Balkan countries have the same culture. In Skopje, in Bitola, they eat as I eat, the plates are the same, the feasts are the same, the religion is the same. Why do we speak of cultural divergences?" He has picked up another slice of cheese pie and is waving it around. "All Balkan people are united in a common culture. The substructure of our cultures is the same, be they Byzantine or Slavic. Nothing divides us. There are others who are interested in dividing us. That is, in two words, my conclusion."

Christ's Great Martyr, Demetrius, a very handsome person, whose soul was even more beautiful, whose words were sweet but whose behavior was sweeter, was the most fragrant blossom of Thessaloniki.

—FROM THE GUIDEBOOK TO THE BASILICA OF ST. DEMETRIUS

I HAVE FOUND a chunk of marble pillar to sit on, here in the crypt of the great Basilica. Somewhere within these vaulted subterranean chambers is the pavement of Demetrius's cell where he was imprisoned and murdered. I had once imagined a golden rope thrown around it to mark the spot, perhaps even a faint stain of blood. The guidebook I consult in the half-light tells me that the Saint was "probably" speared "here" by the little barrel-vaulted chapel under the brick-and-mortar arches. I look around some more; all the arches look the same.

Within minutes of unpacking my bag at the hotel this late afternoon, I was hurrying up the street toward the Basilica on St. Demetrius Avenue. Michalis at the reception desk had informed me that this very evening the crypt in the Basilica was open for a Vespers service. I understood that this happened only occasionally, that I was lucky, and that I'd better get going.

The streets were full of brutal and cacophonous traffic and harsh glare, but when I stepped into the deep shade of the cavernous nave, I passed into another world, that of Orthodox worship, and I instantly felt its peace—the spitting beeswax candles, the whispered repetitions of prayer before the icons, the shadows cast in the half-light of the columns. Demetrius himself was multiplied in frescoes and icons throughout the voluminous space of his church, but I was in a hurry and did not stop to look, only noticing from a quick glance a group of the faithful who were lined up at a glass-encased silver sarcophagus to make the sign of the cross and lean over it with a kiss. I'd read about Demetrius's miraculous appearances at his own silver tomb: an unnamed relative of a prefect of Illyricum during the reign of Emperor Phocas (602–610) had a vision in which he entered the Basilica and, wonderingly, approached the six-columned ciborium, flashing silver. "What, O brethren," he asked the attendants, "is this wonderful work that rises in the middle of the church's length?" And they replied: "We have been told by our fathers that the most glorious martyr Demetrius reposes there in divine fashion." Was this it? Was he in there?

Out of the shadows of the crypt, two altar boys have materialized, fussing with their vestments. One of them, the blond one, suddenly turns to me and, lifting the heavy gilt censer smoking out from all its apertures, solemnly censes me, and I bow my head to receive the gift of the curling smoke.

Earth covers me, and the grave,
but full is the world with my fragrance,
from myrrh gushing by the grace of Christ.
Wherefore, fear not, my birthplace,
possessing me,
for in Christ shall I trample thy enemies
and guard thee and save thee,
who honour me.

— ST. SIMEON OF THESSALONICA

Then I hear the song of a priest reverberating through the crypt, rolling over marble and brick and echoing through the archways the cadences of the opening phrases of the Divine Liturgy. These were the first sounds of the Liturgy in Europe, and they were in Greek. Here it was, the mother text of the Slavs, who would make it their own, even in the zone of their humble New World churches, stumbling sometimes on its archaic language, confused by its protocol of gestures, but sealing their gratitude with a kiss on its velvet, bejewelled cover: God had come in a book.

Converted, the barbarians stopped storming the gates and began to go to church. Perhaps those around Thessalonica lined up with the Greeks in the Basilica that houses Demetrius's ciborium, the silver baldachin raised over a holy place, then waited their turn at the fountains, holding the crude ampullae in which they bore away the healing *myron* exuded from St. Demetrius's bones, sacred efflux of the tomb.

As have streams and generations of foreign visitors to Thessalonica before me, I, too, have come straightaway to the home of St. Demetrius.

Right here on an outside wall of the Basilica, pilgrims would have stopped to consider the mosaic representing the first of Demetrius's miracles—the healing of the paralyzed prefect, Marianos, a miracle celebrated throughout northern Greece and in Constantinople, a miracle "in the mouths of all the people," according to Thessalonica's Archbishop John. Inside, they made their way to the focal point, to the site of Demetrius's powers, the silver ciborium, there to make petitions and light candles in memory of their dead. They came to his home, his repose, to pray, to seek healing, or at least to look around in awe, at the mosaics and frescoes and great pillars, and at the Saint's tomb, covered with large marble tiles and ornamented with jewels and silver.

Sosipatris, Thessalonians called him; compatriot, as they had once called Apollo and Heracles, a veneration that surpassed that of all other saints, Christ Himself included. "The Thessalonians have always been very devout," noted the Romanian historian of their city, Oreste Tafrali. "From the Middle Ages their city has been known as the 'Orthodox city'...Thessalonica possessed the body of St. Demetrius, her pride and glory which attracted a constant stream of pilgrims from all countries." If I were a medieval pilgrim, I would take away as a souvenir tiny moulded figures of the Saint lying in his tomb, his bed. The healing oil and myrrh, filling the whole Basilica with a beautiful fragrance, would work its miracle in my sick and suffering self.

It is told, of an ascetic on the Mount of Solomon, that, when he heard of the miracle of the myrrh-gushing Demetrius, he doubted. There were many other great martyrs who suffered more than St. Demetrius, he thought, yet they were not so honoured by God's grace as this. But one night, as if in a dream, he walked into the Church of St. Demetrius and asked the old man with the keys to open the tomb of the Saint so that he might venerate it. The door opened, and there stood the body of the Saint, shining and fragrant, and from all the

wounds in his holy body where the spears had lanced him there flowed the
miracle of abundant myrrh.

Byzantine Emperor Michael IV, hideously bloated by disease
and prostrated by the loss of Sicily to the Saracens in 1040, spent
much of his time in Thessalonica, "spread-eagled over the tomb
of his beloved St. Demetrius as he implored his intercession." He
was dead within a year. Forty years later, at war with Normans, the
luckier Emperor Alexius Comnenus dreamed he heard the voice of
St. Demetrius address him from an icon in the Great Martyr's sanctuary in Thessalonica. "Cease tormenting yourself and grieve not;
on the morrow you will win." Alexius spent the whole winter in
Thessalonica—from where he raised a credible army by the simple
expedient of confiscating church treasures throughout the empire
and melting down the silver and gold to pay for men and arms—
threw back the Normans and reigned another thirty years. He had
spared, it seems, Demetrius's beautiful silver ciborium.

:: *Preacher among the porticoes*

NEXT DAY, I return to the Basilica with Aristotle Mentzos, amiable
professor of Byzantine archaeology at Aristotle University and
eloquent source of history of Thessalonica and its structures in Late
Antiquity. We meet outside the building near its west entrance,
just steps away from the diabolical fury of traffic on St. Demetrius
Avenue, which in Roman times had been a cobbled street running
along the hot springs that fed the baths. I have asked whether there
is anything left of the city of Thessalonica where Demetrius may
have grown up and lived. There are the exposed sections of the agora,
Mentzos explains, ruins of the northern part of the baths lying on the
north side of the church, remains of the immense palace of Emperor
Galerius Maximianus, farther into the centre of the city—now sand-
wiched between high-rise apartment blocks—and the rotunda, the
temple built by Galerius and probably dedicated to a group of pagan
deities. Galerius was fiercely devoted to the old gods, and his edicts

of persecution against the Christians were issued in 303, caught Demetrius in their net, and were not withdrawn until 311 as Galerius lay dying.

Galerius, surnamed Armentarius, or herdsman, from the original profession of his ancestors, was a gruff, brutal professional soldier from Thrace, who enjoyed keeping bears who "resembled him in both size and viciousness." Constantine, the future emperor who would patronize the Christians, their bishops, and their Church, grew up in the court of Diocletian and his associates, and watched them with loathing, especially Galerius. "Him in particular I remember, with his pitted jaws and livid eyes, exposing me to dangers in battle," he muses in the fictionalized *Emperor* by British writer Colin Thubron. "I picture him on campaign in Persia, squatted among rocks like an ape, picking the diseased skin between his toes. Was that a god?"

"Unfortunately most of the Roman city lies right underneath the present city centre."

We walk down from the Basilica to the forum, then turn and look out toward the excavations (begun in 1962) of what had been the most important public buildings of the Late Roman period—a theatre, galleries, mosaic pavements—now just a portion of gracefully arched arcades and a rubble of brick wall next to a municipal bus station. Mentzos points out the walls of the Assembly with its theatre-like ranges of seats and the lower galleries open to the sea breezes. Was it somewhere here that Demetrius, scion of an eminent Thessalonian family, preached the word of the Christian God in the precincts of the pagans? "Some say in a portico used by coppersmiths, in the basement of the church of the Virgin Mary."

I look over to the red-tiled domes of the lovely, pink-bricked eleventh-century Panagia Halkeon Church, St. Mary of the Coppersmiths, believed also to have been built on the site of a temple to the pagan gods of coppersmithing, Hephaestos and the semi-divine Cabiri (or Kaviros). Interestingly, Reverend Ioannis Tassias, author of my guidebook to the Basilica of St. Demetrius, takes no offence and, in fact, sees a precursor to Demetrius in this "great god," pagan protector of navigators and miners thought to influence idolaters and defend the city: "This shows that the Thessalonians wanted to believe in a god

that would encourage them to fight against the enemies of the city."
Many churches in honour of such gods were erected in the city, only
to be rededicated as Christian temples "profane until now." Did
Demetrius preach to the coppersmiths, acutely aware of the danger
their souls ran?

We have been speaking of Demetrius as of a celebrated historical
personage, but Mentzos admits there is no sure way to know whether
there existed a Demetrius "as a person." His own opinion is that there
did exist a certain Demetrius but "his personality was subsequently
obscured and invested with additional meaning so we cannot easily
distinguish now between what is true and what is legend." Scholars
are not even sure he was a baptized Christian or simply attracted to
Christianity. "His end came when he was debating with other people
subjects of Christianity. He was approached by members of Galerius's
Imperial Guard, arrested, and brought to Galerius."

I read out loud from the guidebook that, like Jesus Christ before
him, Demetrius was betrayed to the governor by his fellow citizens,
"idolaters, having the devil in their hearts and wanting to be
honoured by Caesar." Mentzos adds that excavations have disclosed
a fresco in one of the galleries depicting two men at prayer on either
side of an enthroned Christ, proving, to some people, that this
forum was a Christian place of assembly, just as the narratives of St.
Demetrius's Passion tell it.

As we stroll back toward the Basilica, Mentzos continues the
story: "Galerius, after a brief interrogation, wasn't sure what to do with
Demetrius as he understood he was an important member of the local
society. So he decided to put him away, to jail him, in a certain space in
the subterranean portion of the Roman bath, which was exactly where
the church is situated now." According to the Basilica's own guidebook, the bath was a disgusting hole leaking excrement and full of filth,
home to venomous vermin. When Demetrius made the sign of the cross
and crushed a scorpion ready to sting him, an angel holding a golden
wreath immediately appeared above him and said: "Hail St. Demetrius,
soldier of Christ; be strong and brave and defeat your enemies."

We enter the Basilica. "According to the hagiographic text," Mentzos
relates, "the first church was built by a certain eparch, a local

administrator in the beginning of the fifth century. Of this building we have almost nothing." What excites the archaeologists is the layers of later architectural leavings as one version of the Basilica after another burned down—"thanks to the flames of candles that were constantly burning"—or was shattered by earthquake, until the current restoration.

That there is this Basilica, home, of St. Demetrius at all, after all these centuries of geophysical and political assault—earthquakes, fires, sieges—is a kind of miracle all its own. In fact, there is a miracle recorded of a ghastly conflagration of an early version of the church that, mysteriously, burned in full daylight without damaging any property around it. "All witnessed there the punishment of their sin-hardened ways," the Archbishop wrote of this miracle early in the seventh century. "St. Demetrius took pity on the afflicted Thessalonians, who couldn't bear to see the church in such a lamentable state, ·without a roof, and thanks to the Martyr's intercession this magnificent building, as you see it now, has been gloriously re-established, for the salvation of strangers and Thessalonians and for everyone's joy."

The interior of this seventh-century Basilica was rebuilt most recently after the fire in 1917 and is a hodgepodge of a treasury of the iconography of its Patron Saint. I can only feebly imagine the emotions of Thessalonians at the staggering loss of their 1,400-year-old monument: only five years earlier it had been restored to them as a church when the Turks withdrew. Contemporary photographs show that the roof collapsed into piles of rubble taking stupendous colonnades of mosaic along with it, leaving behind ragged openings in the sooty brick walls and the scorched concave of the apse open to the four winds. Like its original, the Basilica's grand interior is five-aisled, a fitting stage for the "Sunday performance," as Mentzos styles the Divine Liturgy with all its trappings of processionals and ceremonials appropriate to a church that is also a *martyrium*, an ecclesiastical building devoted to the cult of a certain person, a Martyr, a Saint. The belief had grown and spread that Demetrius's tomb was lying in the Basilica in the ground beneath the ciborium. "Now, this belief was extended to the Western Europeans when as Crusaders they occupied

Thessaloniki in 1204. They, too, believed the Saint's tomb was lying below the ciborium. It seems—I'm not sure but it seems—that when they left some twenty years later they took with them some supposed relics from the Saint's body. These relics were deposited in northern Italy in a place called Sassoferrato and returned to the church of Thessaloniki in the 1980s."

At the very centre of the cult was the well deep underneath the present structure of the crypt, which supplied the Roman baths. I ask what it produced. "In the beginning the well produced water, a simple and plain well of water. As the cult progressed and it developed into more complicated patterns, this was turned into a holy fountain and the water was considered turned into *ayesma*, holy water. Eventually, this water was connected with the Saint's tomb and the Saint's body. And if we study the texts we understand that this water had a perfumed smell. It was myrrh, *myron*, scented water."

By this time we have made our way down into the crypt, the same cavern where I had stumbled across the Divine Liturgy, and we quietly review its features, the arches of the old Roman bath, the little chapel, the marble basin that held the Holy Water and the aromatic myrrh that oozed out of the martyr's tomb, which was believed to be in the ground beneath the ciborium, that silver hexagonal, six-columned, domed structure that I had seen in the nave.

"The details of the physical qualities of this liquid, this *myron*, escape us," Mentzos avers diplomatically. There never was a relic of the Saint's body in this *martyrium*; even in Byzantine times the body was not known to lie here. Gradually, though, a belief grew that the Saint's tomb was lying below the ciborium. Yet no one ever actually saw relics; even the great Emperor Justinian's attempt to excavate them was halted by divine command, a voice crying out of a flame, according to a local tradition.

"Today people are praying in this ciborium. To what, exactly?"

"It's a skull. A human skull."

"Really?"

"The remains of Demetrius said to have been deposited in the Abbey of San Lorenzo in Campo, Italy, near Sassoferrato, by the Normans who had occupied Thessalonica in 1185 and sacked it."

Pious Thessalonians believe this skull is the Holy Head of their Guardian. Wrote native son Nikos Pentzikis in *Mother Thessaloniki*: "Into the homes of Christians, the Priest, reading the Prayer Book to himself out loud, 'by the assaults of sorrows is the soul tormented,' brings, in a richly decorated silver casket, the Hallowed Head for them to kiss, the faithful on their knees like children."

:: *Blessed guardian of his city, full of glory*

HE WAS THEIR GUARDIAN and Divine Intervener: with his help, they repeatedly routed Avars and Slavs, the very seas throwing back the barbarian cadavers toward the impregnable walls; the Greek defenders cut off their heads and posted them along the ramparts, then rushed to Demetrius's church to give thanks. But in 904, a Saracen fleet, thwarted at Constantinople, turned their ships around and through the Dardanelles sailed straight for Thessalonica, which they besieged for three days; eventually, the defences crumbled and the Saracens poured through. They plundered and butchered for a full week, littering the streets with the dead, put the city to the torch, and finally re-embarked their ships with more than 30,000 prisoners, "leaving the second city and port of the Empire a smouldering ruin," writes historian John Julius Norwich. "It was more than a disaster; it was a disgrace."

"Where was the Guardian and Protector then?" I ask Mentzos. High up on the east wall of Thessalonica's ramparts is inscribed the boast of the medieval Persian engineer and architect, Hormisdas: *By indestructible walls Hormisdas completely fortified this town.* Mentzos: "We can assume that whatever miracles did take place, took place at the *western* walls." Bristling with some sixty towers, they are extant to a large extent. It was the eastern walls that were most exposed to attacks from the sea.

One night, five hundred years later, asleep in his palace, Ottoman Sultan Murad II dreamed that God appeared to him and held out to him a rose. He smelled, and swooned within, its delightful perfume. When Murad asked God if he could keep it, God told him that the rose was Thessalonica and that he had indeed decreed it should be his. By the end of the fourteenth century, with the Byzantines exhausted by futile efforts to contain Serbian, Bulgarian, and Italian ambitions on the fragmented empire, not even Demetrius could save Thessalonica from the insurgent Ottomans to whom Balkan citadels had fallen one by one. In 1430 Murad's dream of the rose proved more powerful than Thessalonians' of their Athlete: Not even the evocation by their Bishop Symeon of the giant warrior on horseback coming to help them could bolster the Thessalonians' spirit—most of their compatriots had already fled, others wanted to surrender before they starved, and the countryside and villages were already in Turkish hands.

As the Ottomans closed in on them, Thessalonica's last Orthodox Archbishop, Symeon, appealed in vain for his fellow citizens' repentance, without which their Champion could not intervene to save them from the besieging Ottoman armies. He reminded them that the Saint had intervened repeatedly in their long history, "tall and wonderful to behold...and striking terror into those attacking the city." But the starving city agitated for surrender—Ottoman policy treated surrendered populations with leniency, visiting vengeance on those who resisted—and Symeon himself admitted "there was nothing, humanly speaking, to help us out, neither ship nor galley nor allies nor sustenance." The Thessalonians slackened and grew weary, and when Symeon himself, thundering at them yet barely able to stand, died in September 1429, they were overwhelmed a short six months later by the enemy, who pillaged their houses and churches and rounded up all survivors, including clergy, nuns, and children, for the slave markets.

Symeon is said to be the poet who wrote, with unflagging faith, in the voice of his fellow Thessalonians even as many hoped for surrender: *Let the whole territory of Thessaloniki rejoice, let godly Thessaloniki be glad, for the glorious soldier of Christ with thee abides, thy sentry and saviour, crushing thy enemies, heaping riches upon thee, and O, it cries out in thy honour, hail Demetrios.*

In 1495 St. Demetrius's Basilica was turned into a mosque; it was still a mosque, but held Demetrius's tomb, when the historian Arnold Toynbee visited it in 1912, and there "St. Demetrius was still performing the miraculous cures that had attracted the halt and maimed to this spot for centuries. With sublime benevolence, he now cured Christians and Muslims impartially." Not a few months later, Demetrius himself reappeared at the decisive moment in 1912, just before his Feast Day, when Greek soldiers marching north to liberate Thessalonica, saw "with their very own eyes," a vision of the two Great Martyrs, George and Demetrius, ride ahead of their forces and strike the Bulgarian enemy stone blind. Yet, liberated from the Turks and joined with independent Greece, Thessalonica once more seemed deserted by her Guardian as the catastrophic fire ravaged the Basilica in 1917. In 1936 labour organizers—modernity's martyrs—were cast into Thessalonian prisons by Prime Minister General Metaxas, followed by thirty Communists sent to the morgue during a general strike in the God-protected city. In 1963 a socialist parliamentary deputy, Grigorios Lambrakis (immortalized by Yves Montand in the film, Z), was murdered in a Salonica street, run over by a motor vehicle after speaking at a meeting of the local Peace Committee. In 1978 a terrible earthquake shook Thessalonica for two days.

As many historians have noted about Demetrius, he is a "surprising saint," faith in whom must necessarily be a spiritualized faith, for his devotees have from the beginning been deprived of the consolation of his relics. His miracles belong, at the earliest, to the sixth century, and the fragrant and healing *myron* did not arrive until the tenth century. Not even the early hymns dedicated to Demetrius mention his bones. Unlike the unlucky towns and cities of the empire whose martyrs' relics had been summarily removed to Constantinople and its insatiable churches, the home of Demetrius has remained exclusively Thessalonica, his power never transferable from it.

Constantinople boasted a dozen sanctuaries in his name: one was the site of court ceremonials on the Saint's Feast Day, another of funerals of the royal family, and a third was demolished during the construction of the Ottoman Seraglio, but not a single one contained even a piece of his relics. Not even Emperor Maurice (582–602), who had petitioned Thessalonica's Archbishop Eusebius explicitly for a donation of a relic of St. Demetrius, could be satisfied, and it was vulgar of him even to ask. "It is not the practice, O Emperor, of the inhabitants of God-loving Thessaloniki, as it is of course in other areas, to visibly display the bodies of the martyred saints," the sanctimonious Archbishop wrote back. "On the contrary we have established the faith intellectually in our hearts and we shudder at the physical view on account of our deep piety." No, not even Constantinople could have him. Thessalonica was the *martyrium*, and if pilgrims wished to venerate Demetrius at his tomb, they would have to make the trip to Macedonia, and there collect the oil "which is always effecting the most wonderful cures," wrote the emperor's daughter, Anna Comnena, " for those who approach it with faith."

What exactly did the Russian pilgrim Alexander the Scribe see when he wrote at the end of the fourteenth century that he had seen the "holy oil of the martyr saint Demetrius" at a monastery in Constantinople?

Demetrius rests undisturbed in Thessalonica, *present* to the faithful inside his silver ciborium. It had once been furnished with a couch on which he "lay," in the form of his icon. And from this chamber he conducted affairs of the city and supervised the citizens' welfare by way of miracles and healings when it or its citizens were in danger. In the Miracles he "opens the door of his abode when someone knocks, shows himself at the threshold, talks with his visitors, weeps, gets angry, closes the door which is the image of that of the city."

Walking about the Basilica I make my own little venerations (the cramped gesture of the sign of the cross Orthodox-style, thumb, index, and middle fingers pinched together, a swift pucker of a kiss) before the icons that please me, but this feels furtive: there is something going on here that I am not privy to. I go through the motions of my fellow devotees but I do so with a kind of weightlessness, unburdened as I am of Thessalonian history, which the Thessalonians around me have inherited as a catechism of memory, and untouched as I am, too, by the relief of miracle by which *their* Demetrius interceded in the catastrophes that beset them physically and spiritually.

It is as though the Thessalonians have arranged, through prayer and devotion, that Demetrius should cleave to them as their own Divine Guardian against the enemies who assault their souls. How should I, a stranger, view this? How should I join my prayer to theirs? I turned to Anastasia Tourta, then-acting director of the Museum of Byzantine Culture.

We speak in her office, in the splendid, newly expanded museum I had only briefly visited, making a note to return. I begin by remarking how the image of St. Demetrius seems to be everywhere in this city. Referring to the notes I made while walking around the Basilica, I tell her I was struck by the overwhelming preponderance of his representation as a warrior-saint on a horse, looking like a Roman soldier with a weapon of some sort. And that I missed seeing more of him as the white-robed, empty-handed Martyr radiant with love.

In fact, it is not so much the warrior as the Roman aristocrat who is on view in these fifth-century mosaics, according to Tourta, "and they are votive panels, meaning that they were offered to the church in the fulfillment of a vow or promise." Demetrius was not only the protector of the city as a political and social unit, he was also the protector of each one of its citizens, one by one, from the least of them, children, to the political and ecclesiastical leaders. "And he was a healing saint," she adds. "We see a mosaic, a tender image of a mother who brings her children to the Saint for his blessing." And another one, of two children, a boy and a girl, standing, almost embraced, by St. Demetrius, his left hand laid lightly on the girl's shoulder, his right hand raised in a sort of salutation, all three figures staring out from large, round eyes, sharing the same imperturbability of innocence. Elsewhere St. Demetrius embraces the Eparch and the Archbishop of Thessalonica, his arms around their shoulders, all three draped in sumptuous cloaks, a brotherhood of patronage.

Thessalonians have always believed that it was not the power of the state nor the weakness of their enemies that saved them, but the grace of God acting through the benevolent and unflagging gestures of the omnipresent Demetrius.

Demetrius: *athlophoros*, Victorious, *ipermakhos*, Champion, *philopatris*, Lover of the Homeland, *kidemon*, Guardian of his City, *makarios*, Blessed, *theophilestatos*, Beloved of God, *aidimos*, Celebrated in Song; *athlitis*, Champion and Athlete, *panendoxos*, Full of Glory, *o agios tis oikoumenis*, Saint of the Universe.

Saint of the Universe. Here at the seventh-century mosaic of Demetrius with his arm around a deacon, concentric circles of gold mosaic tesserae whirling around his elegant head, we read inscribed below their feet the encompassing prayer: *Blessed martyr of Christ, patron of the city, watch over the citizens and strangers.* Thessalonians and strangers alike are pulled into the embrace of this man of love, whose power is available to any who approach him with devotion, including, why not, far-flung barbarians who light a lamp before his icon as the snow falls on his Feast Day. It is poignant to learn that medieval believers who dreamed of St. Demetrius often explained that they knew it was the Martyr who had visited them "because he looked just like his icon."

By the time he has migrated to the lands of the northern Slavs, he is a young man wearing a greenish brown tunic and white breastplate with a feather pattern, his cloak is green, he is girded with a towel, in his right hand he has a lance, as well as a scroll on which it is written, *O Lord, do not destroy the city and people; if You save the city, I will be saved with them, and if they are lost, I will be lost with them.* In his left hand is a sword in its scabbard, and his knees are bare. So says *An Icon Painter's Notebook: The Bolshakov Edition* (Moscow, 1903), though it is left unspecified which city he is to defend. Is it still only Thessalonica, or has a new, beloved city been erected wherever are found those in prayer: *Blessed martyr of Christ, lover of the city, protect both citizens and strangers?*

"The images are transcendental," Tourta summarizes. "There is a spiritual meaning at the base of the icon, and certainly every period gives a different meaning for this painting, but its meaning is mostly spiritual. For people in the twenty-first century it's not the same as for the people in the seventh or fourteenth. They don't expect St. Demetrius will protect them from invasions because fortunately there are no invasions! But they have the feeling about him as someone who is in the family, a venerated ancestor."

On June 18, 860, two hundred ships from Rus, "fallen on us out of the farthest north," in the words of Patriarch Photius in Constantinople, landed on the shores of the Sea of Marmara. "Why has this thick, sudden hail-storm of barbarians burst forth?" he wondered plaintively, burst forth from their homeland, "far from our country, barbarous, nomadic, armed with arrogance, unwatched, unchallenged, leaderless?" By the thirteenth century, however, before the devastating Mongol attack on Kyiv in 1240, the *Miracles of St Demetrius*, compiled by the Bishop of Thessalonica, John, in the late seventh century, was in circulation in Rus. He had become their venerated ancestor, too. And as his Feast Day eventually came to be celebrated among the Ukrainians, they prepared a lavish dinner: a tableful of fish with horseradish sauce, duck in aspic, eggplant caviar, bread with turnips, mushroom gravy and cutlets, poppy-seed dumplings, with a huge loaf baked from the best flour at centre stage, so to speak. But this is a feast set for the dead, or at least in the event the souls of the family's ancestors show up, in the guise of beggars, orphans, and pilgrims, floating through the village streets on *Dmytra*, the Feast of St. Demetrius.

On the other hand, should the living decide to spend the night in the cemetery and if the shades of the ancestors appear to them in long, white garments, then they will die in the coming year. Obviously, the best place to be on the night of *Dmytra* is at home, opening the feast with a spoonful of *kolyvo*, boiled wheat, the ritual food for the dead, giving thanks for the crops sown in the ancestral soil, "Great and moist Mother Earth, who was originally a Great Goddess." For all their long presence in Byzantine bibliography, there are no Eastern Slavic contributions to Orthodox Liturgy, only these best-embroidered linens, these *knyshi* of filled buns, these *halushky* of boiled dumplings, these fruits of Mother Earth in honour of a warrior in faraway, sea-smitten Salonica.

:: *The Seventh Miracle of St. Demetrius, "Re Onesiphoros, the Sacristan, stealer of candles"*

A CERTAIN ONESIPHOROS, sexton in the Basilica in Thessalonica, was in the habit of substituting small candles for any large ones that had been donated by visitors to the ciborium, as a "cost-saving" measure. He had been warned by the Saint in his dreams to stop this mean-spirited practice: "Brother Onesiphoros, that which you do does not please me. The salvation of a soul pleases me more than a thousand pounds of gold. Do you not realize that the longer the candle which is offered up for sins blazes, the longer it continues [to move] the saints to intercede for sinners? So allow the greater and smaller candles to blaze away, for it is altogether fitting for my house to gleam with candles." But recklessly he took no heed, until one night, unable to control his zeal when a visitor had donated some extra-large candles and had left the church after praying, Onesiphoros rushed into the ciborium in order to extinguish them and substitute smaller ones. Even as his hands moved greedily toward the object of his lust, a loud and terrible voice shouted out from the silver chamber of the Saint, "O, greedy man!" The sacristan was propelled right out of the ciborium in terror. And so we ought to obey the commands given to us by the saints with divine authority. Amen. On a slow Sunday I take a long bus ride to Kastoria, west from Thessalonica almost to the Albanian border. It is full of Byzantine churches, material evidence of the *Oikoumene*, Commonwealth, that had once embraced all the Orthodox Christians in these parts.

Sept. 7.—Sending forward my baggage by the direct road to Kastoria, I begin to descend at 6 through the vineyards of Boghatziko, pass over a fine plain, quite uncultivated, and at 6:45 cross the Injekara...We now cross a plain higher than the level of the river; at its extremity to the right is the Lake of Kastoria, on the margin of which we arrive at 9.30. The waters are stagnant, putrescent at the edge, and entirely covered with a green pellicle...Having skirted the western shore of the lake, we enter some gardens abounding in walnut trees, and halt among them at 10.10, near the gate of the town...

—W.M. LEAKE

Leake mentions a "large monastery" in Kastoria on the far side of the lake (now Lake Orestidha) but doesn't bother with a visit, being preoccupied by the quality of hospitality he is receiving from the local Greek Orthodox priest ("my konak is humble enough") and with consulting his timepiece at every move. But the eleventh-century Mavriotissa Monastery is the reason for my visit, at least the two churches of it that remain. They are famous for their exterior frescoes, and among their figures there is sure to be a Demetrius or two.

The walk from the bus station takes me through the town, a Balkan fur-trade centre for centuries, although there is no fur-trapping here in the denuded hills, only fur factories assembling fashions from fur scraps from Canada and Scandinavia. Naturally, one of the main roads—the lakeside drive—is named for Alexander the Great. But when Leake travelled the toponyms of the region were largely Slavicized: Selitza, Krupitsa, Mount Zmolska, Zagoria.

Just southwest of Kastoria hard by the Albanian border, on a forbidding bastion of rock and pine forest, Mount Grammos, Greeks fell upon Greeks in the final act of brutal civil war in 1949. There were five thousand Communist partisans high up on Grammos when the government bombardments began on August 10; twenty days later, Grammos was their mass grave.

Slavic-speakers from the villages all around the lakes here who had supported the Communist guerrillas—there had been references in Communist manifestos to "self-determination for Macedonian peoples"—fled to Eastern Europe and North America, leaving behind a terrain desolate and depopulated. When rhetorical hostilities flared up again, between Greece and the Former Yugoslav Republic of Macedonia in the 1990s, the Greeks stopped running the bus service between Kastoria and Florina, which is the last town in Greece before the FYROM frontier, a route that had once run through the luckless towns of the civil war, now crumbling and half-deserted. But a street near Kastoria's bus station is called *Grammou*.

The travel guide informs me that the alternative for the slavo-phone villagers had been the "punitive [Greek] government policy of forced assimilation against the Macedonian speakers—as all the lake-dwellers are." I take note of the present tense, and glance around me, not for the first time in Greece, wondering if I have wandered willy-nilly into my own tribal dreamtime.

"There is a lake, named after the place," wrote Anna Comnena in the mid-twelfth century in *The Alexiad*, "and a promontory broadening at the tip and ending in rocky cliffs juts out into it; on the promontory towers and battlements had been built by way of fortifications—hence the name, Kastoria [Latin, *castra*]." Her "accurate description," observed Leake from his vantage point on horseback in nineteenth-century Europe's Balkan back-of-beyond, "shows that no great change has occurred since the twelfth century."

I decide on a short detour to the very modest Byzantine Museum and inquire how I might see the "noteworthy Byzantine churches" mentioned in the guidebook. I am offered the services of Niko, the churches' key-keeper, and off we go, in a chatter of pidgin English and pidgin Greek; this is how I learn that *Evangelismos* means Annunciation, for this is the word Niko uses while pointing at the blotted remains of a fresco in a cramped eleventh-century church, probably some wealthy family's private chapel, which is slowly tilting earthwards under the burden of its art.

Leake didn't much care for Byzantine art, for all the effort he made to see it, tramping through mountain forest to visit the Monastery of St. Athanasius, for instance. The monastery had employed a cele- brated painter to renovate its frescoes: "...the figures themselves are in the usual Greek taste, intolerably stiff and unnatural." I can see what he means as I stand before a monumental Archangel guarding the entrance to a chapel: he's built like a block of wood and holding his drawn sword above his head as though he were wielding an umbrella, but I'm used to this way of depicting saints, the Ukraino- Canado-Byzantine version was my first view of them, and so I dart happily with Niko from one mouldering example to another.

On my own, I set out on a slow almost somnambulant walk along the lake to the monastery. In 1832 Leake noted that of Kastoria's six hundred families, one-tenth were Jewish and the rest were divided equally between Greek and Turkish residents, all of them under the command of Demir Bey, who paid his masters in Istanbul "25 purses a year" for the privilege of extracting and keeping for himself the revenue of the district's fifty villages. From the fishery alone he received twelve purses in rent from a certain Hassan Effendi, who in turn exacted a third of the produce from the town's fishermen, the only ones doing any *work* in these arrangements.

According to Leake, even those who travelled abroad and returned to Kastoria fell under the spell of the powerful effects "of the Turkish system" in which their countrymen had been embedded for four centuries—"a want of energy and an indifference to everything but the vulgar pursuits of life." One wonders if Leake ever managed to have a good time himself, whether, for instance, he would have joined the boisterous crowd of weekenders I see at the lakeside restaurant in the shade of ancient plane trees, the local fish grilling on the fire, the proprietor's barrels of retsina emptying into their glasses?

At the eleventh-century monastery of Panagia Mavriotissa, I marvel at the still-vivid frescoes on the exterior walls, warrior-saints guarding the church against those with impure hearts and sinful thoughts from stepping over the threshold into the sacred space of the chapel. There is indeed a St. Demetrius, his lower extremities whited-out by plaster, his torso girded with gold and red Roman armour, his noble head surmounted by a soft, round coiffure.

I enter the little church to marvel at the interior frescoes. As always in these chapels, beeswax tapers are stacked up for sale (you drop your coins into a little metal box), and you plant them in a round pan filled with sand, in memory of the living or the dead. And, as always, there is some power-hungry church employee or volunteer, usually someone ancient, spidery, and fleet of hand, who comes along a few minutes later, yanks out burning candles by the fistful, blows them out and throws them unceremoniously into a big olive oil can, presumably for recycling.

Thus, having nicely set burning two tapers for my parents, I am sitting meditatively within this ancient little Byzantine church whose frescoed saints and prophets, angels and evangelists and Fathers of the Church have lent their ear for ten centuries to quiet prayer, when in stomps a priest, bloated within his blue cassock, dishevelled and still chewing his lunch. Without so much as a glance in my direction, he grabs all the candles burning in the pan, mine along with several others, in his big fat hand and throws them as though they were garbage into the can already half-full with earlier discards. In my version of the Seventh Miracle of St. Demetrius, as soon as he has stomped out, I scoop out a fistful and light them all again.

Back in Thessalonica, I go for dinner in my favourite taverna around the corner from the rotunda, the brick sarcophagus now consecrated to St. George but built by Emperor Galerius who furiously persecuted Christians in the dying light of the pagan empire. For all his unpromising beginnings—low-born and ferocious—Galerius had nevertheless been favoured by Fortune. By the end of 297 he had won a complete victory over the harassing Persians, captured the harem of Narses, and pushed on from Armenia to take Ctesiphon in Persia together with its enormous wealth. Galerius declared himself a son of Mars and erected an arch here in Thessalonica to commemorate the victory. On my way to the taverna, with hordes of students from the nearby university milling about and cars labouring to get through the intersection, I stood just north of Egnatia Street and peered at the marble reliefs on the piers of a partial arcade with arches, Galerius's triumphal arch, once four pillars supporting a cupola. On the top zone of reliefs, Emperor Galerius enters the city on a horse, while crowds of people are cheering him outside the walls of Thessalonica. In a third zone, Galerius and co-Emperor Diocletian stand full frontal in battle armour alongside a square marble altar stone attended by figures in long white togas. The hero of the Persian wars extends his hand over the charred bones of the sacrificed animal—ritually slaughtered—adding a bouquet of herbs to the flames in a sacrifice of thanks. Emperors and generals exercised political power by the performance of sacrifice, the body of Demetrius crumpled in the baths no exception.

I have the taverna to myself, and I am tapping my foot to music from Greek films while Niko, the proprietor, a particular fan of Melina Mercouri, circles around my table pouring out the house retsina into a glass tumbler. He seems about twenty-five years old, but on a small shelf by the door he has arranged an old oil lamp, an ancient water pipe, a bouquet of dried flowers, and a bleached cloth as though he has laid out a shrine to the irretrievable past. He is very proud of his taverna, its dedication to good Greek cooking, as he is proud of the old photographs that decorate the walls, though he mourns the loss of his beautiful city. ("Everything has changed!")

He disappears behind a curtain to cook my supper—I smell garlic cloves sizzling in the pan—and I flip through the St. Demetrius comic book I've been trying to decode. PALI TA IDIA KANEIS! I read the big red letters inside a jagged yellow word-balloon. I can't translate this but I recognize the story; it is the wretched Onesiphoros, the rotund sexton half-hidden in the shadows of the Basilica of St. Demetrius, spying on the man who's bought the extra-large candles and is now at prayer in front of the icon of Demetrius, tears rolling out of his eyes. In the next panel the bug-eyed, quivering sinner, mere inches from the prize, is thrown as though lifeless to the floor. PALI TA IDIA KANEIS! thunders the Saint from the dark heavens above.

Niko brings me "his" *melitzanosalata*, roasted eggplant dip, rather oleaginous, with a blackened garlic clove and sprig of fresh dill stuck on top. He leans against the door frame into the kitchen, smoking.

I tell Niko what I'm doing here: haunting the Basilica of St. Demetrius and prowling through religious bookstores. And that for a break I visited the Museum of Byzantine Culture and chatted with the young security guard. We stood before a case of silver reliquaries, some in the shape of the Saint's tomb, and simple flask-like ampullae in which pilgrims bore away with them the *lythron*, the soil mixed with the holy blood from the tomb of St. Demetrius. Haltingly, the young guard explained that St. Lupus, one of Demetrius's students who had witnessed his martyrdom, took the Martyr's ring and smeared it with the spilled blood, with which he was then able to perform miracles of healing; and he added shyly that once, and once only, when he was in the presence of this blood himself—standing here, doing his job, guarding the treasures, these reliquaries in the glass cabinets—he smelled the sweetest smell, as though he were standing inside a rose-bush, and knew he was in the presence of the Saint.

Niko leans against the door frame into the kitchen. He's not surprised, he says. While paying their respects in the crypt of the Basilica of St. Demetrius, both his grandfather and father heard the clangourous hoof beats of St. Demetrius's horse clattering over the stones as he descended from the medieval city walls.

He guards us still.

Back in Canada, I will look at the last pages of the comic book—translated by friends—curious about how the story ends. The story is set in October 1965, in Pskov, USSR, north on the Baltic Sea. A group of road workers and a team of atheist archaeologists all suddenly begin to dream of Demetrius, the Holy One. In each dream, he is astride a horse and holds a beautiful chalice he thrusts toward the dreamer, saying: "This chalice contains the blood of Christ, which will bring you peace. To learn who I am, go dig in such-and-such a place." The next day they start digging. In the next dream, he gives himself a name: "I am Dimitri Solunski, and Christ has sent me to you to bring you Love and Peace." On the thirteenth day of their excavations, they unearth a twelfth-century church of Demetrius of Thessalonica; among its buried treasure, a ceramic vessel of great value, identical to the one offered to each dreamer. It is the last page of the comic book, and there is one last message: "The Saint has never stopped helping all those who have called on him," even atheists and Communists in their disbelief.

⸭ *The Passion of Demetrius*

Tis Diocletian's natal day;
Proclaim throughout the bonds of Antioch
A feast, and solemn sacrifice to Jove!
Whoso disdains to join the sacred rites,
Shall feel our wrath in chastisement, or death.

—GEORGE FRIDERIC HANDEL, *Theodora*

::

It was the nineteenth year of Diocletian's reign and the month Dystrus, called
March by the Romans, and the festival of the Saviour's Passion was
approaching, when an imperial decree was published everywhere, ordering
the churches to be razed to the ground and the Scriptures destroyed by fire,
and giving notice that those in places of honour would lose their places, and
domestic staff, if they continued to profess Christianity, would be deprived of
their liberty. Such was the first edict [February 24, 303] against us....Then,
then it was that many rulers of the churches bore up heroically under horrible
torments, an object lesson in the endurance of fearful ordeals.

—EUSEBIUS, *History of the Church*

"WE CELEBRATE FOR SEVEN DAYS," Reverend Dimitrios
Vakaros explained to me, when I had asked him how the church in
Thessalonica would celebrate St. Demetrius's Feast Day. "We celebrate the Holy Week of St. Demetrius the same way we celebrate the
Holy Week of Easter." Since childhood I have known that Easter is the
supreme festival of the church year but I remember it as a festival
of one day, Easter Sunday, when we went to church very early in the
morning with our family's basket full of foods to be blessed for the
main event: Easter Sunday lunch. But a fourteenth-century Greek
bishop had spoken of the Passion Week of Demetrius as the Imitation
of Christ's Passion; and, after the long Ottoman interlude, then wars
and dictatorship in the twentieth-century, thanks to the intensive
efforts of the Metropolitan of Thessalonica, Panteleimon, the Holy
Week of St. Demetrius has been revived.

"On the Friday we have the relics brought into the middle of the
church and we put flowers. We sing some special hymns"—here he
hummed a verse in Greek—"as on Holy Friday for Christ and we make
a procession, the Archbishop and Bishop and priests all singing. We
have the Great Vespers"—the phone rang—"and there's a Great Litany
outside the church in the streets, and the next day, the Feast Day"—
again the phone rang and Fr. Vakaros was occupied some time—"the
bishops from all around the world participate in the Divine Liturgy,
the Doxology [concluding liturgical prayer of praise], because we
celebrate the Freedom of the City, too," the date of Thessalonica's
delivery into the hands of the Greek army from a crumbling Ottoman
authority, and just ahead of the Bulgarian troops.

Thessalonica joineth chorus on the day of thy commemoration, O thrice-
blessed Demetrius, and calleth upon all the surrounding cities to keep thy
splendid festival. And, assembling with them, we praise thy struggles in song.

—FROM LITTLE VESPERS

IN THE HOTEL near the Basilica, I have taken possession of Room
15, which looks out at the backsides of the neighbouring apartment buildings with their glory of clotheslines on the balconies. It

is Sunday afternoon and I eat lunch at an open-air taverna in the old market square.

In 1910 the Romanian Byzantinist, Oreste Tafrali, together with the rest of the scholarly world devoted to the history and archaeology of the "East," was horrified to learn that the Turkish authorities in Thessalonica were intent on the demolition of what was left of the Byzantine walls of that city. While there was still time to study and photograph them, Tafrali rushed to Thessalonica, armed with recommendations from senior scholars to the Turkish authorities, where he was graciously received. "His Excellency the governor of the *vilayet* of Salonica, Ibrahim Pasha...was kind enough to offer us all the facilities we needed for the happy outcome of our mission," he wrote two years later. "A police officer was put at our permanent disposal with orders to accompany us and protect us wherever we went." Alas, the walls were already partly demolished, but he set to work, together with colleagues from the French *lycée* in Thessalonica, to document the walls, especially their inscriptions from the Christian era, and eventually to broaden the task to one of a general description of the city's ancient and medieval monuments, their history and location. This was duly published in Paris in 1913 as *Topographie de Thessalonique*.

In 1910 Tafrali walked the grid-like layout of the streets of Thessalonica much as had its Greek and Roman citizens, from east to west on Vardar Road (now Odos Egnatia) between Vardar and Calamaria Gates, and Midhat Pasha Street (Odos Agiou Dimitriou), which began at Yeni-Kapou Gate and terminated at the gate the Byzantines called that of the archangels; Sabri-Pasha Street bisected these two thoroughfares from the embankment of Freedom Square north to the slopes of the city under its massive walls before turning sharply east at Yacub-Pasha Mosque. Unhappily, Tafrali arrived too late in the history of the city to be able to admire many of its most ancient monuments, although as recently as 1860, "there still existed the ruins of a Roman building called *Las Incantadas* by the Jewish population, a sort of portico of Caryatids" later disassembled and carted off to the Louvre in Paris. Tafrali includes a sketch of this portico while it was still in place, a bizarre juxtaposition of four slender caryatids holding up the sky while half-crumbled Corinthian columns with their capitals frame the ramshackle brick-and-tile hovels of the shantytown beneath.

Back in the hotel lobby, I watch a troupe of Russian monks arrive from Mount Athos, their worldly goods in boxes secured by rope and strapped to their backs. The hotel staff has just enough Russian to say, "There are no rooms." The city today, poised to begin Passion Week, is a magnet of desire, just as it was centuries ago when it also hosted the Demetrius Fair. The monks are turned away.

The great fair in Demetrius's honour traditionally began October 20, gathering together merchants from Syria, Egypt, Greece, Italy, Spain, France, and Russia. They streamed through the gates of Thessalonica's Roman walls and through its grid of Roman streets, converging on the agora or forum, still the focal point of public life and contiguous with the stadium. People crowded the hippodrome for horse races and the stadium for circus games, well into the ninth century. The New Testament Acts of the Apostles mention a theatre; the Byzantines used parts of it to build the city's western wall.

The Romans' water cisterns, public baths, and granaries still functioned. Hulking mansions and hospices and public baths of the medieval city spilled all over the slopes around the Basilica of St. Demetrius. In 1919 archaeological work uncovered a fourth-century crypt containing a baptismal font upheld by columns, and, in nearby graves, the bodies of four bishops, buried seated and fully clothed in their state vestments, which, as the astonished archaeologists stood at the now-gaping tombs, disintegrated in a cloud of dust.

"How do we know a saint?" I ask Simeon Paskhalidis, lecturer in hagiography at Aristotle University. Outside, the campus is a crush of students, lollygagging in clusters and yakking at full volume, but inside this dark-wooded office we sit serenely, and I begin to understand that I am speaking with yet another academician of faith.

"His saintliness is recognized by the devotion of the faithful," he replies, "not bestowed by a bishop or patriarch or even council but by all the people who lived in community with him. He had a public, the poor peasants as well as the local townspeople and functionaries, sometimes all the way up to the emperor. The main idea remains that, if the people of a local church believe that someone is a saint, this is the strongest evidence of his sanctity."

The popularity and power of Saints' Lives, as told and retold, circulated through entire communities and along extended networks. They were bestsellers in Byzantium, and when Alban Butler, an ordained Roman Catholic priest, travelled all over the European continent researching for his blockbuster, *The Lives of the Fathers, Martyrs, and other Principal Saints, compiled from original Monuments and other authentic records, illustrated with the remarks of judicious modern critics and historians* (1756–1759), he was able to compile more than 1,600 Lives. "To Thee, O Lord, the planter of creation," begins a hymn on Sunday of All Saints, "the world doth offer the God-bearing martyrs as the first-fruits of nature." Martyred bodies were the community's gift of gratitude to their Creator.

And there is the poetic or metaphoric "truthfulness" of myth or legend that resonates within the human consciousness in spite of the ravages of science and the archive. Modern scholars may be interested in what the hagiographies reveal about language, folk beliefs, historical persons and places, historical geography, and the social and economic situation of the protagonists, but the ordinary man and woman heard or read in them how God "bent down the heavens" and intervened in the most humble of their lives.

And St. Demetrius, whom all of Thessalonica appears to be gearing up to recall, venerate, petition, and praise, I ask Paskhalidis, how may a stranger like myself, a traveller from Ukrainian-Canadian Orthodoxy, receive his truth?

"St. Demetrius is an ecumenical saint," he answers a little sternly. "All saints of all nations are saints of Orthodoxy. This is the true spirit of Orthodoxy, and the traditions of saints of local and ethnic churches can survive in this ecumenicity. We don't have to consign them to the garbage." The traditions survive when people live together in the belief that these saints do belong to the whole Orthodox world. He illustrates this point with a quotation from the Liturgy in the Byzantine period, the special text or *Apolytikon* for the Feast of St. Demetrius, when one word was changed, but a whole mentality

shifted. It is the same point made by Professor Ivan Biliarsky in
Sofia and Fr. Vakaros down the street in Thessalonica. Once upon a
time in Byzantium, the people sang praises to Demetrius—"You are
the person who fights for us"—not just in Thessalonica but in the
Oikoumene, in the whole Byzantine world.

"In spite of all the libraries lost to fire, war, earthquake and
conquests by Persians, Avars, Arabs and Turks," thousands of Greek
hagiographical texts have survived, wrote Byzantinist J.M. Hussey,
and sometimes in dozens of copies. The sheer variety produced is
astonishing: "from the Passions of martyrs, then the eyewitness
accounts, to the epic novels; there are the Lives of non-martyrs,
usually monks and bishops; the collection of Miracles of healing
saints and other miracle-workers such as St. Demetrius; then the
panegyrics, eulogies...and the homilies in honour of the saints, and
the spiritually instructive narratives; and finally the synaxarions and
menaions, liturgical books in which one finds a Life according to each
day of the liturgical calendar, including odes and other hymns with
their allusions to the saints they exalt."

And then the iconographers read all this and "write" the icons,
sometimes even commanded to do so by the saint himself or herself,
appearing in a dream.

"Please explain the different biographies of St. Demetrius," I
entreat Paskhalidis, thinking of the *Miracles* by Archbishop John
written three hundred years after the Martyr's death, and of
Professor Milosevic's hope of a still-buried marble plaque in the
undisturbed tombs of Sirmium. About 412, Prefect Leontius built a
basilica in honour of St. Demetrius. But what of his relics? Did the
fleeing populace of Sirmium, starving to death under Avar siege and
making for Thessalonica, bear something of their beloved deacon in
their rags and cloths? His bones had been left to mingle with the ashes
of the devastated city, but did they carry his ring, his belt, a corner of
his cloak?

"The problem is that the earliest martyrology we have—the *Syriac
Martyrology*, martyrs' lists based on a Greek original of c. 360—
does not mention any Demetrius associated with Thessaloniki.
Sirmium, on the other hand, was already known to have a local cult

of Demetrius since at least 411 when the *Syriac Martyrology* mentions, for the date of April 9, simply: 'In Sirmium, Deacon Demetrius.' But by the end of the fifth century we do have a basilica dedicated to Demetrius of Thessalonica who is not mentioned in any text, however, until well after the founding of this sanctuary. As for the St. Demetrius relics, we don't have a strong tradition at any time." Even Archbishop John, the Saint's great admirer, writes only that "some say," the sacred relics are buried in the silver ciborium. "According to the Sixth Miracle," Paskhalidis continues, "the Christians of Thessalonica hid their martyrs' relics in many places from fear of the pagans. After many years, they no longer remembered where they had placed them except for St. Matronia from the Diocletian era. No one mentioned Demetrius."

Paskhalidis finishes on a note of light melancholy. In his passion for the Byzantine Demetrius he feels quite alone among the Thessalonians. "Nowadays, right here in Thessalonica, there is not even a very strong belief in the Saint. People believe he was a martyr and protected the city in ancient times, but now? He has become a patron of the whole city, not of individuals. He has become a civic figure."

Much of the liturgical material of the Church's services has been cut out of the modern Greek service, initially because of fear of Turkish repercussions, according to Paskhalidis, who regrets it very much and is still waiting for the restoration of the Byzantine Liturgy as it was last sung in 1453.

Kontakion (Second Tone): *God, who gave you invincible power and with care kept your city invulnerable, royally clothed the Church in purple with the streams of your blood, for you are her strength, O Demetrios.*

"DAY ONE OF ST. DEMETRIUS'S FEAST," I wrote to friends from
the Internet café just down from the Basilica. "One icon procession
done, and three Matins, three Vigils, one Epitaphios, and one Divine
Liturgy to go." I was about to undergo a deep immersion into my
inheritance, that "marvellous and profound ecclesiastical poetry,...
all Canons, Tropars, Kondaks, Irmoses etc.," about which Ukrainian-
Canadian Metropolitan Ilarion wrote so excitedly in 1953. "All this
in our Church is Byzantine and it all remains untouched even up to
our own age!" This is a bit of a stretch, to claim the undiminished
Byzantine in a church established by democratic even anti-clerical
homesteaders in twentieth-century North America, but I was willing
to be swept up in the sheer idea of a Liturgy once sung under the
swollen domes of the churches of Constantinople, Heaven bending
itself down toward us, Cosmos and Creation singing together.

The bulletin posted at the Basilica said that the procession of the
icon of the Virgin would start at 4 P.M. from the famous Byzantine
White Tower down on the waterfront. I arrive at 3:45 and mill about
in the very warm and humid heat in a crowd of matrons, priests, nuns
head to toe in black, soldiers in combat outfits and helmets, shouldering lethal weaponry, and choir boys in runners. I look at nuns
from face to face and am startled to see that they are all young, and
smiling and laughing. Priests rush about opening briefcases to extract
scarlet and gold robes, or stand around shouting into cell phones.
The throng progresses in fits and starts from the White Tower to the
Church of the Nea Panagia.

Once we arrive at the church a thunderous peal of bells joyously
rings out the formal beginning of the procession—the exit of the icon
of the Mother of God from the church, covered in silver plate and
trimmed with white roses and borne by priests and monks. Then we
all form up: clergy and nuns and choirboys, a handful of girls in folk
costume who I never see again, the soldiers, the officers, and the rest
of us. And off we go, uphill to the Basilica, led by the soldiers who are
marching in a modified goose step, rifles bristling with bayonets on
their shoulder. This is the trouble, I fear, with military saints.

We are mostly middle-aged women with a sprinkling of the young with their arms around each other (I follow a young man in dread locks) and the faltering elderly. We are not particularly solemn although the women all around me, walking arm in arm, sing hymns in a minor key to the Panagia (Virgin) and the Saint, in stiff competition with the jolly military music of the male marching band out in front. I keep the back of the icon in view, and the snouts of the rifles in procession behind it. We shuffle and step on each other's heels but nobody loses patience. Every church we pass rings out its rapturous bells while people lean on balconies and make the sign of the cross. Traffic stalls at our passage, giving me an experience of immense and gratifying power.

Outside the Basilica, banners of the Greek flag and the Byzantine double-headed eagle and of St. Demetrius as Guardian-warrior flap on long lines in the forecourt. And an enormous blue incense stand lets off puffs of frankincense as the bells clatter and clamour at our entrance to the Basilica. Inside, city police queue up to venerate the icon, taking care to kiss the Saint and not his horse.

The official title of the Roman emperor was *dominus et deus*, Lord and God; his forehead was crowned with the mystical diadem, borrowed from the (Iranian) Sassanids, symbolic of the sun and eternity. "The public saw [the emperors] robed like religious idols, their heavy brocaded gowns falling in shimmering folds, a golden girdle about their waists, their wrists and ankles sparkling with precious stones; and whoever spoke to them had to perform the rite of *adoratio*, of *proschynesis*, in which the subject prostrated himself upon the ground and kissed the hem of his emperor's cloaks," as the novelist-turned-church historian Henri Daniel-Rops wrote so vividly in *The Church of Apostles and Martyrs.*

We are apparently repeating an ancient repertoire of gestures appropriated directly from the pagans—speeches in praise of the gods, processions in their honour, dedication of monuments inscribed with evocations of their stupendous deeds, sacred songs, and even incense. Like them we ring bells, commission votive plaques, and scatter holy water on loaves and fruits of the field to hallow their importance to our physical being. When we fall asleep in the "presence" of the Saint in his tomb, we hope, as did the ancients, for visions in our sleep. But now we repeat all these in praise of Demetrius, who has proved more powerful than all who went before him, hero, sage, or daemon.

When I walk into the Basilica and up into a side gallery and look down into the nave, I can see the whole assembly as a swirl of movements that together compose the choreography of veneration. Priests enter and exit through the doors of the iconostasis; they put on, they take off vestments. In black stovepipe hats and the gorgeous brocades of imperial red and gold, orange and white, they form parallel lines before the icon of the Virgin, while the firm, unwavering song of the deacons leads us all in our genuflections—the sign of the cross from forehead to breast, the dip with one hand down to the floor—and then the people surge up the centre aisle to the icon, to kiss the silver hand of the Panagia who holds it up in the gesture of the *Hodegetria*, she who shows the way, small, elegant fingers pointing to her baby. *He is the Way.*

The collective memory of St. Demetrius of Thessalonica is 1,697 years old.

:: *October 24*

THE BULLETIN at the church door said 7:30 A.M., and so the bells ring once, twice, and I am there at 7:45, but we are very few, mainly women (all choosing pews on the left), the icon of the Panagia still in front of the altar with her garland of pink and white blossoms. Three cantors sing and chant the text—two elders who mainly thrum while a stocky young man in a yellow and black football sweater, his thick black hair swept back, sings in a high-toned baritone, elegant ascending and descending phrases, keeping the beat with a rhythmic rocking up and down off the balls of his feet. Presently, a young priest, hatless, hair pulled back into a knot at the base of his neck, wearing gold and white vestments, emerges from behind the iconostasis with the censer.

This is a large basilica—five aisles wide—and up and down them all he goes, hell bent for leather, swinging the censer like a yo-yo at the scores of icons distributed throughout the church. The worshippers turn their bodies as they follow his progress, making the sign of the cross when he passes them. He remains expressionless throughout and never makes eye contact. Maybe he isn't the point—his action is? At 8:00 and at 8:30 there is a fusillade of bells.

That evening a multitude of the faithful gather for the service of the Epitaphios, the carrying of the relics of the Saint around the nave. Again I stand in the gallery so I can look down on the proceedings, an excellent vantage point for seeing what mysteries are being performed behind the iconostasis, that exclusively male zone, and for taking note of the fact that the male priesthood is serving an overwhelmingly female community of worshippers.

It is a spectacular service, and from where I stand I see how the entire interior, of bodies and light, colour and textures, moves and flows in an elaborate choreography of ritual and veneration. People enter and leave the Basilica in continuous streams, light their clutches of beeswax tapers, venerate the icons, and line up patiently to approach the icon of the Virgin, still splendid in her border of white and pink flowers. Right behind them a small, grizzled man, I assume a church employee, squirts disinfectant from a spray bottle followed by a swift, discreet swipe of the glass cover, wiping it clean of all its kisses.

Behind the iconostasis perhaps fifty priests, swaddled in their sumptuous vestments, line up with lighted tapers and make their way out into the nave. Here they move about in synchronized patterns performing different tasks—one censes the relics, genuflecting before the Bishop, another refills the incense burners and passes along the gold flasks of blessed water, others, singing the hymns, hold the wicker baskets full of flower petals that the Bishop flings, both hands at once, over the heads of the faithful, and they drift down to the floor, confetti of a celestial wedding. *The Bridegroom cometh.* One poor priest has been assigned throughout the job of managing the Bishop's long red robe, fussing with it as the Bishop stands up, sits down, turns this way and that and back again, oblivious to the frantic efforts of his subaltern to untwist the plush red yardage flowing from his shoulders. The clear and powerful voices of the chanters and priests together in plainsong—the Byzantine style of ecclesiastical music is based on the chants of the synagogues of Jerusalem and Antioch in apostolic times—sounds to my spoiled Slavic ears more Islamic than Orthodox, but I am mesmerized, the ceaseless, powerful drone pinning me breathless to the gallery rail.

The delivery of the Sermon is a signal for a general milling about again, and so I walk out into the nighttime streets—into a traffic jam and sidewalks crammed with shoppers, popcorn sellers, a merry-go-round, and a woman with a huge bouquet of balloons for sale, including one of Tweety Bird. Well, all right: the Feast of St. Demetrius was the occasion all through the Middle Ages and beyond—even the Turks honoured St. Demetrius's tomb and opened it annually—of a huge autumn fair that drew people from all over the Balkans. They probably had their version of Tweety Bird, too.

The twelfth-century traveller, Timarion, who returned to Constantinople after hair-raising adventures in booming, bustling, cosmopolitan Thessalonica, tells his old friend, Kydion, all about it. His purpose had been to pray in the churches, but he made sure to get there in time for the Demetria, the great fair leading up to the Feast Day of St. Demetrius. We may imagine that Kydion, sophisticate of the imperial capital, waits to be amused by his friend's account of how they do things out there in the provinces, so Timarion lays it on a bit thick. "Not only does the native and indigenous throng pour in but also men of every conceivable race and country....In short, the shores of the ocean send pilgrims and sightseers to the martyr, so famous is he in Europe." From his vantage point on a hill overlooking the city, he viewed the panorama of the fair, and exulted in its babel of sounds, the "whinnying horses, lowing cattle, bleating sheep, grunting pigs, and barking dogs." Walking among the hundreds of merchants' booths, his discerning eye noted the brocades and linens "and all the things that merchant ships bring from Italy and Greece," and from Egypt, Spain, and the Black Sea, sent down to the city on the Thermaic Gulf by horse and mule train. Thessalonica's own hinterland is rich, too, with immense vineyards, orchards, and olive groves, which oblige the traveller to ride its roads for hours on end before reaching the city gates.

After all that excitement, he goes to church; after all, as he tells Kydion, "I told you before how pious and holy the object of my trip was."

According to a history of the city of Thessalonica, a religious procession in imitation of the route walked by the Saint on his way to martyrdom was reproduced on the evening of October 25, right down to the closing years of the Byzantine period in the early fifteenth century. All the churches of the city were decorated and brilliantly illuminated as the crowds began their procession in the falling light, led by the Archbishop and clergy and surrounded by cantors and people bearing candles, from the site of a church founded within the galleries of the market. They paused at the Church of the Acheiropoietos (future site of the victory service of Sultan Murad) and then proceeded along the Egnatia Road to the Basilica. Once the crowd had arrived at the Basilica, the Liturgy began and would continue for three days, while the most devout of the people, hands tied behind their backs, paced around the church in imitation of the Saint's ordeal.

Not only was the Saint venerated on his Feast Day but also every Sunday, Wednesday, and, in the Church of the Acheiropoietos, every Friday together with the Virgin. Wednesday was the day of the Saviour's betrayal and also the day when Demetrius was born; Sunday represented his ascension and eternal installation at the side of Christ in Heaven.

One would think, then, that the medieval Thessalonians were a very pious people, that their participation in this pomp and circumstance in honour of their beloved Patron led to the cessation of all disputes, that all discord evaporated as they went about their devotions, their souls in the grip of piety, but their fourteenth-century Archbishop, Gregory Palamas, knew them better. He complained about them in his sermons, that they came only now and then to Mass, and no longer to Vespers and Vigils at all, they had reduced the number of feast days and even had no compunction on those days about committing the sin of *working*. When they did bother coming to Mass, they no longer sang the hymns along with the cantors, they did not pray with any focus on God, and, worse yet, they no longer paid serious attention to the Liturgy, producing scandalous scenes instead: while the priest was officiating, some people chatted together, arranging business deals, and turning the church, this house of prayer, into a marketplace.

The Christian virtues were in full decline, people sought only their own amusement, they hung out at the theatres at the fair to gape at the foolishness of the clowns and acrobats, they loitered at the cabarets profaning their own bodies shamelessly.

But such amusements! Well into the Ottoman era, the great fairs continued to draw the crowds (and fill the coffers of the taxman). The "incessant traveller" of the seventeenth-century, Evliya Celebi, son of the chief jewellery designer in the Ottoman palace, and who roamed the Turkish provinces, described how, at a great market in Macedonia, just north of Thessalonica:

> Once a year, at the time of the cherries, 100,000 men from the Ottoman Empire, Arabia, Persia, India, Samarkand, Balkh, Bokhara, Egypt, Syria, Iraq, the entire West, and generally from the four corners of the world all the merchants of the land and sea, come together at the panegyris [fairs of the Saints]. All types of goods are sold...a great sheep market....There is also a slave market. Thousands of sun-bright and moon-faced beautiful youths and maidens are sold....There are also more than a thousand coffee houses and shops where they sell ices....All the sleight of hand artists and acrobats who exist on the surface of the earth are to be found in the squares and tents....In all the tents and the open market there are, from every land, singers, players of kithara, dancers, wrestlers, athletes, archers, brave and handsome youths, honourable and beloved boys of their era, and even female singers.

:: *October 25*

I ARRIVE AT 9:30 P.M., just as Navy recruits shouldering rifles debouch in front of the Basilica: Demetrius is a matter of State as well as of Church. I see Red Cross nurses; military officers and reservists; cameramen; men in suits in front of the episcopal throne. Nuns gripping candles cram into the side aisles alongside altar boys in sneakers. Workmen hammer away at the processional icons while deacons chant from the Psalter dressed in black with purple neckbands. Four huge wheels of bread are propped up in the centre of the nave. There are priests everywhere. It is all over in fifteen minutes, including the Homily, but not everyone leaves. Small groups sit in huddles in the pews, whispering to each other. Tonight is the Vigil over the tomb of Demetrius.

The rest of the week becomes a blur of Matins, Vespers, another Vigil, and a Divine Liturgy. The red votive lamps that hang suspended on silver chains in front of all the icons, the quivering flames of hundreds of sputtering beeswax candles, the scintillating bronze rings of the enormous chandeliers cast an elaborate pattern of light and colour picked up by the scarlet and gold and white vestments of the priests and the warm amber glow of the gold of the mosaics. The priests pass the Litanies around among themselves while the male choir sings the responses and worshippers whisper along with them. The Lamentations make my hair stand on end. Flowers give off their perfume in the heat and light. There is a "dance" of all the processions up and down the aisles, priests swirling around, genuflecting, embracing, the people themselves in constant motion. I feel like one of those emissaries of a barbarian kingdom who, visiting Constantinople the first time and entering Hagia Sophia, cap in had, looks around in wonderment at the architecture of Paradise and faints.

Finally, on October 26, the people and clergy of medieval Thessalonica moved again in procession through the city, bearing icons past the partly submerged Church of the Kataphyge, or Refuge of the Virgin.

Timarion watched and gaped: "It was a spectacle that gave me no ordinary delight....The chosen leaders...made the procession a marvellous sight, being men all in their prime, all glowing with health...respendent in their silk and studded garments, their hair thick and gold....Beneath them their Arabian horses pranced along, pawing the air and rearing up as though to leave the ground and fly."

The emperor or the governor and his retinue finally arrived at the Basilica, followed by noblemen and noblewomen and surrounded by their horseguards, as well as foot soldiers. The crowd formed up in the passage and greeted them with loud acclamation. They had come for the Divine Liturgy. As had Timarion: "Then from those who had specially practiced the rituals of the festival—what a congregation they had there—there was heard a most divine psalmody, most gracefully varied in its rhythm, order and artistic alternations. For it was not only men who were singing; the holy nuns in the left wing of the church, divided into two antiphonal choirs, also offered up the Holy of Holies to the martyr. And when every part of the spectacle and service had been properly concluded, we too invoked the saint in the customary way, praying to the saint for a safe return..."

Nothing could be more amazing than the fearless courage of these saints under such duress, the stubborn, inflexible endurance in youthful bodies.
— EUSEBIUS, *The History of the Church*

A SECOND EDICT from Diocletian in 303 ordered the arrest and imprisonment of all bishops and priests without option of offering sacrifice. In November 303, on the twentieth anniversary of Diocletian's reign, a third edict granted amnesty to bishops and priests on condition they offered sacrifices. If they refused, they were to be tortured into compliance. Still Diocletian insisted this be a bloodless repression, for he wanted civil order in Rome, not martyrs in Paradise. But the fourth edict in 304 moved to outright repression and, finally, the grim determination of the civil authorities to impose order among the Christians met head on with the equally ghastly resolve of many of the Christians to die the "second baptism" of martyrdom for their refusal to approach the "abomination" of sacrifice in the pagan temples:

> *Then, then it was that many rulers of the churches bore up heroically under horrible torments, an object lesson in the endurance of fearful ordeals; while countless others, their souls already numbed with cowardice, promptly succumbed to the first onslaught. Of the rest, each was subjected to a series of different tortures, one flogged unmercifully with the whip, another racked and scraped beyond endurance, so that the lives of some came to a most miserable end. But different people came through the ordeal very differently: one man would be forcibly propelled by others and brought to the disgusting, unholy sacrifices, and dismissed as if he had sacrificed, even if he had done no such thing; another, who had not even approached any abomination, much less touched it, but was said by others to have sacrificed would go away*

without attempting to repudiate the baseless charge. Another would be picked up half dead, and thrown away as if already a corpse...

Those who died in the faith as "witnesses" to Christ's own Passion, often anonymously, were those "whose names are known only to God." Having died "for the glory of Christ" the Martyr had "fellowship forever with the living God." For those who lived after them, the martyrs also lived on as "mediators" of their prayers to God and there are numerous examples, from the era of persecutions, of martyrs who promised to intercede for the living—even for their own torturers— once they had attained to Paradise that very day of their soul's departure.

As the Jesuit historian of martyrology, Hippolyte Delehaye, wrote of their witness: "All that raises man above himself, this is what the idea of the martyr evokes in us, as it imprinted itself on the Christian conscience during the period when the wood still smouldered at the stake." For months after the first edict, and through several others, the priest, deacons, and bishops of the Christian communities of Thessalonica, as everywhere in the empire, had lived with the imperial command to sacrifice to the emperor, and they had prevaricated or bribed or just waited. The unlucky—or the zealous volunteers—had been seized, tortured, sometimes barbarously executed, then went straight to Heaven. The repressions petered out, flared again; there would be panic and flight, then the incumbent authorities fell afoul of palace or army intrigues, or the Persians burst over the borders again, or the emperor died. But in 304 the situation had become much more dangerous: every citizen of the empire was under order to sacrifice.

But Dimitrie, strengthened by the Holy Spirit, defied the Emperor and remained steadfast in his faith, like a rock hit by the waves. He not only refused to sacrifice to the idols but he urged other Christians boldly to confess their faith, especially a young man, Nestor. Nestor, blessed by Dimitrie, beat the favourite gladiator of Maximilian, the powerful Lyaeus. Maximilian decided to have Dimitrie killed. On the morning of October 26, 304, the

soldiers of the Emperor entered the dungeon where Dimitrie was praying, and
stabbed him to death with their spears.

— REVEREND CEZAR, "The Great Saint Martyr Dimitrie"

"What is a saint for you?" I had asked Simeon Paskhalidis. "A
saint is a man like all the others," he answered, "but he managed to
defeat his humanity, receive gifts from God, such as making miracles,
and left behind holy relics after his death." So it was written of
Demetrius, in one of the Passions, that, while the martyred body of
Demetrius had been discarded by his killers, they were "all-holy" to
his followers. "[They] came at night to the place where the body had
been thrown. There they buried it with a mound of earth so that his
body would not become prey for wild animals....And many signs and
miracles of healing occurred in that place."

Ah, yes, relics, the bones that Demetrius may or may not have left
behind. I might have felt like a swooning Byzantine matron in the
Basilica, succumbing to the incense and candle heat and incessant
male drone of the cantors on Demetrius's and my big day, his Feast
Day, but was he really there? All week I had been feeling with rising
intensity that he was eluding me. In the wake of uncountable others
who had made their way over the centuries to this city to honour
the sacrifice and benevolence of the Wonder-maker of Macedonia,
I repeated the itineraries, the rituals of worship, the prayers. In
Orthodoxy, I knew, the cult of saints believed that men become saints
when God inhabits them, in life and in death. Saints are still "alive" to
us in their coffins and crypts, even as relics, and are one with living
Christians. To the "Church visible" they are the "Church invisible." So
it is possible to communicate with them, and, working as the hands
of God to perform His works, they do deeds of love even after their
death. It has been the *obligation* of Orthodox Christians to direct our
spiritual gaze toward them, who have pleased God, and in the canons
of the Seventh Ecumenical Council it explicitly instructs that we must
"hasten to the saints." Yet, as I stood in Demetrius's house, word-
lessly speaking to the spirit of a man who had once sat here on his
silver couch, who had moved among the sick and healed them, who

had turned ships around in the harbour and caused the fallen walls
of his city to rise again, who had thwarted even an emperor from
shovelling out his grave for the precious relics of his broken bones,
I felt that I was not in the grip of the Saint himself but in that of the
Thessalonians who pressed all around me, devout in their longing.
I was surrounded by his images, but Demetrius himself, I felt, was
elsewhere.

Historians themselves are sometimes at a loss how to "rationally"
interpret the Acts and Lives and Passions of martyrs on the basis of
which faithful Christians go about their festal venerations. As saints,
martyrs have sometimes supplanted the Virgin and Christ himself
in the awestruck imagination of villagers and townspeople who
dreamed of a patron. *Sympolites*, the Byzantines called Demetrius:
co-citizen. Hippolyte Delehaye, in the preface to the 1905 edition of
his *The Legends of the Saints*, refers unabashedly to "recent advances in
scientific hagiography"—scientific! By which he seems to mean skep-
tical hagiography, which has led more than one historian into severe
difficulties with his readers: "[I]f you express doubt about some
marvellous happening, which is well-calculated to enhance the saint's
glory but has been reported by the writer on insufficient evidence,
you are at once suspected of a lack of faith." Delehaye made a distinction, however, between the clouds of "rhetoric" that have vaporized
the martyrs themselves and the thoroughly admirable original,
simple narratives written with a pen "dipped in the blood of the
martyrs," which witnessed to their heroism. As Delehaye concluded,
he was engaged in the discrimination between "materials that the
historian can use and those that he should leave to poets and artists as
their property..."

Yet the "mad professor" of Sremska Mitrovica invoked "science"
as his witness, too, even without evidence. "Science can tell us that
Demetrius from Sirmium is a historical figure while Demetrius from
Thessaloniki always appears in legends. That's not science," he had
argued. "Why do the historical accounts never mention Demetrius of
Thessalonica? Why, when Emperor Justinian [sixth century] asked the
people of Thessalonica, 'What martyrs do you have?' they mentioned
only one woman? How come they didn't say, 'We have Demetrius'? In

the sixth century the people of Thessalonica don't know anything about this supposed Demetrius of theirs!"

I remembered his scorn, his scoffing. What if he is right? The skepticism was bracingly rational, but I preferred the amiable Right Reverend F.G. Holweck, who did not trouble himself with edifying distinctions between history and historiography. Indeed, the "scrupulous adherence to truth" being common to both genres, he was consoled by a reading of the Lives of the Saints as narratives of "spiritual prowess and heroic virtue," in a profane world of "sin and scandal, successful plunders and murders." The scientists of that world were welcome to their lucubrations—their "vehement naturalism"—but Rev. Holweck would approach the Passions of the Saints in a spirit of reverence and discrimination. The rational spirit, alas, had placed itself "outside the circle of spiritual phenomena," and was in no position to dispute the prayer that passes between the brokenhearted and their Saints.

In 303 seven girls from Thessalonica—among whom were three sisters, Agape, Chionia, and Irene—admitted to studying their Scriptures in secret, "considering their own family worse than enemies." When a persecution broke out, they fled to the hills. For refusing to sacrifice and hiding large numbers of copies of the Scriptures, they were eventually martyred at Thessalonica on April 1, 304. Irene was the last to die: "We prefer to be burned alive or to suffer any punishment you choose rather than hand over the books." On that same day, five women and one boy were accused of hiding Christian writings and of having refused to sacrifice once they were arrested; three of them were burned.

We possess few documents on the application of the edict of 304 in the provinces bordering the Danube, but the three sisters of Thessalonica keep reappearing, perhaps precisely because of the paucity of other materials: somehow or other, this story of the Great Persecution in Thessalonica will be told. French historian Paul Allard, writing in 1908, adds one man to the list of several Christian women who were brought before the courts in Thessalonica in March 304, for having refused to obey the newest edict to consume the meat of burned offerings. "The man's name was Agathon; among the women were three sisters who, the year before, had fled into the mountains after hiding several manuscripts of the Scriptures. After a period, they returned home where they were arrested." They were named for Love, Innocence, and Peace: Agape, Chionia, Irene.

The three sisters still speak from a fragment of their interrogation by Dulcetius, governor of Macedonia: "You, Agape, what do you say?" "I believe in the living God and I will not abandon the way of truth." "And you, Irene? Why do you disobey the emperors?" "Because I fear God." "And you, Chionia? What have you to say for yourself?" "I believe in the living God. I have been guilty of no impiety whatsoever." The matter was of the gravest concern: the empire depended on the guarantee of the gods for its economic and spiritual well-being. And here were unbelievers, the Christians, who would not perform the most elementary of acts for the commonweal. Was it so much to ask, that a Christian burn a few (inexpensive) grains of incense on the emperor's birthday? Accept a morsel of sacrificed flesh? The emperor was prepared to pardon anyone on the ground of repentance if he or she should resume "adoring our gods." Edward Gibbon summarized the situation: "If the empire had been afflicted by any recent calamity, by a plague, a famine or an unsuccessful war; if the Tiber had, or if the Nile not, risen beyond its banks; if the earth had shaken, or if the temperate order of the seasons had been interrupted; the superstitious Pagans were convinced that the crimes and the impiety of the Christians, who were spared by the excessive lenity of the government, had at length provoked the Divine justice."

Dulcetius pronounced sentence: "Agape and Chionia, who by their impiety and spirit of opposition have resisted the divine edict of our lords the Emperors and the Caesars, and who are still even today practising the Christian religion, shallow, foolish, and odious to all pious men, will be delivered to the fire. As for Irene, you are to be exposed naked in the brothel, bread will be brought to you every day from the palace but the guards will not release you." Demetrius isn't here. Where there should be a record of him and his sudden and violent end there is nothing. In the roll call of names of those died in 304 in Thessalonica there is no "Demetrius."

*At length, however, on the first of March [305], Diocletian once more
appeared in public, but so pale and emaciated that he could scarcely have
been recognized by those to whom his person was the most familiar. It was
time to put an end to the painful struggle, which he had sustained during
more than a year, between the care of his health and that of his dignity....He
resolved to pass the remainder of his days in honourable repose, to place his
glory beyond the reach of fortune, and to relinquish the theatre of the world
to his younger and more active associates.*

— EDWARD GIBBON

Over the winter of 304–05, Diocletian's health deteriorated, and
on May 1, 305, on a spacious plain before a great parade of troops in
Nicomedia, he addressed them, from a lofty throne, for the last time
as their emperor, and voluntarily abdicated. He removed the purple
robe and left the scene in a covered chariot, headed for his retirement
palace on the Dalmatian coast. Galerius, formerly Caesar and now
in control as the Eastern Empire's new emperor, zealously pressed
on with the persecutions, together with his unflagging second-in-
command, Maximin.

In Salona [Split] Diocletian had laid out, close by his birthplace
on the Dalmatian coast of the Adriatic Sea, ceremonial chambers
and service quarters, rectangular halls and circular vestibules,
Corinthian columns of marble and red granite, statuary in courtyards
and streets intersecting at right angles, with the imperial residential
suite overlooking the sea. The ruins may still be visited. He gardened,
he did some carpentry, he fished: "The little stream of the Hyader...
produces most exquisite trout." When an envoy from Rome travelled
to Salona to entreat the abdicated emperor to resume his office—the
empire was collapsing into civil war—Diocletian simply led him to
his garden. He leaned on his hoe and showed him his cabbages, their
heavy green heads sparkling with the spray from the sea.

The Life and Death of St. Demetrius, a Young Man of Thessalonica, April 304 (Two Versions)

:: *I*

BECAUSE THE ICONS SHOW HIM YOUNG, I imagine Demetrius to be, say, twenty-five years old in the year of his death. He was a Thessalonian born into the Christian faith, of pious parents who made sure all their children, girls and boys, were instructed in the dogma and gestures of that faith. He read Latin as well as Greek codices—Cicero and Virgil, as well as the Gospels—collected in his father's library. When the household gathered to pray, they chanted hymns modelled on the Biblical Psalms—*My soul magnifies the Lord, And my spirit has rejoiced in God my Saviour*—and when they celebrated the Eucharist, they did so communally with fellow Christians.

So, Demetrius in, say, 300: well-born, blooming with youth, gathers with his parents and siblings and a small group of fellow Christians in a large, well-appointed room in the "house of the congregation," perhaps their family home within the walls of Thessalonica turned over to the community for worship. From the late second century Christians had been instructed by *The Epistle of Barnabas* that "you are not to retire by yourself and live alone, as if you were already righteous, but you are to come together in one place and seek the common good."

Ideally, they lived isolated from the non-believers, away from their idolatrous festivals, banquets, and theatres, visited the marketplace only to supply the household's needs, and absolutely did not carry arms. But in the real world there was collaboration, if only the artist and craftsmen employed to depict a pagan deity or the soldier in camp serving under the "protection" of the sculpted eagles, worshipped as idols. How many others, Christians in their hearts, asks a historian of the persecutions, "silently obeyed detested orders?"

This is still the Roman world—the peristyled courtyard, the rose garden with fish pools, the luxurious marble and mosaic floorings in the *triclinium* where the family meals are served them by servants and slaves whose living quarters lie at the back of the house. They pray together, all turned to face the east—the direction from which Christ will return—heads uncovered and arms stretched out as though bearing the sacrificial lamb, faces uplifted to the Lord, and loud in their acclamations for the soul's ascent to and union with God. At the close of the day they sing an evening hymn, *Gracious light of the holy glory of the holy...*

Although "heretical" theologies were already denounced by 180 CE, until 150 CE the only Bible Christians possessed was the Greek Old Testament, and debates among them had been intense about the formulations of their belief. Initially from oral tradition, from circulating Gospels (of Thomas, Judas, and Mary) and Revelations, they had formulated the essentials of their faith and belief, and, if Demetrius's household had a library, he may have read for himself an embryonic Creed in Hermas's *Shepherd*: "First of all, believe that God is one, who created, fashioned and made all things to exist out of nothing;" and from the early martyrs, both Ignatius—"Be deaf when anyone speaks to you apart from Jesus Christ...who was truly raised from the dead, his Father raising him"—and Justin, who asserted that "in the books of the prophets we found proclaimed beforehand that Jesus our Christ would come."

They stand together—for hours—for readings from the Acts and Epistles and Apocalypses of the Apostles and the writings of the Prophets (the canonical New Testament compilation was still a hundred years in the future), a sermon, and intercessory prayer. They conclude with the kiss of peace. *Amen,* they say: So be it. Then their Bishop gives thanks over the bread and wine that the celebrants themselves have brought and all share in the Communion. Demetrius's family was noble: the gifts would be handled in gold and silver vessels reflecting the light of the candles sputtering in bronze candlesticks. They were compassionate, and took up a collection for the poor.

Demetrius prayed aloud, and loudly, but meditated in silence, sitting alone in the garden, always facing east.

Although some Lives of St. Demetrius make him a Roman army officer, *my* Demetrius never had the stomach for the Roman army and the glorification of the martial virtues, nor for their temples. Roman gods may have been appeased by the ritual sacrifice of the animals, but Demetrius's Lord required only a penitent heart. Some fiery bishops encouraged their flock to seek glory in martyrdom— become the Lord's Athlete, seize the palm and crown—but Demetrius was haunted by images of torture and by nightmares of being ripped apart by wild beasts and burning alive at the stake. According to the Church, while his soul rose up to Paradise, borne in the arms of angels, his flesh would feel nothing. Greeted by ranks of seraphim "with acclamations of admiration and triumph," he would take his place in the communion of saints, angels, and the Divine Master Himself, in a glory of light. But he wavered.

Demetrius and his brother and sister catechumens, after three years of preparation and scrutiny, and having prayed and fasted, were exorcized by the Bishop, immersed naked in blessed water, washed of their sins and reborn into their new life "in the name of the Father, and of the Son, and of the Holy Spirit." Their new status in the fellowship of Christians was sealed with a laying on of hands and anointing of the head with oil, a kiss of peace and a first Communion of milk mixed with honey—symbols of the newborn soul—along with the bread and wine.

The hagiographies all say Demetrius was arrested for preaching the faith, and so I begin to imagine him on the last day of his life, one April day of 304, going out to preach.

I imagine that Demetrius emerges from an open portico and turns down the street from his house, his parents' house, which I think of as surrounded by cypresses and tall, ochre-coloured walls, toward the centre of the city, to the forum. He walks down a marble pavement, feet slapping it in thin leather sandals. This is still the age of the draped not sewn garment, white, embroidered folds of linen that sway to the stride of his legs; there is a jewel clasp at his shoulder. It is a hot morning. Some dogs give a perfunctory bark as he passes. There is no wind. I imagine the soft thud of oranges falling off trees in the gardens, but perhaps April is too early for falling oranges. Down the slope to his left lies the sea lacquered by a silver sheen. To his right, up the slope, loom the defensive walls patrolled by archers. He knows there are soldiers at the gates.

Ahead of Demetrius rise the elegant columns, white as chalk, of the temple and the arcades of the forum. It is so hot and airless that sweat beads then dribbles down the back of his neck, across his forehead, along his arms. He glistens, he shimmers. As he leaves the shadows of the houses on the marble pavements and crosses to the paved square of the forum, he walks shimmering in the glare of the sun.

Demetrius is now often afraid. His priest has already been dragged off to the prison cells. The homes of the deacons and subdeacons have been searched and Scriptures seized. But Demetrius enters the forum to preach, as usual, assaulted by the heat, the stench of rotting food and animal blood and excrement, hawkers' lewd banter and shouts. He teaches his listeners what he has been taught, but he himself is imperfect in his understanding. He knows he is not alone—the martyrs have preceded him—but he has not learned the mystery of their joy, their very chains "worn by them as a comely ornament," as was written of their early martyrs by the churches of Lyons and Vienne. There, under the brick arches of the market stalls, surrounded by his audience of townsfolk—the old woman with her fistfuls of mint to sell, her grandson the basket-weaver, the widow with her begging bowl, the blind poet with his, the sailor and fisherman and seamstress—he preaches what he himself has heard preached.

But I say unto you which hear, Love your enemies, do good to them which
hate you,

Bless them that curse you, and pray for them which despitefully use you.

And unto him that smiteth thee on the one cheek offer also the other; and
him that taketh away thy cloak forbid not to take thy coat also....But love ye
your enemies, and do good, and lend, hoping for nothing again; and your
reward shall be great, and ye shall be the children of the Highest: for he is
kind unto the unthankful and to the evil.

Be ye therefore merciful, as your Father also is merciful.

He has a modest but growing reputation as an inspired rhetor.

But this crowd in the forum is smaller than usual, and even most of
these have slipped away as the soldiers of Caesar Galerius approach,
marching lockstep toward him.

They have come to arrest him. They know him. He has already
once, twice ignored the edicts to perform the ritual sacrifice to the
emperor. Others he knows have been brought before the authorities
and questioned. It has just been a question of time, but he has been
steadfast and has not sacrificed. It is unthinkable. Since his baptism,
he has practised the disciplines of fasting, prayer, and alms-giving,
searching for that fixed centre of himself that is oblivious to the flux
of emotions and sensations. Now he will be tested.

The soldiers, helmeted and booted, their round shields held up
against their chests, grab hold of Demetrius. Unarmed, he offers no
resistance, even as they curse him and wrench his arms up behind
his back. They drive him ahead with such force that his feet almost
lift from the ground, and he does not hear the cry of those few of his
followers brave enough to shout "Help!" in the forum as others hide
in the shadows. Then these brave ones, too, fall silent as the soldiers
turn into the street leading to the baths, and Demetrius is no more to
be seen.

He is thrown alone into a cell of the baths. From that moment until
his death, Demetrius lives in total silence. Even the vermin make no
noise. A little light seeps through chinks in the brick wall. Even his
prayers are finally silent.

Outside, some friends stand sentinel in the shadows, anxiously waiting for a sign of his fate.

He is speared to death in the cell. He is one man against half a dozen soldiers. They burst suddenly into the room, blinding him with the shaft of light that strikes him through the open door. He cannot make out their faces but struggles anyway, the only sounds his heavy breaths and groans mingling with theirs as they try to hold him still enough to thrust the sword straight into his heart. For all his prayerful meditation on the glory of the martyrs, his own life is still so fresh and muscular in him, leaping through his blood, that he cries out in disbelief. The soldiers of Galerius leave him to bleed to death on the bare earth where his friends, having bribed a guard, creep in from the night, make him a shallow grave, then slip away, cupping bloodied soil in their hands as though they bear the Eucharist wine and bread.

I HAVE TRAVELLED AND STUDIED, I have filled notebooks and file folders and index cards, I have amassed bibliographies and collected memorabilia and souvenirs, I have taken photographs and written long letters, I have become familiar with the cast of characters associated with his Life—Galerius, Maximin, Nestor, Lyaeus, Leontius—I have visited his "home" and venerated his icons, I have even prayed as I knew how, in pursuit of St. Demetrius, and all the while he eluded me.

He eluded me as a Greek Warrior, then he slipped out of my sight as a Byzantine Saint, Great Martyr, and Miracle-worker of Thessalonica, too. I look again at his icon, which I carry in its blue velvet pouch: he is in fact featureless, or, rather, bears the features of a prototype, young, wise, at peace. But if I could interrogate eyewitnesses to his life, is this the face they would describe? Or would they say he wore a dark beard, that his skin was burnished from the Aegean sun, that he had a loud laugh and was bow-legged from riding his beloved horses so much? Or that he was fat and loved the theatre, until his conversion, of course, and then he became lean and studious?

If he was never a nobleman in his home in the silver ciborium in the great Basilica, if a Demetrius of Thessalonica was never martyred in the city let alone entombed in the crypt, if he was never there, who and where might he have been?

And a vision appeared to Paul in the night; There stood a man of Macedonia,
and prayed him, saying, "Come over into Macedonia and help us."

:: **II**

I PUT DEMETRIUS IN THESSALONICA ANYWAY. Why not? St. Paul
had chosen this bustling port city with a thriving Jewish diaspora as
a good place to bring the good news of the resurrected Christ and to
proclaim him to the Greco-Roman world, still 90 per cent pagan. He
strode about his world with staunchless energy, this little man with a
big, bald head, according to tradition. "His legs were crooked, but his
bearing was noble. His eyebrows grew close together and he had a big
nose. A man who breathed friendliness."

And so, in the spring of 50, Paul and his companions walked to
Thessalonica—they had high hopes for the place—and founded there
a church among the Gentiles. So as not to be a burden on the converts,
Paul settled in at his trade of tent-maker. H.V. Morton, writing a trav-
elogue, *In the Steps of St. Paul*, pictures the tent-maker, already weary
and sweaty from a day's hard labour, nevertheless sitting in the
evening among a circle of his followers and speaking to them. "The
gentleness, the tenderness, and the charm which Paul, a man capable
of so much nervous temper, expended on these simple converts is one
of the most beautiful things in ancient literature."

> *So, affectionately longing for you, we were well pleased to impart to you not*
> *only the gospel of God, but also our own lives, because you had become dear*
> *to us.*

Six months later, however, writing from Corinth, a correspondence
known as The First Epistle of Paul the Apostle to the Thessalonians,
he was responding to reports that some of them still had difficulty
maintaining chastity, while others were obsessively engaged in
various calculations and date-setting for the Second Coming instead
of attending to their practical duties: *Rejoice always,* he wrote, *pray*
without ceasing. A few months later he received another report; the

community was still holding steadfast amidst persecution but had become so excited about the Second Coming (a mere twenty years after the Ascension) that they had abandoned their jobs and were living off the Church's charity. In his reply, Paul reminded them that Jesus Himself had called on his followers to live lives of faithful stewardship and constant vigilance.

The Thessalonian Church survived, even flourished. Demetrius's Church is located somewhere between those first eager, anxious, exultant generations who hurried to a neighbour's home for their ritual meal, confident in the Heavenly banquet being prepared for them any day now, and that later church near the end of the fourth century, when the eastern congregations finally receive a complete eucharistic text, and a pattern of churches was laid down on the travel routes of the Mediterranean and centred in cities. On a map, they looked like a constellation of the Milky Way, thick clusters of dots in southern Spain, North Africa, Campania south of Rome, Egypt, Phoenicia and Judea, and in Galatea in what is now Turkey.

One hundred and fifty years after Paul, a theologian from Carthage, Tertullian (c. 155–222), was able to boast with gusto in his *Apology* addressed to the Roman governors: "We came but yesterday, and already we occupy your land, all your domains, your cities, your suburbs, your forts, your townships, your assemblies, your barracks. We have your tribes, your collegia, your court, your senate, and your forum. The temples? These you may keep."

Then came the Edicts of Diocletian.

February 23, the feast of Terminalia, 303: Diocletian published his first edict "everywhere," ordering all copies of Christian Scriptures surrendered and burned and all worship meetings prohibited. Christians in the public service were dismissed and the manumission of Christian slaves was abolished. Incensed, a local Christian and eminent citizen tore the edict down from the wall; he was seized and roasted alive, "in accordance with the law."

But in 304 the law hardened: every citizen of the empire was under order to sacrifice.

Animals had been sacrificed to pagan gods throughout the empire on auspicious occasions. A portion of each sacrificial offering was used ceremoniously and the rest sold in meat markets to the public. Clearly, Christians should spurn idolatrous offerings. How, though, to defy that other idol, the emperor, whose public cult created a community of all the peoples of the empire?

For all its inclusive severity, the edict of spring 304 was difficult to enforce in a systematic way, given the absence of accurate registers of the population. Wielding newly compiled registers, street by street, soldiers called on residents to stand forward and sacrifice, but there is some evidence that a whole household could be registered as having discharged their obligation if one member undertook to do it. In the wealthier Christian households, that "member" may have been a servant or slave. Did it matter to the head of household that the servant or slave may have been a Christian himself and risked the fires of Hell if he sacrificed?

And it is here that I sense hidden the other story of my Demetrius.

Neither Christians quite nor quite idolaters,
Using our crosses and our images,
We are trying to build the new life
Whose name is not yet known.

— KOSTIS PALAMAS

In the comic book I bought in Thessalonica, looking for the Saint, a young and beardless Demetrius in a simple cloak pinned at the throat is standing in a field outside the city walls, gesturing to a group of rough-hewn men who look to be farmers or labourers. He is radiant with compassion. He says to them: "We cannot see the invisible God— this is why he made himself human....This is what St. Paul means when he says that 'and the Word became Flesh.'"

I have been obsessed by that young man in the cloak, handsome, articulate, well-shod. A missionary among the poor, he is a well-born citizen whose name has not in fact come down to us. He has divided up his inheritance among the poor of Thessalonica, and he has their riveted attention. So now I turn mine to those rustic labourers and slaves who form his audience. My Demetrius is among them, listening to the preacher's words: *Blessed are you poor, for yours is the kingdom* of God. *Blessed are you who hunger now, for you shall be filled.* "Whoever says he loves God," the young preacher goes on, "must not nurture evil thoughts about or have bad feelings in his heart even for his enemy. Whoever has money and personal possessions and does not share with the poor, the love he says he feels for God is a lie."

Demetrius cannot believe his ears. His master is a Christian, the whole household where he labours has been converted, but it is crumbs the master doles out to his slaves at the *agape* meal.

And so Demetrius weeps with relief. St. Paul himself had said to the Thessalonians: "But we were gentle among you, even as a nurse cherisheth her children." He comes again and again to this field near the sea, on a fixed day before it is light, before he is missed in the house, as do other slaves and servants, some with their children, and some peasants driven off their land and now begging in the city, a demobilized soldier, an old woman from the marketplace, the widow who sells the wild herbs she gathers from the wasteland. Wool-workers, cobblers, and laundresses. The unmarried and orphaned. None are wise or influential, many are despised and count for nothing. Demetrius's own poor parents sold him into slavery, and he has no idea where he was born or who his people are. His loneliness has been his own to bear.

They sing a morning prayer: *Helper of those who turn to you, light of those in the dark, creator of all that grows from seed, promoter of all spiritual growth, have mercy, Lord, on me, and make me a temple fit for yourself.* They are all nobody's people, they will become each other's. Where three of them are gathered, the young rhetor has said, "There is the church."

Liturgy means "work of the people," an action done in common: "Let *us* pray to the Lord." So they stand and sing in alternate verses a hymn to Christ, and bind themselves by a solemn oath, never to commit any fraud, theft, or adultery, then exchange a kiss of peace, "after which it was their custom to separate, and then reassemble to partake of food—but food of an ordinary and innocent kind," in the report of a governor sent off to Rome. Their utensils are carved crudely of wood and they eat from a common bowl.

How they loved one another! For the first time in his young life, the slave Demetrius feels he has been unburdened, for an hour, a day, and another day: God loves him more than he himself knows how to love, but he will try—he will share his bread with the beggar at the door, give up his sleeping place to the young, feverish cook's help, say prayers for the departed soul of the master's mother.

So my Demetrius is a pious young Christian who loves Jesus Christ with all his heart, with all his mind, with all his soul. And now, on market errands, he has heard of the edict that all residents must sacrifice at the temple, and the master of the household has assembled everyone, including the servants, and has turned to him, Demetrius, and told him that he must go to the temple and make the sacrifice and come back with the certificate that will protect them all from harassment and worse. No one will bother him. He's a man of no importance. Go.

Demetrius goes.

I think of him dragging his feet along the street. He is trying to imagine what will happen when he gets to the temple. He has never seen this sacrifice, only seen and heard the bellowing animals driven through the market streets before the priests—the beauty of them, their horns gilded, their sleek hides groomed like a coiffure over their superb flesh—not the blow of the axe or knife that fells them and opens up their throats to the streams of their blood. He knows of the dutiful son of a local patriarch who slaughtered fifty-one bulls and thirty-eight goats at his father's tomb. Wild animals are slaughtered in the arena along with gladiators. This endless bloodletting: Christians have urged prayer with a pure heart instead. When they break bread and drink wine in remembrance of the risen Christ, he knows now that, after Christ's perfect sacrifice, there can be no more.

But he has another memory, too, that of the smell of the roasting meat, portions of which will soon be distributed among the pagan faithful, most especially the poor whose only chance comes once a year to eat a bit of meat and stave off hunger—that nagging, enervating hunger of the poor who do not quite starve. Demetrius has never tasted roasted meat, though he has salivated at the smell, and vomited.

It is noon, he is sweating from the sun that blazes like fire in the firmament, it is the Sixth Hour, the hour when Christ died on the

Cross and the lambs of Passover bled to death in the synagogues all over the Promised Land. Then his friends received His dead body from the tree and laid Him in the tomb. And when the mourning women—Mary Magdalene, Joanna, Mary, the mother of James, and others—came there with spices for his shroud, they found two men in shining garments standing by the rock at the empty tomb. Imagine their perplexity, their alarm. Yesterday, the tomb was filled with the reek and pitch of death, and now the tomb is empty and they are standing in the light of the angels. *And it came to pass, as they were much perplexed thereabout, behold, two men stood by them in shining garments: And as they were afraid, and bowed down their faces to the earth, they said unto them, Why seek ye the living among the dead? He is not here, but is risen.*

Demetrius tries to imagine what would move him to do his duty to the emperor and the indifferent gods. But he literally cannot imagine himself making the requisite gestures, not even the least grain of incense dropped onto the fire, even in mockery or deception. He wonders if there is perhaps some part of his heart that God has left as it were uncreated from which he can invoke the energies of Isis and Serapis, but the thought makes him tremble. He refuses to sacrifice.

He has found his courage. The preacher has taught that the immortal souls of martyrs take precedence over all other souls and are received immediately in Heaven. The doors of Paradise will open for him just beyond the city walls. And this day of his death is his true birthday, the day of his Passion.

He dies under torture. The soldiers drag his body out onto a small wasteland and leave him in the weeds. His master makes no enquiries, but the household does pray for his soul for a few prayer meetings. His body lies unclaimed. Under cover of dark, however, the slaves and servants of the house bury him hastily there where he lies. It is only to keep the dogs away: already the ground seems a kind of charnel house strewn with the remnants of the unluckier dead, whose exposed remains are all that the "beasts and the fire had left, part torn, part charred" before these, too, will be burned to ashes and swept into the sea. They will come back when it is safer to rebury him in the hallowed ground outside the city gates. When it finally is safer, in the year 311, they, too, are dead or have scattered or have forgotten the spot in the weeds. Demetrius's grave is unknown.

...Concerning the ritual of reading the names of the deceased, what can be more useful or suitable; what can be more worthy of admiration?

—ST. EPIPHANIUS

EDMONTON, NOVEMBER 2, 2002, the Saturday before the Feast of St. Demetrius, "Soul Saturday," one of several celebrated during the Orthodox liturgical year in memory of all the dead. I looked for a Mass this morning and found it at my childhood church, St. John's. There were about ten of us, including the two priests, who were in purple vestments for we were in mourning. As snow fell outside, a soft light filtered through the stained-glass windows, while inside the candles flickered blue, green, red in their votive cups.

Two cantors have also joined us. One, a janitor by trade, is tall and bony, with a pitch-perfect baritone of a glass-like clarity. The other, a retired priest, small, pink-faced and white-haired, sings with a youthful, unquavering tenor. Together, their voices take up the Trisagion hymn, "Holy God, Holy Almighty, Holy Immortal, have mercy on us," in the simple melody I learned as a child, and I am so grateful for their gift of this that I weep.

This Liturgy is so intimate. We few have gathered as though on behalf of everybody else and create a little space of prayer and reflection inside a day—Saturday—usually spent rushing around. We have dropped out of it as though from another planet, to land here, repeating ancient gestures from another civilization.

As for St. Demetrius, he is here as Patron of the Dead. Today the first name of everyone who died this year in the parish is read out. We sing *Vichnaia pamiat'*, Eternal Memory. I have no idea who these people were, but that is not the point. Like them, and their forebears, I was baptized into this church, and this morning we've each agreed to gather as the *community* that remembers them in this service. And so the dead linger on for a little while longer because we stand here, holding a candle, and hear their names: Paraska, Anna, Dmytro, Steven, Sophie, Nestor, Jason...

Finally, we are silent. We blow out our candles. The priests withdraw behind the icon screen and close the Royal Doors. There is some rustling of garments, tinkling of silver plate behind the icon screen, and then the sanctuary, too, is silent.

"Speech is the organ of the present world," wrote St. Isaac the Syrian. "Silence is a mystery of the world to come."

I linger awhile, loitering in the silence of this space, as though this church already stands at the threshold of the mystery. Certainly, as a building, it has been blessed, consecrated, and set aside as sacred space, "the place where God's glory dwells," I read somewhere, and so the utter loveliness of this "other Heaven" and the admonition to stand here "with reverence and awe" holds me a few minutes more.

And the tongue is a fire, St. James wrote. It once sent me out into the world. Now I look around and see it burn without a flicker in the red lamp hanging on its gold chain before the Royal Doors. It burns in olive oil and it never goes out.

ANY BOOK THAT TAKES A DECADE to write is not the work of a solitary artist in an isolated garret with a license to print money.

In the first instance, I am grateful for the financial support of the Alberta Foundation for the Arts early in the project; and for the appointment as writer-in-residence at the Saskatoon Public Library and the University of Alberta, and as the Haig-Brown writer-in-residence at Campbell River, BC, as the manuscript developed. The University of Alberta residency also made it possible for me—with the generous assistance of the university librarians—to access obscure materials hidden away in far-flung collections or, in several instances not so hidden, right in the university library's own excellent collection of texts related to Byzantine and Balkan Studies.

In Saskatoon, I lived with the family of Val Veillard, Bob Eaton, and Oliver Eaton, and to them I owe not only their welcome but also their willingness to hear me out as I thought aloud about my writing difficulties. Thanks also to the Saskatchewan Writers Guild program of Artist Colonies: repeated stays in the colony at St. Peter's Benedictine Abbey, Muenster, SK, provided me not only the peace and quiet to write but also the community and encouragement of other writers and of the brothers themselves, who prayed five times a day, sometimes even for us writers. And to Andreas Schroeder and Sharon Brown, for the refuge of their writer's cabin on the sea at Robert's Creek, BC, and for their hospitality at their table.

While the book was still taking shape in the form of notes and outlines, I benefited from the conversation of friends and fellow writers who were my "sounding board" as I struggled mightily to wrest control of my material. I thank David C. Carpenter and Honor Keever, Teri Degler, Sandra Campbell, Susan Crean, Ron Evans, Susan Feldman, Linda Goyette, Mary Ann Hushlak, Bohdan Krawchenko, Ruth and Trevor McMonagle, Roger Murray, Andriy Nahachevsky, Ana Olos, Erna Paris, Olya and Marko Pavlyshyn, Marusia and Roman Petryshyn, Tom and Eva Radford, Robert Richard, Rhea and Ted Sampson, Joan Skogan, Natalka and Bohdan Somchynsky, Alex Stein, and Diana and Robert Stevan.

While the book was still very much a work-in-progress, I was grateful to Jennifer Barclay, David Margoshes and Shelley Sopher, Valerie Miner, and Lisa Solod Warren for invitations to submit to literary anthologies; and especially to CBC *Ideas* producer Kathleen Flaherty, for collaboration on two radio documentaries as well as unflagging enthusiasm for the ideas driving them and the book.

Crucial to the book's evolution was the fellowship of Rev. Don Aellen, V. Rev. Fr. Walter Makarenko, Fr. Taras Makovsky, Nancy Mattson and Mike Bartholomew-Biggs, V. Rev. Fr. Georg Podtepa, Marianna Savaryn, Fr. Myroslav Tataryn and Marusia Truchan, and Fr. Demetrius Wasylyniuk, OSB.

Specific informants in the course of my travels are named in the book. But I want to name here the friends who acted beyond the call of obligation while I visited them: Kaja and Bozidar Andrejevic, Galina Avramova, Ileana Cura, Petar Gramatikoff, Ljubica Janeslieva, Slavica Janeslieva, Sonja Liht, Vesna Lopicic, Olgica Marinkovic, Milan Nikolic, Stephanie Sampson, Bosa Stojanovic, Zdenka Vukobrat, and Diana Yankova.

Without the editorial—literary and intellectual—intervention, first, of the inestimable Barbara Pulling, then, very timely, of Curtis Gillespie and Mark Morris, and finally of the acutely insightful John Eerkes-Medrano, this book may have ended up as a misbegotten draft in the proverbial drawer. For the encouragement of her final edit, I thank Meaghan Craven.

For their years-long encouragement and *esprit de corps*, and for intelligent and sympathetic scrutiny, I am forever in the debt of Nena and Miki Andrejevic-Jocic, Denis and Kathie Bell, Ted Bishop, Debbie Bryson, Duane Burton, Anne Campbell, Chrystia Chomiak, Serhiy Cipko and Jacqueline Tait, Caterina Edwards, Brian Fawcett, Liz Grieve, Jim Harding and Jan Stoody, Trevor Herriot, John-Paul Himka, Kitty Hoffman, Lenore LeMay, Debbie and Heather Marshall, George and Julia Melnyk, Olenka Melnyk, Rae Parker, Srdja and Darka Pavlovic, Lloyd Ratzlaff, Lida Somchynsky, Eugenia Sojka, Frank Sysyn, Betsy Warland, Katherine and Jim Woodward, Irene Zabytko, and, especially, the wonderfully patient and provocative Eve Zaremba.

For her unsparing interrogations of my ideas and assertions, for the sense of urgency she imparted to the project, for the deep recognition of our resemblance, and for the shared attachment to her birthplace, Thessalonica, I am deeply grateful for the friendship of Smaro Kamboureli.

Finally, I thank my relations—Janice Kostash, John Hannigan, Elizabeth Kostash, Louise Kostash, Lydia Semotuk, and Verna Semotuk—for their unconditional, unwavering, and unstinting solidarity and love, even as I moaned and groaned, fumbled and flip-flopped, pontificated and importuned, and generally held forth: even when I lost faith, they knew there would be a book.

Earlier versions of sections of *Prodigal Daughter: A Journey to Byzantium* have appeared in *AWOL: Tales for Travel-Inspired Minds*, eds. Jennifer Barclay and Amy Logan (Toronto: Vintage Canada, 2003), *Listening with the Ear of the Heart: Writers at St. Peter's*, eds. Dave Margoshes and Shelley Sopher (Muenster, SK: St. Peter's Press, 2003), *Desire: Women Write About Wanting*, ed. Lisa Solod Warren (Berkeley, CA: Seal Press, 2007), and *Locating the Past / Discovering the Present: Perspectives on Religion, Culture, and Marginality*, eds. David Gay and Stephen R. Reimer (Edmonton: The University of Alberta Press, 2010). Portions have also been broadcast on CBC Radio's *Ideas* program, as *Pursuing Demetrius* (2001) and *Six Things You Need to Know About Byzantium* (2007).

ACKNOWLEDGEMENTS

PART ONE: *Demetrius among the Slavs*

:: **Prologue**

page 13, paragraph 2, line 4: "betray our entire history and one's nation!"
Metropolitan Ilarion, "Universal Tragedy," May 15, 2003.

page 16, paragraph 2, line 11: "beyond the eastern Mediterranean hinterland."
Fletcher, *The Barbarian Conversion*, xi.

page 17, paragraph 2, line 7: "earns almost universal respect." Adler, "They
can't do anything to me," *LRB*, January 20, 2005.

page 18, paragraph 3, line 16: "whether we were in heaven or on earth."
Zenkovsky, *Medieval Russia's Epics*, 67.

:: **Byzantium on the Prairies**

page 23, paragraph 5, line 9: "to the Lord and ask his counsel." Kelley, *An
Iconographer's Patternbook*, iv.

page 24, paragraph 2, line 14: "by grace and divine power." Quoted in
Florovsky, "On the Veneration of Saints," http://www.orthodoxinfo.com/
general/florov_veneration.aspx

page 25, paragraph 1, line 7: "who is what he ought to be" Cavarnos, *Orthodox
Iconography*, 47–48.

:: **Hiking for Demetrius**

page 31, paragraph 4, line 7: "the wall paintings are in almost good shape." *The
Byzantine Churches of Kandanos*, 154.

page 33, paragraph 1, line 1: "ravines and the desolate areas." *The Byzantine Churches of Kandanos*, 17.

:: *Mother Thessaloniki*

page 37, paragraph 1, line 1: "a Ladino greeting outside a synagogue." Fermor, *Roumeli*, 228.

page 38, paragraph 2, line 8: "sabres, daggers and pistols…" de Jongh, *The Companion Guide to Mainland Greece*, 204–05.

page 39, paragraph 1, line 7: "creation for the benefit of the Moslems." Kiel, "Notes on the History," 142.

page 39, paragraph 2, line 16: "ginger and other burning spices." Cited in Vacalopoulos, *A History of Thessaloniki*, 112.

page 40, paragraph 1, line 6: "the poor most of whom are dying." In Mazower, *Salonica*, 111.

page 41, paragraph 2, line 4: "gathered from Demetrius's tomb." Muir Mackenzie and Irby, *Travels in the Slavonic provinces*, 52, 55, 57.

page 41, paragraph 2, line 7: "Salonica than Paul himself." Clarke, *Bulgaria and Salonica in Macedonia*, 8.

page 41, paragraph 2, line 4: "knelt in the courtyard to pray." Morton, *In the Steps of St. Paul*, 245.

page 42, paragraph 1, line 21: "the manners of England are the best." Fraser, *Pictures from the Balkans*, 190.

page 42, paragraph 2, line 8: "sprinkled the races of civilized Europe." Cited in Todorova, *Imagining the Balkans*, 122.

page 43, paragraph 2, line 4: "We do seek her! We do seek her!" In Herzfeld, *Ours Once More*, 136.

page 43, paragraph 3, line 7: "to stay here [Belgrade] a few months." In Wolff, *Inventing Eastern Europe*, 42.

page 43, paragraph 3, line 15: "an absolute scoundrel, a drinker of blood." My translation of J. Philémon, in V. Colocotronis, *La Macédoine et l'héllenisme*, 347.

page 44, paragraph 1, line 1: "dervishes danced, close to the church of the Martyrs" Nikos Pentzikis, *Mother Thessaloniki*, 74–75.

page 44, paragraph 3, line 15: "near woods and swamps." Fine, *The Early Medieval Balkans*, 27.

page 45, paragraph 2, line 3: "a servile state by conquest in the 9th c." *The Canadian Oxford Dictionary*, 2001.

page 45, paragraph 3, line 6: "English, *slave*, Dutch, *slaaf*." Conte, *Les Slaves*, 89.

page 45, paragraph 4, line 15: "constantly changing his place of abode." Fine, *The Early Medieval Balkans*, 28–29.

page 45, paragraph 4, line 20: "their private parts they enter into battle with their opponents." http://www.clas.ufl.edu/users/fcurta/Procopius.htm

page 46, paragraph 1, line 3: "when it is easy to cross over the rivers on the ice." In Whittow, *The Making of Byzantium*, 69.

:: **Miracles on the Ramparts**

page 49, paragraph 1, line 6: "like a rock that did not move." Apostolos Vacalopoulos, *A History of Thessaloniki*, 19.

page 51, paragraph 3, line 13: "to write all the required books." Lemerle, *Les plus anciens recueils, Vol. I Le texte*, 205.

page 51, paragraph 4, line 5: "meaning of the Demetrian legend." Lemerle, *Les plus anciens recueils, Vol. I Le texte*, 162.

:: **History is the Dogma of Scars**
page 52, title: The title of this chapter is taken from Marshall McLuhan.

page 55, paragraph 4, line 4: "one continuous martyrdom" H.N. Brailsford, *Macedonia*, 61.

page 56, paragraph 1, line 8: "during the time of Turkish atrocities." John Foster Fraser, *Picture from the Balkans*, 12.

page 56, paragraph 2, line 5: "bullet through the jaw, dripping blood." In Clark, *Why Angels Fall*, 136.

page 57, paragraph 2, line 3: "and superhuman strategic insight." Mazower, *Salonica*, 275.

page 57, paragraph 3, line 3: "horror one can never easily forget." Karakasidou, *Fields of Wheat*, n285.

page 57, paragraph 5, line 2: "imagined community of the Hellenes." Karakasidou, *Fields of Wheat*, 148.

page 57, paragraph 5, line 4: "eternal enemies of the Greek nation." Cited in Chatzopoulos, "The Bulgarians in the Greek Textbooks," 273.

page 57, paragraph 5, line 8: "traumatized [their] Greek sentiment." Karakasidou, *Fields of Wheat*, 236.

page 58, paragraph 1, line 2: "Saint Dimitrios had triumphed again—over the Slavs." Mazower, *Salonica*, 280.

page 58, paragraph 6, line 2: "Slavonic population stops everywhere short of the sea." Muir Mackenzie and Irby, *Travels in the Slavonic provinces*, 66.

page 59, paragraph 2, line 19: "we natives of Thessaloniki?" Ioannou, *Refugee Capital*, 150.

:: *Demetrius among the Macedonians*

page 62, paragraph 1, line 5: "nothing could grow or reach maturity." Rose, *A Handbook of Greek Mythology*, 92.

page 62, paragraph 2, line 9: "pagan goddess of the fruits of the earth?" Nilsson, *A History of Greek Religion*, 109.

page 62, paragraph 2, line 12: "Athenians of old called the dead 'Demeter's people." Harrison, *Prolegomena*, 267.

page 62, paragraph 2, line 14: "a Church of St. Demetrius on the site of her temple." Farnell, *The Cults of the Greek States*, 48, 45–46.

page 63, paragraph 1, line 4: "make cakes for the sacrifices out of its produce." Miller, *Greece Through the Ages*, 98.

page 63, paragraph 1, line 9: "the abundance of their fields." MacMullen, *Christianity and Paganism*, 158.

page 64, paragraph 3, line 2: "the earth and the sea, and everything that is essential to us." In Tafrali, *Thessalonique au quatorzième siècle*, 134.

page 66, paragraph 2, line 1: "We get lost in the concrete and glass, / worship new gods." Wagner, *This Hot Place*, 49.

page 67, paragraph 1, line 11: "at the festival called the Chthonia." Detienne, "The Violence of Wellborn Ladies," 141.

page 69, paragraph 3, line 5: "faithful on Kasim's Feast Day." Cited in Lewis, *The Emergence of Modern Turkey*, 121.

page 70, paragraph 3, line 8: "adorned in its Justinianea Prima days." Muir Mackenzie and Irby, *Travels in the Slavonic provinces*, 161.

page 70, paragraph 3, line 11: "even produce a map." Maas, *Cambridge Companion*, 355.

page 71, paragraph 1, line 3: "no weariness ever overtook him." This text is part of the Internet Medieval Source Book. The sourcebook is a collection of public domain and copy-permitted texts related to medieval and Byzantine history. http://www.fordham.edu/halsall/source/procop-anec1.html

page 73, paragraph 1, line 9: "A map whose dimension is time, not space." Reed, *Salonica Terminus*, 181.

page 74, paragraph 4, line 8: "monumentally vainglorious buildings." Sam Vakunin, "Where Time Stood Still," unpaginated.

page 75, paragraph 1, line 2: "populous and blessed in every way." Procopius, *The Buildings*, 227. http://www.clas.ufl.edu/users/fcurta/Procopius.htm

page 77, paragraph 3, line 10: "pretensions to Hellenic descent." Kitto, *The Greeks*, 154.

page 80, paragraph 2, line 17: "The orphan of Banitsa would not be coming home." In 2003 the Greek government announced it would allow those "ethnic" Macedonians who had been expelled or forced to flee from Greece after 1949—28,000 of them children—to enter Greece, correcting a 1982 law on repatriation that had been applied only to those "Greek by genus." According to the 2003 U.S. Department of State's country report on human rights practices for Greece, "there were occasionally complaints that the state limited the right of some individuals, particularly Muslims and Slavo-Macedonians, to speak publicly and associate freely on the basis of their self-proclaimed ethnic identity....A number of citizens identified themselves as Turks, Pomaks, Vlachs, Roma, Arvanites (Orthodox Christians who speak a dialect of Albanian), or 'Macedonians' or 'Slavomacedonians.' The Government formally recognizes only the 'Muslim minority' (see Section 2.c.), and does not officially acknowledge the existence of any ethnic groups, principally Slavophones, under the term 'minority.' However, the Government has affirmed an individual right of self-identification....The Government does not recognize the Slavic dialect spoken by 10,000 to 50,000 persons in the northwestern area of the country as 'Macedonian,' a language distinct from Bulgarian. The minority's use of the term 'Macedonian' has generated strong objections among the 2.2 million non-Slavophone inhabitants of the northern region of Macedonia, who use the same term to identify themselves." http://www. state.gov/g/drl/rls/hrrpt/2003/27840.htm

:: *Demetrius among the Serbs*

page 86, paragraph 2, line 13: "radiation of the aggressor's bombs." "The Lethal Rays of Irony," in Colovic, *When I Say Newspaper*, 33.

page 87, paragraph 3, line 4: "otherwise they will all be scattered for the year." Notes taken during a telephone conversation, December 2000.

page 89, paragraph 4, line 2: "another drink, from barley." Barišić, "Priscus comme source," 62. My translation.

page 90, paragraph 2, line 14: "the plentiful harvest of the vines." Rouillard, *La vie rurale*, 199.

:: *Demetrius among the Bulgarians*

page 94, paragraph 1, line 15: "called themselves Saint Dimitar and Saint Georgi." Popov, *The Twin Saints*, 170 ff.

page 98, paragraph 1, line 3: "Iliev's paper, "Price and Prejudice."" http://www.cas.bg/uploads/files/Sofia-Academic-Nexus-WP/Ilya%20Iliev.indd.pdf

page 99, paragraph 1, line 7: "but honest, cleanly and chaste." Muir Mackenzie and Irby, *Travels in the Slavonic provinces*, 65.

page 99, paragraph 2, line 2: "The Proper Use of Ancestors." Iliev, "The Proper Use of Ancestors," 8–17.

page 101, paragraph 3, line 13: "occupies its due place in Europe." http://www.clio.uni-sofia.bg/EN/departments.html#bghist

page 102, paragraph 3, line 4: "a plundered treasure, / bone and stone." Tsanko Lalev, "Excavations," Belin Tonchev, trans. http://www.geocities.com/sulawesiprince/bulgaria/excavations.html

page 106, paragraph 1, line 5: "which annoyed and appeased the neighbouring villages." Andreevski, "Love Letters," 82.

page 106, paragraph 2, line 10: "out through their opened gates and routed them." Cecaumenus, in *Documents and Materials*, 16–17.

:: *Who is He Killing?*

page 108, paragraph 4, line 5: "somewhat downcast armour-plated soldier." Bozhkov, *Bulgarian Contributions*.

page 110, paragraph 1, line 2: "walls of the city in the year 1207." Grabar, *La peinture réligieuse*, 300–01. My translation.

page 112, paragraph 2, line 7: "rebellion against Emperor Isaac II in 1185." Magoulias, *O City of Byzantium*, 204.

page 114, paragraph 3, line 6: "the light of the candles in a benevolent way." Radeva, *Legends of the Kingdom*, 3–5.

page 115, paragraph 1, line 8: "death was wrapped in a shroud of mystery." Radeva, *Legends of the Kingdom*, 6–8.

page 115, paragraph 2, line 9: "before his life ended miserably." Choniates, *O City of Byzantium*, 338.

page 117, paragraph 1, line 7: "urinating round about the sacred floor..." Choniates, *O City of Byzantium*, 167 ff.

page 117, paragraph 3, line 6: "removed himself from us." Cited in Stephenson, *Byzantium's Balkan Frontier*, 290.

page 117, paragraph 5, line 5: "leaped with joy at rebellion." Choniates, *O City of Byzantium*, 206.

page 118, paragraph 4, line 7: "God's almost total abandonment of us."
Choniates, *O City of Byzantium*, 168.

page 119, paragraph 3, line 2: "headed for Turnovo." Radeva, *Legends of the Kingdom*, 11.

page 120, paragraph 1, line 6: "blood made the church turn scarlet." In Colombo and Roussanoff, *The Balkan Range*, 56.

page 122, paragraph 9, line 6: "the Great Saint the anchor of your faith." Pentzikis, *Mother Thessaloniki*, 80.

:: **Letting Go**

page 124, paragraph 2, line 3: "pure Hellenic blood flows in [their] veins." Cited in Charanis, "On the Demography of Medieval Greece," 195.

page 124, paragraph 2, line 8: "our whole land has become slavicized." Cited in Hrushevsky, *History of Ukraine-Rus*, 127.

page 124, paragraph 2, line 14: "it was an empty vision..." Cited in Vryonis, "Recent Scholarship on Continuity," 246.

page 125, paragraph 1, line 7: "the gentleman from Constantinople." Bon, *Le Péloponnèse byzantin*, 134.

page 125, paragraph 2, line 6: "Greece's connection with the Hellenes and the Olympians." Leake, *Travels in the Morea*, v.

page 125, paragraph 3, line 7: "strangest hotchpotch of colours." Rambaud, *Études sur l'histoire byzantine*, 264.

page 125, paragraph 4, line 5: "'those nasty little Slavs.'" Cheetham, *Medieval Greece*, vii.

page 125, paragraph 5, line 2: "masters of the whole country." Cited in Cheetham, *Medieval Greece*, 16.

page 126, paragraph 1, line 4: "like liquid across blotting paper." Fermor, *A Time of Gifts*, 227.

page 126, paragraph 2, line 3: "an accursed people." Cited in Charanis, "The Chronicle of Monemvasia," 149.

page 126, paragraph 3, line 6: "murmur indignantly and endure." Obolensky, *The Byzantine Commonwealth*, 52.

page 127, paragraph 1, line 9: "dangerous romantic twaddle." Kark, *Attic in Greece*, 88.

page 127, paragraph 2, line 5: "has been called the "reconquista."" Vryonis, "Review Essay," 427.

page 128, paragraph 1, line 2: "precipices of the southern slope." Runciman, *A Traveller's Alphabet*.

page 128, paragraph 1, line 8: "had been reduced to its bare walls." Leake, *Travels in the Morea*, 202–03.

page 128, paragraph 1, line 12: "screaming at them above the wind." Andrews, *The Flight of Ikaros*, 68.

page 128, paragraph 2, line 9: "settled in it with their own bishop." Cited in Charanis, "The Chronicle of Monemvasia," 148.

page 129, paragraph 2, line 11: "in Sclavinica terra." In Kalligas, *Byzantine Monemvasia*, 42.

page 129, paragraph 3, line 5: "whence their comfort is." In Kalligas, *Byzantine Monemvasia*, 45

page 129, paragraph 4, line 4: "sheepfold is made of iron." Ritsos, "from Romiosini," 195.

page 130, paragraph 1, line 2: "tells us from the fifteenth century." Cited in Charanis, "The Chronicle of Monemvasia," 159.

page 130, paragraph 2, line 2: "took Greece [Graeciam] from the Romans." Cited in Hrushevsky, *History of Ukraine*, 127.

page 130, paragraph 3, line 12: "the second half of the seventh century." Bon, *Le Péloponnèse byzantin*, 175.

page 130, paragraph 3, line 15: "his magisterial *A History of Europe*." Pirenne, *A History of Europe*, 29.

page 132, paragraph 2, line 2: "Greek, facing the stars?" Karouzos, "Triplets for Beautiful Mystras," 104.

page 132, paragraph 3, line 11: "sacrifice horses to the Sun." Pausanias, *Guide to Greece*, 73.

:: **Lord, have Mercy**

page 136, paragraph 6, line 4: "the day's single genuine emotion." Katerina Anghelaki-Rooke, unpublished in English translation.

:: **Return to Canada**

page 137, paragraph 1, line 11: "St. Demetrius, whom God has sent upon us!" In Zenkovsky, *Medieval Russia's Epics*, 52.

:: *Interlude*

page 144, paragraph 3, line 5: "only as an appendage of the social process." Cited by Rose, "A Use for the Stones," 21.

page 144, paragraph 4, line 10: "amelioration of the human condition." Emberley, *Divine Hunger*, 21.

page 145, paragraph 1, line 1: "in a sickened world." Emberley, *Divine Hunger*, 21.

page 145, paragraph 1, line 10: "Everything else is postmodern chatter." Adapted from Philip Jenkins, "Europe's Christian Comeback," June 2007, www.foreignpolicy.com

page 146, paragraph 1, line 4: "joy at the triumph of life." Cited in Ware, *The Orthodox Way*, 87.

page 146, paragraph 1, line 5: "Nietzsche who is dead." Jason DeBoer, "Sublime Hatred: Nietzsche's Anti-Christianity," www.absinthe-literary-review.com

page 146, paragraph 1, line 27: "egoistic self to a "new life."" James, *The Varieties Of Religious Experience*, 57, 110, 110, 175.

page 149, paragraph 2, line 9: "something bigger than ourselves." Tom Hayden, *The Lost Gospel*, 175.

page 149, paragraph 2, line 13: "the Christianization of reason." Vladimir Lossky, *Orthodox Theology*, 38.

page 149, paragraph 3, line 3: "the settling of self into the world." McKay, *Vis à Vis*, 22, 23.

:: *Opening: The Mad Professor of Sirmium*

page 152, paragraph 3, line 4: "successful investigations of the road" Popovic, "A Survey of the Topography and Organization," 121.

page 152, paragraph 4, line 2: "hand over Sirmium to barbarians?" Blockley, *The History of Menander*, 141.

page 153, paragraph 2, line 7: "a strong effort to meet the crisis." Blockley, *The History of Menander*, 217–19.

page 153, paragraph 4, line 5: "abandon any part of the Roman state." Blockley, *The History of Menander*, 219–21.

page 153, paragraph 5, line 10: "their lives and one cloak each." Blockley, *The History of Menander*, 241.

page 154, paragraph 1, line 5: "the wretches had had only cats to eat." In Mirkovic, "Sirmium—Its History," 56.

page 154, paragraph 5, line 9: "as the Passion of St. Demetrius has it." Skedros, *Saint Demetrios*, 149.

page 155, paragraph 5, line 6: "more than me is not worthy of me.'" Allard, *La persécution*, 294.

page 156, paragraph 1, line 5: "a holy place indeed." Popovic, "Sirmium: A Town of Emperors and Martyrs."

page 156, paragraph 1, line 10: "the sanctuary of St. Demetrius" Zeiller, *Les origines chrétiennes*, 83.

:: *Slavs in Byzantium*

page 158, paragraph 2, line 10: "Thessalonians speak pure Slavic." Kantor, *Medieval Slavic Lives*, 11.

page 159, paragraph 1, line 15: "verbal exchanges of pidgin tongues." Tachiaos, *Cyril and Methodius*, 16.

page 159, paragraph 7, line 5: "the Word was God," and so forth." Kantor, *Medieval Slavic Lives*, 67.

page 160, paragraph 3, line 7: "while the devil was shamed." Kantor, *Medieval Slavic Lives*, 69.

page 161, paragraph 3, line 11: "sing unto the Lord a new song." Kantor, *Medieval Slavic Lives*, 71.

page 162, paragraph 2, line 6: "like us was born a human being." Ware, *The Orthodox Way*, 78.

page 163, paragraph 3, line 9: "How should suicides be buried?" Fletcher, *The Barbarian Conversion*, 367.

page 164, paragraph 1, line 2: "words that heal our hearts and minds." http://www.mymacedonia.net/language/slavonic.htm

page 164, paragraph 2, line 12: "all at once "by a saint." Fine, *The Early Medieval Balkans*, 135.

page 164, paragraph 2, line 15: "have set this gospel in gold..." Kijuk, *Medieval and Renaissance Serbian Poetry*, 7.

page 164, paragraph 3, line 7: "the peoples of Eastern Europe." Obolensky, *The Byzantine Inheritance*, 149–51.

page 165, paragraph 2, line 12: "also western Europe knew it." Ševčenko, *Byzantium and the Slavs*, 5.

page 165, paragraph 2, line 20: "from Byzantium to the West" Ševčenko, *Byzantium and the Slavs*, 6.

page 167, paragraph 1, line 9: "saints and of religious service." Cited in Colombo and Roussanoff, *The Balkan Range*, 62.

page 167, paragraph 2, line 6: "*onion, cabbage,* and *fried eggs.*" Ševčenko, *Byzantium and the Slavs*, 12.

page 168, paragraph 3, line 2: "the faith and to give them a law." Tapkova-Zaimova, "Les légendes sur Salonique," 134.

page 169, paragraph 1, line 2: "celebrate thy most sacred memory." Nichoritis, "Unknown Stichera," 79–85.

page 169, paragraph 2, line 9: "within it through your prayers..." Obolensky, "The Cult of St. Demetrius," 12.

page 169, paragraph 4, line 11: "the National Library of Sofia." Nichoritis, "Unknown Stichera," 79.

page 170, paragraph 3, line 5: "the fact that we do not read books?" Cited in Colombo, *The Balkan Range*, 51.

page 171, paragraph 4, line 5: "other Christian nations have known thee." Cited in Zenkovsky, *Medieval Russia's Epics*, 71.

page 173, paragraph 1, line 9: "truth constructs knowledge." Aquilina, *Fathers of the Church*, 101.

page 180, paragraph 1, line 10: "feted as a saint above the apostles..." Magdalino, "The Byzantine Holy Man," 54–55.

:: *The Byzantine Saint*

page 184, paragraph 4, line 15: "desire still gnaws at me and time eats me" In Kornakov, *Makedonski Manastiri*, 112.

page 186, paragraph 2, line 12: "as extolled by a princess herself" Serafimova, *Medieval Painting in Macedonia*, 42.

page 186, paragraph 3, line 6: "with the Quadrivium of sciences" Comnena, *The Alexiad*, 17.

page 187, paragraph 1, line 1: "art of Renaissance Italy." See for example Rice, *The Beginning of Christian Art*.

page 189, paragraph 4, line 5: "There the sunrise warms the soul" In Miladinov, *Collected Works*.

page 190, paragraph 2, line 11: "how to write by holding their hands." Cited in Colombo and Roussanoff, *The Balkan Range*, 44.

page 191, paragraph 1, line 1: "understanding came down upon my people" Cited in Fletcher, *The Barbarian Conversion*, 364.

page 191, paragraph 1, line 5: "forced to live with frogs in the mud." Ševčenko, "Three Paradoxes," 229.

page 191, paragraph 1, line 12: "from the lack of culture." In Kosev and Hristov, *Documents and Materials*, 41.

page 193, paragraph 3, line 10: "icon of St. John the Baptist" In October 2009 a fire destroyed much of the monastery treasures including the library and archives, but sparing the icons. Reconstruction of the konak began in 2010.

page 199, paragraph 2, line 5: "'Might is right.'" An Internet search (June 2010) did not turn up any such museum, although Brussels does boast an Orthodox Church Museum.

page 202, paragraph 3, line 7: "ourselves justly flowed by blood!" "Speeches to Montenegrins before battles against Turks, 1796," http://www.rastko.rs/rastko-cg/povijest/sveti_petar-1796e.html

page 205, paragraph 3, line 6: "the Serbs consider their own." Colovic, *The Politics of Symbol*, 126.

page 210, paragraph 1, line 2: "the saint of the known world." Obolensky, *The Byzantine Inheritance*, 20.

:: *The Guardian Saint*

page 214, paragraph 5, line 5: "If they must perish, I shall perish also." Cormack, *Writing in Gold*, 67.

page 215, paragraph 4, line 5: "in the abode of the dead." Toynbee, *Constantine Porphynogenitus*, 536.

page 219, paragraph 1, line 7: "Demetrius reposes there in divine fashion." In Mango, *Art of the Byzantine Empire*, 129.

page 220, paragraph 3, line 5: "mouths of all the people" Lemerle, *Les plus anciens recueils, Vol. I Le texte*, 234.

page 220, paragraph 4, line 7: "pilgrims from all countries." Tafrali, *Thessalonique au quatorzième siècle*, 130.

page 221, paragraph 1, line 2: "the miracle of abundant myrrh" "The Life of St. Demetrios of Thessalonica," http://fr-d-serfes.org/lives/stdemetrios.htm

page 221, paragraph 2, line 4: "he implored his intercession." Norwich, *Byzantium: The Apogee*, 286.

page 221, paragraph 2, line 9: "on the morrow you will win." Comnena, *The Alexiad*, 169.

page 222, paragraph 2, line 3: "both size and viciousness." Norwich, *Byzantium: The Early Centuries*, 133.

page 222, paragraph 2, line 11: "Was that a god?" Thubron, *Emperor*, 23.

page 223, paragraph 1, line 3: "profane until now." Tassias, *St. Demetrius*, 106.

page 224, paragraph 2, line 12: "for everyone's joy." Lemerle, *Les plus anciens recueils, Vol. I Le texte*, 192–93.

page 224, paragraph 3, line 9: "open to the four winds." See, for instance, Papachatzis, *Monuments of Thessaloniki*, 83.

page 226, paragraph 1, line 6: "on their knees like children." Pentzikis, *Mother Thessaloniki*, 119.

page 226, paragraph 2, line 14: "was a disgrace." Norwich, *Byzantium: The Apogee*, 110.

page 226, paragraph 3, line 4: "*completely fortified this town.*" Cited in Papachatzis, *Monuments of Thessaloniki*, 22.

page 227, paragraph 1, line 1: "he had indeed decreed it should be his." In Mazower, *Salonica*, 28.

page 227, paragraph 2, line 10: "nor allies nor sustenance." Balfour, *Politico-historical Works*, 157–59.

page 227, paragraph 2, line 15: "for the slave markets." Balfour, *Politico-historical Works*, 240.

page 227, paragraph 3, line 6: "*thy honour, hail Demetrios.*" In Pentzikis, *Mother Thessaloniki*, 59.

page 228, paragraph 1, line 2: "cured Christians and Muslims impartially." Toynbee, *Constantine Porphyrogenitus*, 537.

page 228, paragraph 1, line 7: "the Bulgarian enemy stone blind." Clogg, "The Byzantine Legacy," 267.

page 228, paragraph 2, line 3: "the consolation of his relics." Lemerle, *Les plus anciens recueils, Vol. II Commentaire*, 76.

page 228, paragraph 2, line 10: "power never transferable from it." Skedros, *Saint Demetrios*, 121.

page 229, paragraph 1, line 5: "our deep piety." Skedros, *Saint Demetrios*, 87.

page 229, paragraph 1, line 10: "approach it with faith." Comnena, *The Alexiad*, n93.

page 229, paragraph 2, line 3: "a monastery in Constantinople?" Majeska, *Russian Travellers*, 164.

page 229, paragraph 3, line 8: "the image of that of the city." Lemerle, *Les plus anciens recueils, Vol. I Le texte*, 88.

page 231, paragraph 1, line 12: "looked just like his icon." Cormack, *Byzantine Art*, 76.

page 231, paragraph 2, line 9: "which city he is to defend." Melnick, *An Icon Painter's Notebook*, 306.

page 232, paragraph 1, line 1: "unwatched, unchallenged, leaderless?" In Mango, *The Homilies*, 82–84.

page 232, paragraph 2, line 7: "originally a Great Goddess." Bilaniuk, "The Notion of Religion," 44.

page 232, paragraph 2, line 9: "Eastern Slavic contributions to Orthodox Liturgy," Ševčenko, *Byzantium and the Slavs*, 165.

page 233, paragraph 1, line 14: "with divine authority. Amen." Lemerle, *Les plus anciens recueils, Vol. I Le texte*, 96–97.

page 233, paragraph 2, line 8: "at 10.10, near the gate of the town…" Leake, *Travels in Northern Greece*, 323.

page 235, paragraph 1, line 1: "name, Kastoria [Latin, *castra*]." Comnena, *The Alexiad*, 181.

page 235, paragraph 1, line 4: "since the twelfth century." Leake, *Northern Greece*, 330.

page 235, paragraph 3, line 5: "intolerably stiff and unnatural." Leake, *Northern Greece*, 320.

page 236, paragraph 1, line 3: "vulgar pursuits of life." Leake, *Northern Greece*, 325.

page 237, paragraph 1, line 3: "low-born and ferocious" Orr, *The History*, 138.

:: **The Passion of Demetrius**

page 240, paragraph 2, line 9: "in the endurance of fearful ordeals." Eusebius of Caesarea, *The History of the Church*, 258.

page 242, paragraph 2, line 12: "protect us wherever we went." Tafrali, *Topographie de Thessalonique*, C–D.

page 242, paragraph 3, line 14: "carted off to the Louvre in Paris." Tafrali, *Topographie de Thessalonique*, 122.

page 243, paragraph 1, line 3: "hovels of the shantytown beneath." Tafrali, *Topographie de Thessalonique*, 123.

page 243, paragraph 4, line 8: "disintegrated in a cloud of dust." Morton, *In the Steps of St. Paul*, 243.

page 245, paragraph 2, line 2: "Persians, Avars, Arabs and Turks" Hussey, "The Place of Byzantium," 345–46.

page 248, paragraph 3, line 10: "vividly in *The Church of Apostles and Martyrs*." Daniel-Rops, *The Church of Apostles*, 407.

page 248, paragraph 4, line 4: "and even incense." Lane Fox, *Pagans and Christians*, 89.

page 251, paragraph 3, line 5: "up to the Feast Day of St. Demetrius." Baldwin, *Timarion*, 15, 44.

page 251, paragraph 3, line 21: "before reaching the city gates." Baldwin, *Timarion*, 43, 44–45.

page 252, paragraph 1, line 1: "history of the city of Thessalonica" Vacalopoulos, *A History of Thessaloniki.*

page 252, paragraph 2, line 5: "at the side of Christ in Heaven." Tafrali, *Thessalonique au quatorzième siècle*, 139ff.

page 252, paragraph 3, line 15: "into a marketplace." Tafrali, *Thessalonique au quatorzième siècle*, 148.

page 253, paragraph 3, line 12: "their era, and even female singers." Cited in Vryonis, "The *Panegyris*," 217–18.

page 254, paragraph 4, line 6: "to leave the ground and fly." Baldwin, *Timarion*, 46.

page 255, paragraph 1, line 6: "to the saint for a safe return..." Baldwin, *Timarion*, 49.

page 256, paragraph 1, line 2: "as if already a corpse..." Eusebius, *The History of the Church*, 259.

page 256, paragraph 2, line 4: "forever with the living God." Frend, *Martyrdom and Persecution*, 15.

page 256, paragraph 3, line 4: "still smouldered at the stake." Delehaye, *Les origines du culte*, 1.

page 257, paragraph 1, line 2: "stabbed him to death with their spears." Pamphlet translated from the Romanian by Eugene Giurgiu.

page 257, paragraph 2, line 10: "miracles of healing occurred in that place." In Skedros, *Saint Demetrios*, 153.

page 257, paragraph 3, line 19: "hasten to the saints." Paevsky, "The Basis for the Veneration," unpaginated.

page 258, paragraph 2, line 14: "you are at once suspected of a lack of faith." Delehaye, *The Legends of the Saints*, ix.

page 258, paragraph 2, line 20: "poets and artists as their property..." Delehaye, *The Legends of the Saints*, xii.

page 259, paragraph 2, line 12: "outside the circle of spiritual phenomena," Holweck, *Biographical Dictionary*, iii.

page 259, paragraph 3, line 4: "they fled to the hills." Lane Fox, *Pagans and Christians*, 424.

page 259, paragraph 3, line 8: "rather than hand over the books." In Frend, *Martyrdom and Persecution*, 15.

page 260, paragraph 1, line 4: "Agape, Chionia, Irene" Allard, *La persécution*, 282–83.

page 260, paragraph 2, line 6: "guilty of no impiety whatsoever." Cited in Daniel-Rops, *The Church of Apostles*, 417–18.

page 260, paragraph 2, line 21: "provoked the Divine justice." Gibbon, *The Decline and Fall*, 208.

page 260, paragraph 3, line 7: "guards will not release you." Cited in Allard, *La persécution*, 288.

page 261, paragraph 1, line 8: "younger and more active associates." Gibbon, *The Decline and Fall*, 133.

page 261, paragraph 3, line 8: "produces most exquisite trout." Gibbon, *The Decline and Fall*, 136.

:: **The Life and Death of St. Demetrius, a Young Man of Thessalonica, April 304 (Two Versions)**

page 263, paragraph 1, line 2: "seek the common good." Ferguson, *Early Christians Speak*, 67.

page 263, paragraph 2, line 8: "silently obeyed detested orders?" Le Blant, *Les persécutions et les martyrs*, 21.

page 263, paragraph 4, line 9: "made all things to exist out of nothing;" Ferguson, *Early Christians Speak*, 19.

page 264, paragraph 3, line 14: "Himself, in a glory of light." Le Blant, *Les persécutions et les martyrs*, 104.

page 265, paragraph 3, line 10: "churches of Lyons and Vienne." In Fremantle, *A Treasury*, 178.

page 266, paragraph 4, line 1: "as your Father also is merciful." King James Bible, Luke 6:27–30, 35–36.

page 268, paragraph 1, line 2: "Come over into Macedonia and help us." King James Bible, Acts 16:9.

page 268, paragraph 2, line 8: "man who breathed friendliness." Johnson, *A History of Christianity*, 4.

page 268, paragraph 3, line 10: "things in ancient literature." Morton, *In the Steps of St. Paul*, 249.

page 268, paragraph 4, line 2: "because you had become dear to us." King James Bible, 1 Thess. 2:7–8.

page 269, paragraph 3, line 7: "These you may keep." Cited in Johnson, *A History of Christianity*, 75.

page 270, paragraph 4, line 4: "Whose name is not yet known." Palamas, "A Hundred Voices."

page 271, paragraph 3, line 2: "a nurse cherisheth her children." King James Bible, 1 Thess. 2:7.

page 271, paragraph 4, line 3: *"make me a temple fit for yourself."* Cited in Ferguson, *Early Christians Speak*, 133.

page 271, paragraph 5, line 6: "ordinary and innocent kind" Cited in Johnson, *A History of Christianity*. 71.

page 273, paragraph 1, line 12: "He is not here, but is risen." King James Bible, Luke 24:5-6.

page 273, paragraph 4, line 9: "ashes and swept into the sea." In Fremantle, *A Treasury*, 181–82.

About the Bibliography

IN 2000, when I realized there was no course in Byzantine Studies I could enroll in at a Canadian university, I moved to Toronto for six months, obtained a card to the Robarts Library at the University of Toronto, and systematically began my own course of studies by indiscriminately reading one book after another from the stacks until I began to "get the picture." The classic and established studies by Norman Baynes, Robert Browning, J.B. Bury, Averil Cameron, Charles Diehl, John Fine, Joan Hussey, Romilly Jenkins, Alexander Kazhdan, Ernst Kitzinger, Henry Maguire, Cyril Mango, Donald Nicol, David Talbot Rice, Sir Steven Runciman, Warren Treadgold, and Mark Whittow occupied me until I was ready to read more narrowly.

The history of Byzantine-Slav relations was hugely important for my topic. The works of Peter Charanis, Francis Dvornik, Dimitri Obolensky, Ihor Ševčenko, Paul Stephenson, and Speros Vryonis covered the gamut of discussion and dispute from Rus to Bulgaria, Macedonia to Constantinople, the Peloponnese to Thessalonica, Obolensky's canonical *The Byzantine Commonwealth* being the most comprehensive.

As I zeroed in on the character and life of St. Demetrius of Thessalonica, I came across the essential work of Paul Lemerle, Michael Vickers, and James Skedros, each working with the medieval texts of the Demetrian "legend." Vasilka Tapkova-Zaimova's work proved a gold mine of its Bulgarian version, while Robin Cormack and Ruth Macrides each examined it from the point of view of a religious and patriotic cult. For the significance of its iconography, I read Christopher Walter, André Grabar, and, again, Robin Cormack.

For historical accounts of Demetrius's city, Thessalonica, I fell gratefully on Oreste Tafrali's and Apostolos Vacalopoulos's early work. Anthony-Emil Tachiaos has written copiously of the Slav-Greek encounter in medieval Thessalonica. Mark Mazower's *Salonica, City of Ghosts: Christians, Muslims and Jews 1430–1950*, is a recent marvelous exposition of its intercommunal history.

The fraught territories known collectively as the Balkans were vividly represented by early modern writers such as H.N. Brailsford and the travellers G. Muir Mackenzie and A.P Irby, but these have come under more dispassionate scrutiny in the work of others, such as Michael Herzfeld and Maria Todorova; to my mind, the compact but judicious survey history, *The Balkans*, by Mark Mazower, remains the best summary of Greek-Slavic-Turkish shared histories in the region.

Finally, to situate the story of St. Demetrius in the context of the early Christian Church, I found the work of Eusebius of Caesarea, Hippolyte Delehaye, Henri Daniel-Rops, and Robin Lane Fox to be, if not the most authoritative, at least the most compelling in their storytelling. The most authoritative is the prolific and provocative Peter Brown, for his work on early Christianity in the Late Roman Empire.

I also read avidly, and with relief, more strictly literary works, such as the Byzantine classics by Anna Comnena, Michael Psellus, and Constantine Porphyrogennetos; the popular histories, such as John Julius Norwich's *Byzantium*; and historical fiction, such as Colin Thubron's *Emperor*. Modern travel writers have revisited Eastern and southeastern Europe in the wake of the revolutionary changes of 1989–1991: Victoria Clark's *Why Angels Fall: A Journey Through Orthodox Europe*, William Dalrymple's *From the Holy Mountain: A Journey in the Shadow of Byzantium*, Fred Reed's *Salonica Terminus: Travels into the Balkan Nightmare*, and Patricia Storace's *Dinner with Persephone: Travels in Greece*.

:: **Reference**

Benedictine Monks of St. Augustine's Abbey, Ramsgate, eds. *The Book of Saints*. London: Adam and Charles Black, 1939.

Bowersock, G.W., Peter Brown, and Oleg Grabar, eds. *Late Antiquity: A Guide to the Postclassical World*. Cambridge, MA: Belknap Press of Harvard University Press, 1999.

Holweck, Reverend F.G. *Biographical Dictionary of the Saints*. St. Louis: B. Herder Book Co., 1924.

Kazhdan, Alexander, editor-in-chief. *The Oxford Dictionary of Byzantium*. New York: Oxford University Press, 1991.

Maas, Michael. *Cambridge Companion to the Age of Justinian*. Cambridge: Cambridge University Press, 2005.

Pétain, Abbé. *Dictionnaire hagiographique ou Vies des saints et des bienheureux honorés en tout temps et en tous les lieux depuis la naissance du christianisme jusqu'à nos jours*. Paris: Ateliers catholiques du Petit Montrouge, 1850.

Les RRPP Bénédictins de Paris. *Vies des saints*. Paris: Éditions Letouzey et Ané, 1952.

Rose, H.J. *A Handbook of Greek Mythology*. London: Methuen and Co., 1928. First published 1958.

Thurston, Herbert and Donald Attwater, eds. *Butler's The Lives of the Saints*. New York: P.J. Kennedy and Sons, 1956.

:: Early Church

Aquilina, Mike. *The Fathers of the Church: An Introduction to the First Christian Teachers*. Huntingdon, IN: Our Sunday Visitor, 1999.

Beatrice, Pier Franco. *Introduction to the Fathers of the Church*. Translated by Placid Solari. Venice: Edizioni Instituto San Gaetamo, 1987.

Le Blant, Edmond. *Les persécutions et les martyrs aux premiers siècles de notre ère*. Paris: Imprimerie Nationale, 1893.

Brown, Peter. *The Cult of the Saints: Its Rise and Function in Christianity*. Chicago: University of Chicago Press, 1981.

Daniel-Rops, Henri. *The Church of Apostles and Martyrs*. Translated by Audrey Butler. London: J.M. Dent & Sons, 1960.

Delehaye, Hippolyte. *Les légendes grecques des saints militaires*. Paris: Librairie Alphonse Picard et fils, 1909.

———. *Les origines du culte des martyrs*. Bruxelles: Société des Bollandistes, 1933.

———. *The Legends of the Saints*. Translated by Donald Attwater. New York: Fordham University Press, 1962. First published 1905.

Eusebius of Caesarea. *The History of the Church*. Translated by G.A. Williams. Revised and edited with a new introduction by Andrew Louth. London: Penguin, 1989.

Ferguson, Everett. *Early Christians Speak: Faith and Life in the First Three Centuries*. Abilene, TX: ACU Press, 1999.

Fletcher, Richard. *The Barbarian Conversion: From Paganism to Christianity*. New York: Henry Holt and Company, 1997.

Fremantle, Anne, ed. *A Treasury of Early Christianity*. New York: Mentor Books, 1953.

Frend, W.H.C. *Martyrdom and Persecution in the Early Church: A Study of a Conflict from the Maccabees to Donatus*. Oxford: Blackwell, 1965.

Johnson, Paul. *A History of Christianity*. Harmondsworth: Penguin, 1978.

Lane Fox, Robin. *Pagans and Christians: Religion and the Religious Life from the Second to Fourth Century A D*. San Francisco: Harper & Row, 1986.

MacMullen, Ramsay. *Christianity and Paganism in the Fourth to Eighth Centuries*. New Haven: Yale University Press, 1997.

Musurillo, Herbert, ed., intro., and trans. *The Acts of the Christian Martyrs*. Oxford: Clarendon Press, 1972.

Orr, James. *The History and Literature of the Early Church*. London: Stoughton, 1908.

Patlagean, Evelyne. "Ancient Byzantine Hagiography and Social History." In Stephen Wilson, ed. *Saints and Their Cults: Studies in Religious Sociology*. Cambridge: Cambridge University Press, 1983.

Rice, David Talbot. *The Beginning of Christian Art*. London: Hodder & Stoughton, 1957.

Ware, Bishop Kallistos. *The Orthodox Way*. New York: St. Vladimir's Seminary Press, 1999.

:: *Iconography*

Belting, Hans. *Likeness and Presence: A History of the Image before the Era of Art*. Translated by Edmund Jephcott. Chicago: University of Chicago Press, 1994.

Cavarnos, Constantine. *Orthodox Iconography*. Belmont, MA: Institute for Byzantine and Modern Greek Studies, 1977.

———. *Guide to Byzantine Iconography*. Boston: Holy Transfiguration Monastery, 1993.

Cormack, Robin. *Writing in Gold: Byzantine Society and Its Icons*. London: George Philip, 1985.

———. *Byzantine Art*. Oxford: Oxford University Press, 2000.

Grabar, André. *La peinture réligieuse en Bulgarie*. Paris: Librairie Orientaliste, 1928.

———. "Le trône des martyrs." *Cahiers archéologiques* VI (1952): 31–41.

Kelley, Fr. Christopher, trans. and ed. *An Iconographer's Patternbook: The Stroganov Tradition*. Torrance, CA: Oakwood Publications, 1992.

Kitzinger, Ernst. *Byzantine Art in the Making*. Cambridge, MA: Harvard University Press, 1977.

Maguire, Henry. "Disembodiment and Corporality in Byzantine Images of the Saints." In Brendan Cassidy, ed. *Iconography at the Crossroads*. Princeton: Princeton University Press, 1993.

Melnick, Gregory, trans. and ed. *An Icon Painter's Notebook: The Bolshakov Edition*. Torrance, CA: Oakwood Publications, 1995. First published by Sergei Bolshakov as *Iconographic Patternbook*, Moscow, 1903.

Onasch, Konrad, and Anne Marie Schnieper. *Icons: The Fascination and the Reality*. Translated by Daniel Conkiln. New York: Riverside Book Company, 1997.

Popov, Rachko. *The Twin Saints in the Bulgarian Folk Calendar*. Summary. Sofia: Publishing House of Bulgarian Academy of Sciences, 1991.

Walter, Christopher. *The Warrior Saint in Byzantine Art and Tradition*. Aldershot: Ashgate Publishing, 2003.

:: *Byzantium*

Arnott, Peter. *The Byzantines and Their World*. New York: St. Martin's Press, 1973.

Blockley, R.C., ed. and trans. *The History of Menander the Guardsman*. Liverpool: Francis Cairns, 1985.

Bon, Antoine. *Le Péloponnèse byzantin jusqu'en 1204*. Paris: Presses universitaires de France, 1951.

Brown, Peter. *The World of Late Antiquity*. London: Thames & Hudson, 2002.

Bury, J.B. *Selected Essays*. Edited by Harold Temperley. Amsterdam: Adolf M. Hakkert, 1964.

Byron, Robert. *The Byzantine Achievement*. London: Routledge and Kegan Paul, 1987. First published 1929.

Cameron, Averil. *The Mediterranean World in Late Antiquity 395–600*. London: Routledge, 1999.

Charanis, Peter. "The Chronicle of Monemvasia and the Question of the Slavonic Settlements in Greece." *Dumbarton Oaks Papers* 5, 139–66. Cambridge, MA: Harvard University Press, 1950.

———. "On the Demography of Medieval Greece: A Problem Solved." *Balkan Studies* 20 (1979): 195.

Choniates, Niketas. *O City of Byzantium, Annals of Niketas Choniates*. Trans. Harry J. Magoulias. Detroit: Wayne State University Press, 1984.

Clogg, Richard. "The Byzantine Legacy in the Modern Greek World: The Megali Idea." In Lowell Clucas, ed. *The Byzantine Legacy in Eastern Europe*. Boulder: East European Monographs, 1988.

Comnena, Anna. *The Alexiad of Anna Comnena*. Translated by E.R.A. Sewter. Harmondsworth: Penguin, 1987.

The Cultural Association of Kandanos. *The Byzantine Churches of Kandanos*. Chania: Epikoinonia, 1999.

Dennis, George, trans. *Strategikon of Maurice: Handbook of Byzantine Military Strategy*. Philadelphia: University of Pennsylvania Press, 1984.

Diehl, Charles. *Études Byzantines*. New York: Burt Franklin, 1905.

———. *Byzantium: Greatness and Decline*. Translated by Naomi Walford. New Brunswick, NJ: Rutgers University Press, 1957.

Downey, Glaville. *Constantinople in the Age of Justinian*. New York: Dorset Press, 1960.

Geanakoplos, Deno J., ed. *Byzantium: Church, Society and Civilization Seen Through Contemporary Eyes*. Chicago: University of Chicago Press, 1984.

Hackel, Sergei, ed. *The Byzantine Saint*. Crestwood, NY: St. Vladimir's Seminary Press, 2001.

Hussey, Joan. "The Place of Byzantium in the Medieval World." In J. Hussey, D. Obolensky, and S. Runciman, eds. *Thirteenth International Congress of Byzantine Studies*. Oxford: Oxford University Press, 1967.

Jones, A.H.M. *Constantine and the Conversion of Europe*. Harmondsworth: Penguin, 1972.

Jones, Prudence and Nigel Pennick. *A History of Pagan Europe*. London: Routledge, 1995.

Kalligas, Haris. *Byzantine Monemvasia: The Sources*. Monemvasia: Akroneon, 1990.

Magdalino, Paul. "The Byzantine Holy Man in the Twelfth Century." In Sergei Hackel, ed. *The Byzantine Saint*. Crestwood, NY: St. Vladimir's Seminary Press, 2001.

Magoulias, Harry J., trans. and ed. *O City of Byzantium: Annals of Niketas Choniates*. Detroit: Wayne State University Press, 1984.

Majeska, George P. *Russian Travellers to Constantinople in the Fourteenth and Fifteenth Centuries*. Washington, DC: Dumbarton Oaks Research Library and Collection, 1984.

Mango, Cyril. *Byzantium: The Empire of New Rome*. New York: Charles Scribner's Sons, 1980.

———. *The Art of the Byzantine Empire*. Toronto: University of Toronto Press, 1986.

———. *The Homilies of Photius, Patriarch of Constantinople*. Cambridge, MA: Harvard University Press, 1958.

Norwich, John Julius. *Byzantium: The Early Centuries*. London: Penguin, 1990.

———. *Byzantium: The Apogee*. London: Penguin, 1993.

———. *Byzantium: The Decline and Fall*. London: Penguin, 1996.

Pausanias. *Guide to Greece*. Vol. 2. Translated and edited by Peter Levi. Harmondsworth: Penguin, 1979.

Rouillard, Germaine. *La vie rurale dans l'Empire byzantin*. Paris: Librairie d'Amerique et d'Orient, 1953.

Runciman, Sir Steven. *A Traveller's Alphabet: Partial Memoirs*. New York: Thames & Hudson, 1991.

Stratos, Andreas. *Byzantium in the Seventh Century* I, II, III. Amsterdam: Adolf M. Hakkert: 1978.

Toynbee, Arnold. *Constantine Porphyrogenitus and His World*. Oxford: Oxford University Press, 1973.

Vryonis, Speros, Jr. "Recent Scholarship on Continuity and Discontinuity of Culture: Classical Greeks, Byzantines, Modern Greeks." In Speros Vryonis Jr., ed. *The "Past" in Medieval and Modern Greek Culture*. Malibu, CA: Undena Publications, 1978. 237–49.

———. "The *Panegyris* of the Byzantine Saint." In Sergei Hackel, ed. *The Byzantine Saint*. Crestwood, NY: St. Vladimir's Seminary Press, 2001.

Whittow, Mark. *The Making of Byzantium, 600–1025*. Berkeley and Los Angeles: University of California Press, 1996.

:: *Thessalonica*

Andreevski, Petre. "Love Letters." Translated and edited by Ewald Osers. *Contemporary Macedonian Poetry*. London: Forest Books, 1991.

Baldwin, Barry, trans. and ed. *Timarion*. Detroit: Wayne State University Press, 1984.

Balfour, David. *Politico-historical Works of Symeon, Archbishop of Thessalonica (1416/17 to 1429): Critical Greek Text with Introduction and Commentary*. Vienna: Verlag der Österreichischen Akademie de Wissenschaften, 1979.

Cecaumenus. Collected in *Documents and Materials on the History of the Bulgarian People*. Kosev, D. and H. Hristov, eds. Sofia: Bulgarian Academy of Sciences, 1969.

Colocotronis, V. *La Macédoine et l'héllenisme: étude historique et ethnologique*. Thessaloniki: Société d'études macédoniennes, 1989. First published 1919.

De Jongh, Brian. *The Companion Guide to Mainland Greece*. London: Collins, 1979.

Fermor, Patrick Leigh. *Roumeli: Travels in Northern Greece*. London: Murray, 1966.

———. *A Time of Gifts: On Foot to Constantinople, from the Hook of Holland to the Middle Danube*. Harmondsworth: Penguin, 1983.

Hasluck, F.W. *Christianity Under the Sultans*. Vol. I. Oxford: Clarendon Press, 1929.

Ioannou, Yorgos. *Refugee Capital*. Translated by Fred Reed. Athens: Kedros, 1997.

Kiel, M. "Notes on the History of Some Turkish Monuments in Thessaloniki and their Founders." *Balkan Studies* 11 (1970): 123–48.

Kitto, H.D.F. *The Greeks*. Harmondsworth: Penguin, 1978.

Mazower, Mark. *Salonica: City of Ghosts*. New York: Alfred A. Knopf, 2004.

Morton, H.V. *In the Steps of St. Paul*. London: Rich & Cowan, 1936.

Papachatzis, Nikos. *Monuments of Thessaloniki*. Translated by Chris Markham. Thessalonica: Molhos Editions, n.d. 12th edition.

Pentzikis, Nikos. *Mother Thessaloniki*. Translated by Leo Marshall. Athens: Kedros, 1998.

Procopius. *The Buildings, Book IV Part 1*. Cambridge: Loeb Classical Library, 1940. http://penelope.uchicago.edu/Thayer/E/Roman/Texts/Procopius/Buildings/4A*.html

Spieser, Jean-Michel. "Les ramparts de Thessalonique." *Byzantinoslavica* LX (1999): 557–74.

Tafrali, Oreste. *Thessalonique au quatorzième siècle*. Paris: Librairie Paul Gethner, 1913.

———. *Topographie de Thessalonique*. Paris: Librairie Paul Gethner, 1913.

Tapkova-Zaimova, Vasilka. "Les textes démétriens dans les recueils de Rila et dans la collection de Macaire." *Cyrillomethodianum* V (1981): 113–19.

Vacalopoulos, Apostolos. *A History of Thessaloniki*. Translated by T.F. Carney. Thessalonica: Institute for Balkan Studies, 1963.

:: **St. Demetrius**

Allard, Paul. *La persécution de Dioclétien et le triomphe de l'église* Tome I. Rome: L'Erma di Bretschneider, 1971. First published 1908.

Barišić, Franjo. "Les Miracles de St-Démétrius comme sources historiques (résumé)." In *Čuda Dimitrija Solunskog kao istoriski izvori*. Belgrade: Serbian Academy of Sciences, 1953. 145–53.

Cormack, Robin. "The Making of a Patron Saint: The Powers of Art and Ritual in Byzantine Thessaloniki." In Irving Lavin, ed. *World Art: Themes of Unity in Diversity*. Vol. 3. University Park, PA: Pennsylvania University Press, 1989. 547–52.

Detienne, Marcel. "Culinary Practices and the Spirit of Sacrifice." In Marcel
Detienne and Jean-Pierre Vernant, eds., and Paula Wissing, trans. *The
Cuisine of Sacrifice Among the Greeks*. Chicago: University of Chicago Press,
1989. 2–21.

———. "The Violence of Wellborn Ladies: Women in the Thesmophoria," in
Marcel Detienne and Jean-Pierre Vernant, eds., and Paula Wissing, trans.
The Cuisine of Sacrifice Among the Greeks. Chicago: University of Chicago
Press, 1989. 129–47.

Farnell, Lewis Richard. *The Cults of the Greek States*. Vol. iii. Oxford: Clarendon
Press, 1907.

Frendo, Joseph. "'The Miracles of St. Demetrius' and the Capture of
Thessaloniki." *Byzantoslavica* (1997): 206–20.

Georgoudi, Stella. "Sanctified Slaughter in Modern Greece: The 'Kourbania' of
the Saints." In Marcel Detienne and Jean-Pierre Vernant, eds., and Paula
Wissing, trans. *The Cuisine of Sacrifice Among the Greeks*. Chicago: University
of Chicago Press, 1989. 183–261.

Harrison, Jane. *Prolegomena to the Study of Greek Religion*. New York: Meridian
Books, 1957.

Hemmerdinger-Iliadou, Démétrius. "L'enkomion de Saint-Démétrius par Jean
archevêque de Thessalonique." *Balkan Studies* i (1960).

Kylymnyk, Stepan. *Calendar Year in Ukrainian Folklore/Ukraïns'kyi rik u
narodnikh zvycha´i'akh v istorychnomu osvitlenni*. Vol. v. Winnipeg:
Proceedings of the Ukrainian Research Institute of Volyn, 1963.

Lemerle, Paul. "Saint-Démétrius de Thessalonique." *Bulletin de correspondence
hellénique* 77 (1953): 660–94.

———, trans. and ed. *Les plus anciens recueils des miracles de Saint Démétrius
et la pénétration des Slaves dans les Balkans. Vol. i Le texte*. Paris: Éditions du
Centre National de la Recherche scientifique, 1979.

———, trans. and ed. *Les plus anciens recueils des miracles de Saint Démétrius et
la pénétration des Slaves dans les Balkans. Vol. ii Commentaire*. Paris: Éditions
du Centre National de la Recherche scientifique, 1981.

Lewis, Bernard. *The Emergence of Modern Turkey*. Oxford: Oxford University
Press, 1963.

"The Life of St. Demetrios of Thessalonica." *The Orthodox Word*. Platina, CA: St.
Herman of Alaska Brotherhood. http://fr-d-serfes.org/lives/stdemetrios.
htm

Macrides, Ruth J. "Subversion and Loyalty in the Cult of St. Demetrios."
Byzantinoslavica 51 (1990): 189–97.

Mirkovic, Miroslava. "Sirmium—Its History From The I Century AD to 582 AD." In Vladislav Popovic, ed. *Sirmium: Archaeological Investigations in Syrmian Pannonia*. Belgrade: Archaelogical Institute, 1971.

Nichoritis, K. "Unknown Stichera to St. Demetrius by St. Methodius." In Anthony-Emil Tachiaos, ed. *The Legacy of Saints Cyril and Methodius to Kiev and Moscow*. Thessalonica: Hellenic Association for Slavic Studies, 1992. 79–85.

Nilsson, Martin. *A History of Greek Religion*. Oxford: Oxford University Press, 1925.

Popovic, Vladislav, ed. *Sirmium: Archaeological Investigations in Syrmian Pannonia*. Belgrade: Archaeological Institute, 1971.

———. "Sirmium: A Town of Emperors and Martyrs." In Dragoslav Srejovic, ed. *Roman Imperial Towns and Palaces in Serbia*. Belgrade: Serbian Academy of Sciences and Arts, 1993.

———. "A Survey of the Topography and Urban Organization of Sirmium in the Late Empire." In Vladislav Popovic, ed. *Sirmium: Archaeological Investigations in Syrmian Pannonia*. Belgrade: Archaeological Institute, 1971. 119–29.

Radeva, Zhivka, ed. *Legends of the Kingdom of Tarnovo*. Sofia: Slavena, 2000.

Skedros, James. *Saint Demetrios of Thessaloniki*. Harrisburg, PA: Trinity Press International, 1999.

Tapkova-Zaimova, Vasilka. "Les légendes sur Salonique—ville sainte—et la conversion des Bulgares." In Anthony-Emil Tachiaos, ed. *The Legacy of Cyril and Methodius to Kiev and Moscow*. Thessalonica: Hellenic Association for Slavic Studies, 1992.

Tassias, Ioannis C. Very Rev. Archimandrite. *St. Demetrius*. Thessaloniki: n.d.

Vickers, Michael. "Sirmium or Thessaloniki? A Critical Examination of the St. Demetrius Legend." *Byzantinische Zeitschrift* 67 (1974): 337–50.

Woods, David. "Thessalonica's Patron: Saint Demetrius or Emeterius?" *Harvard Theological Review* 93 (2000): 221–34.

Zeiller, Jacques. *Les origines chrétiennes dans les provinces danubiennes de l'Empire romain*. Paris: 1918.

:: **Byzantium and the Slavs**

Barišić, Franjo. "Priscus comme source de l'histoire ancienne des Slaves du sud (résumé)." *Zbornik Radova* 21. Belgrade: Byzantine Institute, 1952. 62.

Bozhkov, Atanas. *Bulgarian Contributions to European Civilization*. Translated by David Mossop. Sofia: Bulvest, 2000.

Charanis, Peter. "Ethnic Changes in the Byzantine Empire in the Seventh Century." *Dumbarton Oaks Papers* 13, 35–44. Cambridge, MA: Harvard University Press, 1959.

———. "The Chronicle of Monemvasia and the Question of the Slavonic Settlements in Greece," *Dumbarton Oaks Papers* 5, 139–66. Cambridge, MA: Harvard University Press, 1950.

Cheetham, Nicolas. *Medieval Greece*. New Haven: Yale University Press, 1981.

Clark, Victoria. *Why Angels Fall: A Journey Through Orthodox Europe From Byzantium to Kosovo*. London: Picador, 2001.

Clucas, Lowell, ed. *The Byzantine Legacy in Eastern Europe*. Boulder, CO: East European Monographs, 1988.

Dvornik, Francis. *The Slavs: Their Early History and Civilization*. Boston: Academy of Arts and Sciences, 1959.

———. *The Slavs in European History and Civilization*. New Brunswick, NJ: Rutgers University Press, 1962.

———. *Byzantine Mission Among the Slavs, SS Constantine, Cyril and Methodius*. New Brunswick, NJ: Rutgers University Press, 1970.

Franklin, Simon. *Byzantium-Rus-Russia: Studies in the Translation of Christian Culture*. Aldershot: Ashgate Publishing Company, 2002.

Gimbutas, Marija. *The Slavs*. London: Thames & Hudson, 1971.

Kantor, Marvin. *Medieval Slavic Lives of Saints and Princes*. Ann Arbor: University of Michigan Press, 1983.

Kark, Ruth. *Attic in Greece*. London: Warner Books, 1995.

Katrij, Julian J. *A Byzantine Rite Liturgical Year*. Translated by Fr. Demetrius Wysochansky. Toronto: Basilian Fathers Publication, 1992.

Kijuk, Predrag R. *Medieval and Renaissance Serbian Poetry*. Belgrade: Serbian Literary Quarterly, 1987.

MacLear, Rev. G.F. *Conversion of the West: The Slavs*. London: Society for Promoting Christian Knowledge, 1879.

Obolensky, Dimitri. "The Cyrillo-Methodian Heritage in Russia." *Dumbarton Oaks Papers* 19, 47–65. Cambridge, MA: Harvard University Press, 1965.

———. *The Byzantine Inheritance of Eastern Europe*. London: Variorium Reprints, 1982.

———. *The Byzantine Commonwealth: Eastern Europe 500–1453*. London: Phoenix Press, 2000.

Rambaud, Alfred. *Études sur l'histoire Byzantine*. Paris: Librairie Armand Colin, 1912.

Ševčenko, Ihor. "Three Paradoxes of the Cyrillo-Methodian Mission." *Slavic Review* 2 (1964): 220–36.

———. *Byzantine Roots of Ukrainian Christianity*. Cambridge: Harvard University Press, 1984.

———. *Byzantium and the Slavs in Letters and Culture*. Cambridge: Harvard Ukrainian Research Institute, 1991.

Soulis, George. "Cyril and Methodius and the Southern Slavs." *Dumbarton Oaks Papers* 19, 21–38. Cambridge, MA: Harvard University Press, 1965.

Stephenson, Paul. *Byzantium's Balkan Frontier*. Cambridge: Cambridge University Press, 2000.

Tachiaos, Anthony-Emil. *Cyril and Methodius of Thessalonica: Acculturation of the Slavs*. Crestwood, NY: St. Vladimir's Seminary Press, 2000.

Vlast, A.P. *The Entry of the Slavs into Christendom*. Cambridge: Cambridge University Press, 1970.

:: Early Slavs/Rus

Barford, P.M. *The Early Slavs*. Ithaca, NY: Cornell University Press, 2001.

Bilaniuk, Petro B.T. "The Notion of Religion of the Pre-Christian and Christian Eastern Slavs VI to XII Centuries." In *Studies in Eastern Christianity*. Vol. 5. Munich-Toronto: Ukrainian Free University Series, 1998.

Conte, Francis. *Les Slaves: aux origins des civilisations d'Europe centrale et orientale (VIe–XIIIe siècles)*. Paris: Albin Michel, 1986.

Cross, Samuel Hazzard, and Olgerd P. Sherbowitz-Wetzov, trans. and eds. *The Russian Primary Chronicle*. Cambridge: Medieval Academy of America, 1953.

Hrushevsky, Mykhailo. *History of Ukraine-Rus*. Translated by Marta Skorupsky. Toronto: Canadian Institute of Ukrainian Studies, 1997.

Kosev, D. and H. Hristov, eds. *Documents and Materials on the History of the Bulgarian People*. Sofia: Bulgarian Academy of Sciences, 1969.

Plokhy, Serhii. *The Cossacks and Religion in Early Modern Ukraine*. Oxford: Oxford University Press, 2001.

Poppe, Andrzej. "St. Vladimir as a Christian." In John Breck, ed. *The Legacy of St. Vladimir*. Crestwood, NJ: St. Vladimir's Seminary Press, 1990.

Zenkovsky, Serge A., ed. and trans. *Medieval Russia's Epics, Chronicles, and Tales*. New York: Dutton, 1963.

:: Balkans

Bakić-Hayden, Milica. "Nesting Orientalisms: The Case of Former Yugoslavia." *Slavic Review* 54 (Winter 1995): 917–31.

Bracewell, Wendy and Alex Drace-Francis. "South-Eastern Europe: History, Concepts, Boundaries." *Balkanologie* 3, 2 (1999): 47–66.

Brailsford, H.N. *Macedonia: Its Races and Their Future*. London: Methuen, 1906.

Chatzopoulos, Constantinos K. "The Bulgarians in the Greek Textbooks of History of the Second Half of the 19th Century." *Balkan Studies* 39 (1998): 273.

Clarke, James F. *The Pen and the Sword: Studies in Bulgarian History*. Edited by Dennis Hupchick. New York: East European Monographs, Columbia University Press, 1988.

————. *Bulgaria and Salonica in Macedonia*. New York: American Board of Commissioners for Foreign Missions, 1895.

Colombo, John Robert and Nikola Roussanoff, eds. *The Balkan Range: A Bulgarian Reader*. Toronto: Hounslow Press, 1976.

Crampton, R.J. *A Short History of Pre-modern Bulgaria*. Cambridge: Cambridge University Press, 1987.

Fine, John V.A., Jr. *The Early Medieval Balkans*. Ann Arbor: University of Michigan Press, 1983.

————. *The Late Medieval Balkans*. Ann Arbor: University of Michigan Press, 1987.

Fraser, John Foster. *Pictures from the Balkans*. London, Paris, New York, and Melbourne: Cassell and Company, Limited, 1906.

Herzfeld, Michael. *Ours Once More: Folklore, Ideology and the Making of Modern Greece*. New York: Pella Publishing Company, 1986.

Hupchick, Dennis P. and Harold E. Cox. *The Palgrave Concise Historical Atlas of the Balkans*. New York: Palgrave Macmillan, 2001.

Iliev, Ilia. "The Proper Use of Ancestors." *Ethnologia Balkanica* 2 (1998): 8–17.

Jelavich, Barbara. "The British Traveller in the Balkans: The Abuses of Ottoman Administration in the Slavonic Provinces." *Slavonic and East European Review* 33 (1954–1955): 396–413.

Karakasidou, Anastasia. *Fields of Wheat, Hills of Blood: Passages to Nationhood in Greek Macedonia*. Chicago: University of Chicago Press, 1997.

Leake, W.M. *Travels in the Morea*. Vol. 1. Amsterdam: Adolf Hakkert, 1968. First published 1830.

————. *Travels in Northern Greece*. Vol. 1. Amsterdam: Adolf Hakkert, 1967. First published in 1835.

Mazower, Mark. *The Balkans*. New York: Modern Library, 2000.

Miller, Helen Hill. *Greece Through the Ages: As Seen by Travelers from Herodotus to Byron*. New York: Funk and Wagnalls, 1972.

Muir Mackenzie, G. and A.P. Irby. *Travels in the Slavonic provinces of Turkey-in-Europe*. London: Daldy, W. Isbister & Co., 1877.

Reed, Fred. *Salonica Terminus: Travels in to the Balkan Nightmare*. Vancouver: Talonbooks, 1996.

Reid, Graham W., trans. *Contemporary Macedonian Poetry*. Edited by Sitakant Mahapatra and Jozo T. Boskovski. New Delhi, India: Prachi Prakashan, 1981.

Serafimova, Aneta. *Medieval Painting in Macedonia*. Skopje: Ministry of Information, 2000.

Todorova, Maria. *Imagining the Balkans*. New York: Oxford University Press, 1997.

Tsvetkov, Plamen. *A History of the Balkans: A Regional Overview from a Bulgarian Perspective*. Vol. 1. New York: Edwin Mellon Press, 1993.

Vakunin, Sam. "Where Time Stood Still: Skopje, a City of Extremes." *Central Europe Review* 2, 26 (July 3, 2000): unpaginated.

Vryonis, Speros, Jr. "Review Essay." *Balkan Studies* 2 (1981): 427.

:: *Miscellaneous*

Adler, Jeremy. "They can't do anything to me." *London Review of Books*: January 20, 2005.

Andrews, Kevin. *The Flight of Ikaros: Travels in Greece during a Civil War*. Harmondsworth: Penguin, 1984. First published 1959.

Colovic, Ivan. *When I Say Newspaper*. Belgrade: Samizdat/FreeB92, 1999.

———. *The Politics of Symbol in Serbia*. Translated by Celia Hawkesworth. London: Hurst & Co., 2002.

Doniger, Wendy. *Splitting the Difference*. Chicago: University of Chicago Press, 1999.

Emberley, Peter. *Divine Hunger: Canadians on Spiritual Walkabout*. Toronto: HarperCollins Canada, 2002.

Florovsky, Fr. Georges. "On the Veneration of Saints," http://www.orthodoxinfo.com/general/florov_veneration.aspx

Gibbon, Edward. *The Decline and Fall of the Roman Empire*. abr. D.M. Low. New York: Harcourt, Brace and Co., 1960.

Hayden, Tom. *The Lost Gospel of the Earth*. Brooklyn: Ig Publishing, 2007.

Ilarion, Metropolitan. "Universal Tragedy: 500th Anniversary of the Fall of Byzantium." Rep. *Visnyk/The Herald*: May 15, 2003.

James, William. *The Varieties of Religious Experience: A Study in Human Nature*. New York: Collier Books, 1961.

Karouzos, N.D. "Triplets for Beautiful Mystras." In Philip Sherrard, ed. *The Pursuit of Greece*. London: John Murray, 1964.

Kornakov, Dimitar. *Makedonski Manastiri*. Skopje: Matica Makedonska, 1995.

Lossky, Vladimir. *Orthodox Theology: An Introduction*. Crestwood, NY: St. Vladimir's Seminary Press, 1978.

Mansel, Philip. *Constantinople: City of the World's Desire, 1453-1924*. New York: St. Martin's Press, 1995.

McKay, Don. *Vis à Vis: Field Notes on Poetry & Wilderness*. Kentville, NS: Gaspereau Press, 2001.

Miladinov, Konstantine. *Collected Works*. Translated and edited by Peggy and Graham Reed. Skopje: Miska Press, 1980.

Paevsky, Reverend L. "The Basis for the Veneration of Saints." *The Russian Pilgrim*. Vols. 2 and 3. St. Petersburg: 18?, unpaginated.

Palamas, Kostis. "A Hundred Voices." In Aristides E. Phoutrides, trans. *A Hundred Voices and Other Poems from the Life Immovable*. Cambridge, MA: Harvard University Press, 1921.

Pirenne, Henri. *A History of Europe*. Vol. I. Translated by Bernard Miall. New York: Doubleday Anchor, 1958.

Ritsos, Yannis. "from Romiosini." In Kimon Friar, ed. and trans. *Modern Greek Poetry*. New York: Simon and Shuster, 1993.

Rose, Jacqueline. "A Use for the Stones," *London Review of Books*. April 20, 2006. 21.

Thubron, Colin. *Emperor*. Harmondsworth: Penguin, 1978.

Wagner, Bernadette, L. *This Hot Place*. Saskatoon, SK: Thistledown Press, 2010.

Wolff, Larry. *Inventing Eastern Europe: The Map of Civilization on the Mind of the Enlightenment*. Stanford: Stanford University Press, 1994.